Corrective Vision:
Explorations in
Moral Theology

Richard A. McCormick, S.J.

Sheed & Ward

Sheed & Ward™ is a service of The National Catholic Reporter Publishing Company.

Library of Congress Cataloguing-in-Publication Data
McCormick, Richard A., 1922-
    Corrective vision : explorations in moral theology / Richard A.
McCormick.
       p.   cm.
    Includes bibliographical references (p.   ) and index.
    ISBN 1-55612-601-8 (alk. paper)
    1. Christian ethics--Catholic authors. 2. Catholic Church--
Doctrines. 3. Bioethics. 4. Christian ethics--History--20th century.
I. Title.
BJ1249.M239   1994
241'.042--dc20   93-21332
                                         CIP

Published by: Sheed & Ward
                  115 E. Armour Blvd.
                  P.O. Box 419492
                  Kansas City, MO 64141

To order, call: (800) 333-7373

Cover design Copyright© 1994 by Mark McIntyre, S.J.

Contents

Acknowledgements

"Moral Theology: 1940-1989," *Theological Studies* 50 (1989) 3-24. "Moral Theology for the Year 2000," Campion College, University of Regina, Saskatchewan. "Self-Assessment and Self-Indictment," *Religious Studies Review* 13 (1987) 37-39. "How My Mind Has Changed," *The Christian Century* 107 (1990) 732-736. "Discernment in the Moral Life," Center for Ethics Studies, University of Marquette. "The Search for Truth in the Catholic Context," *America* 155 (1986) 276-281. "Theologians and the Magisterium," in *Present and Future Challenges Facing Catholic Universities,* St. Paul University, Ottawa, Canada, 1989. "Theology as a Public Responsibility," *America* 165 (1991) 184-189, 203-206. "L'Affaire Curran II," *America* 163 (1990) 127-132, 142-143. "The Shape of Moral Evasion in Catholicism," *America* 159 (1988) 183-188. "Theology and Bioethics," *Hastings Center Report* 19 (1989) 5-10. "The Malaise in Bioethics," in *Beyond Principlism: Currents in U.S. Bioethics,* Park Ridge Center, 1993. "Hidden Persuaders: Value Variables in Bioethics," The Poynter Center, Indiana University, 1993 and *America* 168 (1993) 7-13. "Who or What is the Preembryo?" 1 (1991) 1-15. "A Middle Ground on Abortion?" *Second Opinion* 10 (1989) 41-50. "Surrogacy: A Catholic View," *Creighton Law Review* 25 (1992) 1617-1634. "The Cruzan Decision: Missouri's Contribution," *Midwest Medical Ethics* 5 (1989) 3-6. "The Case of Nancy Cruzan: A Reflection," *Midwest Medical Ethics* 6 (1990) 10-12. "Moral Considerations' Ill-Considered," *America* 166 (1992) 210-214.

For Charles E. Curran and Richard P. McBrien,
my colleagues, co-authors, and friends
whose courage, competence and compassion are
a gift to the Church and the world.

Introduction

I have entitled this volume of essays *Corrective Vision*. I borrow this phrase from my colleague and friend William F. May, the Cary Maguire University Professor at Southern Methodist University. May, in his wonderful study *The Physician's Covenant*, notes that corrective vision is a fair descriptor of the goal of ethics. I do not wish to annex May into my interpretation of the phrase; for there may be divergences in our understanding. I borrow the phrase to state in shorthand what I take to be the major contribution of moral-theological reflection: opening peoples' eyes to dimensions of reality they may have missed. If moral theology does not do this, it is utterly dispensable.

It is important to underline this aspect of moral reflection at this time in ecclesial history. In a restorative atmosphere there is the tendency to collapse genuine clarification of a teaching into mere repetition of it, which, of course, clarifies nothing. Such "teaching" is a travesty of the teaching-learning process of the Church and trivializes moral theology.

It is with thoughts such as these that I have gathered these essays. Even if they provoke mostly enlightened disagreement, they will have achieved one of the most cherished goals of moral reflection: corrective vision, at least of this author.

A few notes about the essays in this volume. All of them have appeared before substantially as they are here. But they have appeared in sources as disparate as *Second Opinion, Christian Century, Religious Studies Review, Hastings Center Report, America, Theological Studies, Midwest Medical Ethics,* and several books. Even I have trouble rescuing them from salvage piles in my office. That has led me to accept the usefulness of gathering them under one cover.

Second, two of the essays ("L'Affaire Curran II," and "Theology as a Public Responsibility") were co-authored with my colleague the ecclesiologist Richard P. McBrien. I have taken the editorial liberty, with McBrien's approval, to change the original "we" to "I." This is done not to sever McBrien from the thoughts expressed, but for editorial consistency.

Finally, I wish to express deep gratitude to Donna Shearer for her expertise and generosity in bringing this volume to presentable form.

Richard A. McCormick, S.J.
August 1993

CHAPTER 1

Moral Theology from 1940 to 1989: An Overview

In 1940, the first volume of *Theological Studies* carried a section entitled "Recent Canon Law and Moral Theology: Some Important
Items."[1] These thirty-one pages were unsigned but research reveals
that they were actually authored by William McGarry, S.J. John C.
Ford, S.J., beginning with volume 2, continued these critical surveys,
through volume 6 (1945). Gerald Kelly, S.J., began his contribution
with volume 8 (1947), and produced an annual "Notes on Moral Theology" through volume 14 (1953). Volume 15 (1954) saw the beginning of the rich and rewarding collaborative authorship of Ford and
Kelly, as well as the first appearance in *Theological Studies* of John R.
Connery, S.J. Connery and John J. Lynch, S.J. (along with three surveys by Joseph Farraher, S.J., one by Kelly, one by Ford-Kelly, and
several by Robert Springer) carried the "Moral Notes" into the mid-
sixties. The present author began his contributions in 1965 and concluded them in 1987.

I mention this forgettable bit of history because by perusing the
"Notes on Moral Theology" from the beginning—as I did in preparing
this overview—one gets a fairly clear picture of moral theology then
and now, its strengths and weaknesses, as well as its methods and priorities. I say this with confidence because from the very outset these
surveys ranged over moral studies in Latin, French, German, Spanish,
Italian and English, from *Angelicum* and *AAS*, through *Nouvelle revue
théologique, Periodica*, and *Studia Moralia* to *Rázon y fe* and *Stimmen
der Zeit*. However, an overview of moral theology during these five
decades would be incomplete without mention of theologians such as

Francis Connell, C.S.S.R., Joseph Duhamel, S.J., Paul McKeever, Franciscus Hürth, S.J., Edwin Healy, S.J., and a host of others.

It is easy to caricature and no serious scholar with an ounce of self-knowledge and a sense of history will do so. With that caveat in mind, it can be pointed out that in the forties and fifties Catholic moral theology was the stepchild of the *Institutiones Theologiae Moralis* of Genicot, Noldin, Prummer, Aertnys-Damen, et al. Concretely it was all too often onesidedly confession-oriented, magisterium-dominated, canon law-related, sin-centered, and seminary-controlled. In many books and articles Bernard Häring has excoriated this as "legalism." Yet, when reading the Ford-Kelly review of this literature, one must immediately add qualifiers that provide perspective to each of these sweeping indictments. Thus: very pastoral and prudent; critically respectful; realistic; compassionate; open and charitable, well informed. Indeed the two dominant American moral theologians of the forties and fifties (Ford and Kelly) had such towering—and well deserved—reputations that most of us regarded their agreement on a practical matter as constituting a "solidly probable opinion." It is easy to understand why their experience, wisdom and prudence were treasured by everyone from bishops, college presidents, moral theologians, physicians, priests, and students to penitents and counselors.

All of us, however—the present author being *facile princeps*—bear the restricting marks of the cultural contexts in which we work. So, along with truly prophetic and pathbreaking studies that are still urgently relevant,[2] one finds during these earlier years discussions that strike us now as downright quaint. For instance, there is debate about knitting as servile work,[3] of organ-playing at non-Catholic services,[4] of calling non-Catholic ministers for dying non-Catholic patients,[5] of steady dating among adolescents,[6] of the gravity of using "rhythm" without a proportionate reason.[7] It is to the everlasting credit of theologians like Ford, Kelly, Connery, and Lynch that they brought an uncommon common sense to such "problems" that dissipated them before they could seriously quiver the ganglia of the Catholic conscience.

A few examples are needed to jar the unexposed and possibly incredulous post-conciliar Catholic. In 1946 *Theological Studies*—under the editorship of the renowned John Courtney Murray, S.J.—carried an article on fasting. It concluded as follows:

> In conclusion, then, just how much is allowed at breakfast and at collation for a person who is fasting but needs something extra? Some authors say sixteen ounces in all; one or two authors seem to suggest even more. As things stand at present, if one should

be asked how much over the two-ounce/eight-ounce limit is permitted nowadays, it appears that one should reply: First, if a person can conveniently fast on that amount, absolutely nothing extra; otherwise, whatever is really necessary, up to around sixteen ounces; these sixteen ounces can be divided as the person requires—into four for breakfast and twelve for collation, into six and ten, into eight and eight, and so on. However, if the person needs much more than sixteen ounces, or if the mathematical juggling would make him scrupulous, he should be dispensed completely.[8]

If this citation seems extreme, one has only to recall that at the fourteenth annual convention (1959) of the Catholic Theological Society of America, the moral seminar spent the better part of an hour wrangling over whether chewing gum broke the Eucharistic fast. I remember this well because I walked out.

Another example is a paper delivered at the same meeting of the C.T.S.A. by Anthony F. Zimmerman, S.V.D. Zimmerman concluded:

> These and other documents of the Holy See have convinced me that "rhythm" cannot be recommended as a Christian solution for overpopulation. In my opinion Rome has spoken and the case is settled. For we are not allowed to promote the ideal of a small family in a nation, in opposition against the Church's ideal of the large family. But "rhythm" could not be promoted as a means of solving a national overpopulation problem without setting up the small family as a new ideal for that nation.[9]

That conclusion was recognized even then as quite preposterous and I remember distinctly John C. Ford's immediate and magisterial refutation of it. It began: "Rome has not spoken." Today, of course, the refutation would remain vigorous though it might well take a different analytic form.

My final example of how moral theology was pursued by the manuals that constituted the inherited *Weltanshauung* for the forties and fifties is taken from a standard manual of moral theology. Antonius Lanza and Petrus Palazzini, Roman theologians of indisputable stature, discussed the morality of dancing, and specifically of "masked balls." I cite them in the original to forestall questions about authenticity. In other words, one has to see it to believe it.

> Similiter choreae larvatae faciliorem praebent ruinae occasionem: non enim desunt qui ideo faciem tegunt ut pudoris freno non amplius retenti, incogniti ea faciant, quae cogniti facere non auderent. Verum hodie res in multo peius abierunt cum choreis recentioribus: one stoep [sic], paso doble, turquey-trot, pas de

l'ours, spiru, charleston, fox-trot, rumba, carioca, boogie-woogie, samba, etc.[10]

One trembles to think of how these worthies might descend upon today's mores.

Elsewhere I have summarized the perspectives and cultural context of pre-Vatican II moral theology as follows:

> For many decades, even centuries, prior to Vatican II Catholic moral theology conceived its chief task as being the training of priests to hear confessions. Within the sacramental perspectives of the times the confessor was viewed as exercising a fourfold office: father, teacher, judge, physician. Specially necessary to effective ministry were charity (of a father), knowledge (of a teacher and judge), prudence (of a physician) . . .
>
> The knowledge required of a confessor included many things, but above all knowledge of God's law *as proposed by the Church,* i.e., the Church's magisterium. At this period of time, for many understandable sociological reasons, the Church's magisterium was understood in a highly authoritarian and paternalistic way. One did not question ordinary noninfallible teaching. Dissent was virtually unknown and would certainly have been extremely risky.[11]

In the remainder of this overview, I will touch on two points: 1. Significant developments in moral theology over the past fifty years. "Significant" refers in general to factors that affected moral theology, and especially to those that altered the cultural variables that framed the moral agenda of the first twenty years of *Theological Studies'* existence and led to the types of moral concerns and judgments I have cited above. 2. Where we are now.

SIGNIFICANT DEVELOPMENTS

Symptoms abound that there were deep stirrings of dissatisfaction with the brand of theology contained in the *Institutiones theologiae moralis.* One was the growing popularity of Bernard Häring's *The Law of Christ.* Another was the appearance in 1952 of G. Gilleman's *Le primat de la charité en théologie morale. Essai methodologique.*[12] Or again, I shall never forget the shock waves produced by Daniel Callahan in 1964. Ford and Kelly had just published their volume *Contemporary Moral Theology II: Marriage Questions.* It was a haven of moderation against those we used to call *strictiores.* Callahan described the revered authors as "loyal civil servants" and "faithful party workers" and their work as "years behind the (theological) revolution now in progress."[13] Gerald Kelly, I am told by reliable sources, was at his typewriter about to respond, but experienced chest pains in his agitation.

In retrospect I think Callahan was correct. I do not believe that "revolution" is too strong a word for the developments that have occurred in moral theology in the last thirty years. Different authors might well produce different litanies of the revolutionary phases or ingredients. However, I am reasonably confident that the following ten items would appear in one way or another on many lists.

1. VATICAN II AND ECCLESIOLOGY

The Council said very little directly about moral theology. Yet what it said about other aspects of Catholic belief and practice had an enormous influence on moral theology. These "other aspects of Catholic belief and life" are largely though not exclusively ecclesiological. For Vatican II was above all an ecclesiological council. There are many ways of wording this, I am sure. One could, for example, speak of it as the Council of the Holy Spirit to highlight the pervasiveness of the Spirit in the Council's formulations.

Richard McBrien, in a talk to moral theologians at Notre Dame (June, 1988) neatly summarized in six points Vatican II's major ecclesiological themes.

The Church as mystery or sacrament. The Church is a sign as well as an instrument of salvation. As a sacrament, it causes by signifying. As McBrien notes, this powerfully suggests the need to be attentive to justice issues *within* the Church as well as outside. It is this principle of sacramentality that undergirds the statement of the U.S. Catholic Bishops' pastoral letter *Economic Justice For All:* "All the moral principles that govern the just operation of any economic endeavor apply to the church and its agencies and institutions; indeed the church should be exemplary" (para. 347).

The Church as People of God. All the faithful (not just the hierarchy and specialists) constitute the Church. This has immediate implications for the elaboration and development of moral doctrine, for consultative processes, for the free flow of ideas in the Church.

The Church as servant. Besides preaching of the Word and celebration of the sacraments, the Church's mission includes service to human needs in the social, political and economic orders. This suggests that these orders are also ecclesiological problems and that moralists and ecclesiologists must be closely cooperative. It also suggests that moral theology following John Courtney Murray, must continue to probe the relationship between civic unity and religious integrity.

The Church as collegial. The Church is realized and expressed at the local (parish/diocese/region/nation) level as well as the universal. The collegial nature of the Church helps to raise and rephrase the question of the use and limits of authority in the moral sphere, and the meaning of subsidiarity and freedom in the application of moral principles and the formation of conscience.

The Church as ecumenical. Being the whole Body of Christ, the Church includes more than Roman Catholics. The obvious implication is that Catholic officials and theologians must consult and take account of the experience, reflection and wisdom resident in other Christian churches.

The Church as eschatological. The Church is a tentative and unfinished reality. It is *in via.* A *fortiori* its moral and ethical judgments are always *in via* and share the messy, unfinished and perfectible character of the Church itself.

I believe McBrien is absolutely correct when he asserts that these ecclesial metaphors affect both the substance and method of moral inquiry in very profound and practical ways.

2. KARL RAHNER AND FUNDAMENTAL FREEDOM

When I began theological studies toward the priesthood in 1950, Karl Rahner was a "corollary" at the end of our theses on grace, creation, the sacraments, Christology. Not for long, however. During the next thirty-five years he became the most prolific and greatest theologian of the century, and arguably of several centuries.

One of his key contributions to moral theology was his anthropology, and specifically his recovery of the notion of the depth of the moral act.[14] Rahner argued that the human person was, as it were, constructed of various layers of freedom. At the center was the area of core or fundamental freedom which enabled a person to dispose totally of her/himself. Other layers were more or less peripheral. The use of core freedom is the area of grave morality—of total self-disposition, of radical conversion, of truly mortal sin. Actuations of this intensity of freedom may be called "fundamental options" precisely because of their depth, stability and permanence. The notion of *option fundamental* pervades Rahner's writings on grace, sin, conversion, the moral life in general, and above all his presentation of the *Spiritual Exercises* of St. Ignatius.

Such an anthropology has enormous repercussions on some very basic concepts of moral theology: sin, conversion, virtue, serious matter, priorities in the moral life, confession, temptation, laws of the Church, spiritual discernment, to mention but a few. Systematic theologians began to use this anthropology in their presentations of Catholic teachings,[15] but it was domesticated in moral theology largely through the writings of Josef Fuchs, S.J., and his disciple Bruno Schüller, S.J.[16]

Unfortunately, the notion of fundamental freedom can be and has been misunderstood, misrepresented and abused.[17] Perhaps that is the unavoidable fate of the attempt to rethink the depth and complexity of the human person. Be that as it may, I believe that moral theology, largely through the pioneering work of Rahner, has been forever altered. We can no longer think of the moral-spiritual life in terms of the clear and distinct categories that were generated by an anthropology that conceived of freedom exhaustively as freedom of choice. Things are just not that simple.

3. MORAL NORMS AND REVISION OF METHOD

In 1965 Peter Knauer, S.J., published his seminal essay on the principle of double effect.[18] When I drove Josef Fuchs, S.J., from O'Hare airport that year, I asked him about the article. His reply: "Very interesting." Very interesting indeed! It proved to be the opening shot in a twenty-five-year discussion of the proper understanding of moral norms within the community of Catholic moral theologians. Specifically, it concerned the method for determining the morally right and wrong in concrete human conduct. At the risk of oversimplification, Knauer's basic thesis could be worded as follows: the causing or permitting of evils in our conduct is morally right or wrong depending on the presence or absence of a commensurate reason. When such a reason is present, the intention bears on it, not on the evil—and therefore the evil remains indirect. Knauer was on to something, yet he filtered it through traditional categories. The result was provocative, yet a bit untidy and unsettling. That is the way it is with many beginnings.

In 1970 Germain Grisez wrote of Knauer that he "is carrying through a revolution in principle while pretending only a clarification of traditional ideas."[19] Grisez was, I believe, right. That "revolution in principle" gradually led to a vast literature that huddles under the umbrella-term "proportionalism."

Unless I am badly mistaken, I can detect the general shape of this *Denkform* as early as 1951 in the work of Gerald Kelly, S.J. In commenting on a piece by William Conway in *The Irish Theological Quarterly* (wherein Conway considered some procedures involving mutilation as not evils) Kelly wrote:

> For my part, I prefer to say that there are some physical evils that are naturally subordinated to higher ends, and we have a right to cause these evils in order to obtain these ends. Thus, the bodily member is subordinated to the good of the whole body, and one has a right to remove this member where this is necessary for the good of the whole. The principle of the double effect is not required to justify this act; but the reason for this is not that the amputation is not an evil, but rather that it is an evil that one has a right to cause.

> In summary, let me suggest that the principle, evil is not to be done in order to obtain good, is not an absolutely universal principle. It refers absolutely to moral evil. As for physical evils, it refers only to those which lie outside the scope of the agent's direct rights (e.g., death of an innocent person); it does not refer to evils that one has a right to cause (e.g., self-mutilation to preserve life or health; the death of an enemy soldier or an unjust aggressor.)[20]

Kelly was not at that time what is now known as a proportionalist. But those paragraphs indicate that, with a few minor analytic moves, he would be.

So-called proportionalists include some of the best known names in moral theology throughout the world, though some are less explicit about their method: Josef Fuchs, S.J., Bruno Schüller, S.J., Franz Böckle, Louis Janssens, Bernard Häring, Franz Scholz, Franz Furger, Walter Kerber, S.J., Charles Curran, Lisa Cahill, Philip Keane, Joseph Selling, Edward Vacek, S.J., David Hollenbach, S.J., Maurice de Wachter, Margaret Farley, James Walter, Rudolf Ginters, Helmut Weber, Klaus Demmer, Garth Hallett, S.J., and on and on. The leading published opponents of this methodological move are Germain Grisez, John Finnis, Joseph Boyle, William May and the late John R. Connery, S.J.[21]

It is impossible in a brief space to give a fair summary of this development or an adequate account of the differences that individual theologians bring to their analyses, or of the objections lodged against them. However, common to all so-called proportionalists is the insistence that causing certain disvalues (ontic, nonmoral, premoral evils) in our conduct does not *ipso facto* make the action morally wrong as certain traditional formulations supposed. The action becomes morally wrong when, all things considered, there is no proportionate reason. Thus just as not every killing is murder, not every falsehood a lie, so not every artificial intervention preventing (or promoting) conception is necessarily an unchaste act. Not every termination of a pregnancy is necessarily an abortion in the moral sense.

This approach to moral norms has two interesting characteristics:

A. It contrasts markedly with earlier official understandings (e.g., *Humanae vitae*) which regarded some of the actions in question as intrinsic moral evils (i.e., under no circumstances could they be justified).

B. It touches the lives of people in very concrete ways. One may, and I do, suspect that this is why it is so strongly resisted. The twenty-five-year discussion has been well summarized recently by Bernard Hoose, himself a proportionalist.

4. THE BIRTH CONTROL COMMISSION AND *HUMANAE VITAE*

I put these two together because only when *Humanae vitae* is seen in light of the previous consultations does it yield the full dimensions of the problem. The Commission for the Study of Population, Family and Birth (what is widely referred to as the "Birth Control Commission") voted by a heavy majority for a change in Church teaching on contraception. So did the subsequently added (1966) cardinals and bishops. On Sunday, June 26, 1966, after the Commission had completed its work, Canon Pierre de Locht of Brussels, a member of the Commission, wrote in his diary:

> It will not be possible any longer to reaffirm the general condemnations of contraception. I do not understand what excuse he [the pope] can use to impose on the church his own personal option. The research he set in motion does not make sense if he does not take it into account. Why, then, would he have asked for it? Will he accept our conclusions only if they lean toward a reaffirmation?[23]

De Locht's statement summarizes the authority problem that *Humanae vitae* raised in 1968.[24] Paul VI had enlarged the Birth Control Commission and supported its work. Indeed, in 1966, under mounting pressure to issue a statement he had intervened, almost agonizingly, with a kind of delaying plea. He said he was not ready to make his final statement. "The magisterium of the Church," he said, "cannot propose moral norms until it is certain of interpreting the will of God.

And to reach this certainty the Church is not dispensed from research and from examining the many questions proposed for her consideration from every part of the world. This is at times a long and not an easy task."[25]

Yet *Humanae vitae* appeared in 1968. The problem is obvious. I wrote at that time:

> If in February, 1966, the pope needed the studies of the commission to achieve (*raggiungere*) the certainty necessary to propose moral norms, and if having received the majority report of the commission he achieved or maintained a certainty contrary to it, then perhaps we need a long, long discussion about the nature of the magisterium.[26]

This is exactly what de Locht meant when he wrote that "the research he set in motion does not make sense if he does not take it into account."

The firestorm that greeted *Humanae vitae* over twenty years ago is familiar to readers of *Theological Studies* and many others. There is no need for repetition here. What needs to be emphasized, however, is the enormous influence of this event on subsequent moral theology. Theologians became freshly aware of the inadequacy of a heavily juridical notion of the moral teaching office, and correspondingly they became more sensitive to their own responsibilities, especially their occasional duty to dissent in light of their own experience with the faithful and reflection on it. Non-reception became overnight a live theological issue. Questions were raised about the formation of conscience, about the response due to the ordinary magisterium, about the exercise of authority in the Church, about consultative processes and collegiality, about the meaning of the guidance of the Holy Spirit to the pastors of the Church. Contraception, as a moral issue, was virtually smothered in the ecclesiological tumult. The pope had been convinced by a minority of advisors from the commission that any qualification of the condemnation of *Casti connubii* would compromise papal teaching authority. Just the opposite has proved to be the case.

I can think of no moral issue or event in this century that impacted so profoundly on the discipline of moral theology. The reason for this was not only or primarily the sheer day-to-day practicality of the problem, but the fact that *Humanae vitae* was perceived by many to be the symbol of a takeback of important things that had happened in Vatican II. Bernard Häring once remarked to me that he thought we had learned more from *Humanae vitae* than we (as Church) had suffered. He was referring, of course, to the place and exercise of authority in Christian morality. The lesson we learned had chiefly to do with limits. In a sense Paul VI, without really wanting to, or realizing that he was doing so, put Vatican II on the scales by testing it on a single burning issue.

5. THE EMERGENCE OF FEMINISM

This is surely one of the "signs of the times" of which John XXIII and Vatican II spoke. Its full effect on moral theology is probably still ahead of us. Prior to Vatican II, the Catholic Theological Society of America was an all-male club and even earlier, an all-seminary club. Now women are in positions of leadership in the C.T.S.A. It was not until 1971 that a woman (J. Massingberd Ford) first authored an article for *Theological Studies*.[27] Now it is common to see such fine scholars as Lisa Cahill, Catherine LaCugna, Leslie Griffin, Elizabeth Johnson, Marjorie O'Rourke Boyle, Anne Carr, Sandra Schneiders and Carol Tauer in these pages. In the field of moral theology the work of Griffin, Cahill, Tauer, Anne Patrick, Sidney Callahan, Christine Gudorf, Margaret Farley, Judith Dwyer, Eileen Flynn, Diana Bader, Corrine Bayley, Barbara Andelson, Elizabeth McMillan—to mention but a few—has been very effective and deeply appreciated.

The presence of women in the moral theological enterprise should have an obvious impact in several key areas of moral concern. Two that stand out are the place of women in the Church and in society, and the theology of marriage and sexuality. But even beyond such issue-areas, the theological contributions of women will be a constant reminder that Catholic Christianity is still male-dominated and bears its own share of the blame for what an early version of the proposed pastoral on women called a pervasive sin of sexism in the Church.[28]

6. THE MATURATION OF BIOETHICS

Within the Catholic community there had been for some years standard texts in medical ethics. One thinks of those authored by Charles J. McFadden, O.S.A., Gerald Kelly, S.J., Thomas O'Donnell, S.J., and Edwin Healy, S.J.[29] As LeRoy Walters has noted of these texts, "the general approach to medical ethics was based on the standard textbooks of moral theology."[30]

The years 1969 and 1971 represented something of a turning point. In 1969 Daniel Callahan and Willard Gaylin founded the Institute of Society, Ethics and the Life Sciences, now more economically referred to as the Hastings Center. In 1971 André Hellegers founded the Joseph and Rose Kennedy Institute for the Study of Human Reproduction and Bioethics (now known as the Kennedy Institute of Ethics) at Georgetown University. These sister institutes brought physicians, scientists, philosophers, theologians and lawyers together for the systematic and interdisciplinary study of the emerging problems in bioethics. The result was not only a fresh awareness of the breadth and complexity of the problems created by technology, but a huge outpouring of literature that attempted to wrestle with them. Bioethics had been born as a large and loosely but well-enough defined subspeciality of ethics. Since then Centers for Bioethics have sprung up all over the country and the world.

The significance of this for moral theology should not be lost. I will note three aspects. First, it became clear that it is impossible for any one theologian to be a truly reputable expert in all fields of moral theology in our day. Many of us are asked to teach, write, or lecture "on the moral aspects of . . ." virtually anything; naively we used to think we could do that. To persist in such thoughts merely proliferates banality and incompetence, and threatens our theological credibility in the process. The present lacuna of moral-theological competence in certain areas of applied ethics should not tempt us to fill it with instant ethical energy, but long-run incompetence. It should rather function as a challenge.

And that leads directly to my second point. If bioethics establishes any kind of paradigm, it tells us that we need in law, business and politics—to mention but three areas—truly *well-trained* and *experienced* persons who are ready to *specialize* in the ethical dimensions of the professions, that is, limit themselves to such areas in a way that allows them to emerge as nationally recognized experts.

Finally, what is increasingly obvious in medicine—and I would guess, therefore, in the areas of law, business and politics—is that an ethics of medicine can degenerate into a lifeless and detached body of knowledge that one dusts off now and then when faced with a nasty dilemma. That is the result of identifying ethics with "dilemma ethics." What we have come to see as essential to a genuine ethic is a formational dimension and therefore a spirituality of and for the professional person. When that is in place, decisional ethics will have a nourishing and supportive context and it will certainly flourish. Otherwise it remains sparetime aerobics. By "spirituality" I do not mean, for example, a parallel-track, off-time retreat each year or two. I mean an approach to the profession developed from within its institutional ambience that views and lives the practice of medicine as a truly Christian vocation.

7. THE INFLUENCE OF LIBERATION THEOLOGY

Liberation theology has the Vatican worried. That may be in our time the surest sign of its vitality and importance. In 1970 Gustavo Gutiérrez published in *Theological Studies* what he called "Notes for a Theology of Liberation."[31] With that article the Peruvian theologian alerted North America, as well as the world, that something terribly exciting was afoot in Latin America. In introducing the article Walter Burghardt, S.J., referred to it as "theological dynamite." For a world sadly anesthetized to exploding automobiles and body counts on an almost daily basis, *theological* dynamite would seem to be a relatively cozy and comfortable threat.

Try again. Burghardt was prescient. Liberation theology is here—or, more accurately, there—to stay *pace* Andrew Greeley. I am not interested in this overview in reviewing its salient features, and its vast literature, or critiquing its sometimes overreaching claims. Others (theologians such as Roger Haight, S.J., and Alfred Hennelly, S.J., for example) are more competent to do so and indeed have done it. I simply want to point to it as a "significant development." The term "significant" cries out for specification. Exactly how has liberation theology affected moral theology? In many ways I am sure. But I will list three.

First there is the demolition of the "separatist mentality." That refers to the approach that conceives of basic Christian realities such as faith, hope and love—i.e., salvation—as exclusively or at least one-sidedly other-worldly realities. In other words, there is a radical continuity (even partial identification) between the eschatological promises and hope (the Kingdom) and human liberation from systemic oppression. This entails a profound readjustment of our assessment of political and economic activity. These can no longer be viewed simply as "worldly" or secular pursuits. As Gutiérrez words it: "There are not, then, two histories, one profane and one sacred, juxtaposed or interrelated, but a single human progress, irreversibly exalted by Christ, the Lord of history. His redemptive work embraces every dimension of human existence."[32]

Second, as Gutiérrez and others such as Segundo and Sobrino make very clear, the Church's mission of charitable action is not merely that of social critique; it provokes all Christians to participate actively in construction of a just order. Only so will the people of Latin America (and elsewhere) believe the message of love at the center of the Christian idea. Paul VI put it this way in 1971: "It is to all Christians that we address a fresh and insistent call to action . . . It is not enough to recall principles, state intentions, point to crying injustices and utter prophetic denunciations; these words will lack real weight unless they are accompanied for each individual by the livelier awareness of personal responsibility and by effective action."[33]

Third, the theology of liberation is a constant reminder of the primacy of social concerns in our conception and presentation of the moral-spiritual life, and therefore of moral theology. This is a necessary corrective to the individualism of the West since one form of that individualism is overemphasis on the personal (especially sexual) dimensions of the moral life. Paul VI in *Octogesima adveniens* emphasized this: "These are questions that because of their urgency, extent and complexity must, in the years to come, take first place among the preoccupations of Christians . . ."[34] Moral theology, in other words, cannot be equated with the problems and priorities of the western industrialized democracies. We need other cultures to give us critical perspective on our own cultural and theological "locked-in syndrome."

8. THE PERSON AS CRITERION OF THE MORALLY RIGHT AND WRONG

Vatican II (*Gaudium et spes,* 51) asserted that "the moral aspect of any procedure . . . must be determined by objective standards which are based on the nature of the person and the person's acts." The official commentary on this wording noted two things: 1. In the expression there is formulated a general principle that applies to all human actions, not just to marriage and sexuality (where the passage occurred). 2. The choice of this expression means that "human activity must be judged insofar as it refers to the human person integrally and adequately considered."[36]

The importance of this can hardly be exaggerated. If "the person integrally and adequately considered" is the criterion of moral rightness and wrongness, it means a different (from traditional) type of evidence is required for our assessment of human actions. For instance, in the past the criteriological significance of sexual conduct was found in its procreativity (*actus per se aptus ad procreationem*). Deviations from this finality and significance were viewed as morally wrong and *the* decisive factor in judging conduct. In my judgment these perspectives continued to appear in *Humanae vitae* and "The Declaration on Certain Questions Concerning Sexual Ethics."

However, Vatican II adopted the broader personalist criterion. As Louis Janssens words it: "From a personalist standpoint what must be examined is what the intervention as a whole means for the promotion of the human persons who are involved and for their relationships."[37] This commits us to an inductive method in moral deliberation about rightness and wrongness in which human experience and the sciences play an indispensable role.

9. THE CURRAN AFFAIR

Prior to the removal of Charles Curran's canonical mission to teach on the pontifical faculty at Catholic University of America, Bishop Matthew Clark (Curran's ordinary) wrote on March 12, 1986:

> If Father Curran's status as a Roman Catholic theologian is brought into question, I fear a serious setback to Catholic education and pastoral life in this country. That could happen in two ways. Theologians may stop exploring the challenging questions of the day in a creative, healthy way because they fear actions which may prematurely end their teaching careers. Moreover, able theologians may abandon Catholic institutions altogether in order to avoid embarrassing confrontation with church authorities. Circumstances of this sort would seriously undermine the standing of Catholic scholarship in this nation, isolate our theological community and weaken our Catholic institutions of higher learning.[38]

Both things have begun to happen and thus the Curran affair ranks among the most significant developments in moral theology in the past fifty years. For instance, after the appearance of *Donum vitae* (the C.D.F.'s instruction on reproductive technology), I publicly but respectfully disagreed with a few of the instruction's conclusions. A young theologian told me that he agreed with me but added: "Will I get clobbered if I say so?" Such an attitude is understandable but profoundly saddening, especially in a church that rightly claims divine guidance. One would think that the promised guidance of the Holy Spirit would be the most solid basis for welcoming challenge and disagreement. It takes little imagination to see how the climate of fear may lead theologians to "stop exploring the challenging questions of the day," or to hedge his/her bets. This is especially the case if the individual has dependents. And sadly, these are the very people whose experience and reflection is so essential in approaching such questions.

As for abandonment of Catholic institutions, that has not happened yet. But what has begun to happen, I fear, is the gradual and impoverishing isolation of Catholic University. Over and over again I have heard theologians state that in the present circumstances they would recommend Catholic University to neither aspiring professors nor students. I emphasize that this is not a threat of mine: it is a report. But the report is threatening.[39]

There is a single theological issue in play in the Curran case, but one with many ramifications. That issue: public dissent from some authoritative but noninfallible teaching. The teaching in question, as Curran has repeatedly emphasized,[40] has these characteristics: 1. Distant from the core of the faith; 2. Based on natural law; 3. Involved in such particularity and specificity that we should not realistically expect the same level of certitude enjoyed by more general norms.

The C.D.F. has denied the legitimacy of such dissent. This collides in principle with its acceptance by the American bishops in 1968. In this matter I stand by what I wrote in 1986:

> The implications of the Congregation's approach should not be overlooked. The first is that, to be regarded as a Catholic theologian, one may not dissent from *any* authoritatively proposed teaching. The second is that "authentic theological instruction" means presenting church teaching and never disagreeing with it, even with respect and reverence. Third, and correlatively, sound theological education means accepting, uncritically if necessary, official Catholic teaching. The impact of such assertions on the notion of a university, of Catholic higher education, of theology and of good teaching are mind-boggling. All too easily, answers replace questions and conformism replaces teaching as "theology" is reduced to Kohlberg's preconventional level of reasoning (obey or be punished).[41]

10. THE "RESTORATION"

The description is that of Cardinal Joseph Ratzinger.[42] It refers in a very general way to the attempt to "tighten things up" in the Church, especially by authoritative intervention into theological work considered suspect or dangerous. Cardinal Ratzinger has made no secret of the fact that moral theology heads his list. This restoration has taken two forms, one direct, the other indirect. The direct form involves the withholding of the canonical mission, the withdrawal of the *imprimatur*, dust-up actions and letters to bishops and theologians.

The indirect form is found above all in the appointment of bishops and the criteria of suitability for such appointment. Further symptoms of this "restoration" are seen in the failure of the synodal process and of the International Theological Commission. These were designed as vehicles for episcopal and theological collegiality but have fallen a good deal short of these expectations and are widely dismissed as tokenisms.

The theological implications of this restoration are profound and far-reaching. I once listed them as ten "confusions" and have found no persuasive reasons for modifying this listing.[43]

One can, of course, challenge the idea that we are involved in a "restoration." Most would ridicule that challenge as unreal. What I think is beyond challenge is that, if we are, then these confusions will be exacerbated.

The above represent ten significant developments since 1940 that relate to moral theology.

WHERE WE ARE NOW

Once again, I shall work in tens in this section. There are ten points that can describe where we now are in moral theology and I shall refer to them as "ages," as "we are in the age of . . ."

1. THE AGE OF SETTLING

Charles Curran and this author have attempted, in our *Readings in Moral Theology,* to identify some of the areas of both importance and debate in contemporary moral theology. It is somewhat risky and difficult to assess the outcomes of these discussions, and for two reasons. First, they are still ongoing. Second, we are associated with an identifiable point of view. For instance, where dissent is concerned, we both would accept its legitimacy and even necessity in some cases. Or again, where moral norms are concerned, we would reject the notion of intrinsic evil *as this was understood in manualist presentations* and would accept *some form* of proportionalism.

My acquaintance with the literature leads me to believe that most theologians share similar perspectives.[44] Indeed, if this were not the case, one has to wonder why Cardinal Ratzinger (and even John Paul II) has aimed his guns in this direction. So the first thing that might be said about "where we are" is that there has been a quiet theological (even if not magisterial) settling, and a move to other issues in some of these matters. There are several possible readings of this. One is that a significant consensus has developed. Another is that a stand-off has been reached and further discussion appears non-productive. Still another is that people are just bored with some of these concerns. I shall leave the decision to the judicious reader.

2. THE AGE OF SPECIALISTS

I have already touched on this. Suffice it to note that the theologian should not aspire or be expected to be *uomo universale*. It would be unrealistic to expect Daniel Callahan to be a hands-on expert in the field of international relations, or Bryan Hehir to be a standout bioethicist. These people have established reputations in the fields of their competence and have done outstanding work. Without specialization they would hardly have the influences they have.

3. THE AGE OF JUSTICE

There has been a sea-change of moral consciousness during the past fifty years. During that period we gradually began to speak of sin not simply as the isolated act of an individual, but as having societal structural dimensions. We began to see that the sins and selfishness of one generation became the inhibiting conditions of the next. The structures and institutions that oppress people, deprive them of rights and alienate them are embodiments of our sinful condition. The notion of systemic violence and social sin entered our vocabulary and is so much a part of it now that John Paul II uses it freely. For instance, in *Sollicitudo rei socialis* he states:

> If the present situation can be attributed to difficulties of various kinds, it is not out of place to speak of "structures of sin," which, as I stated in my Apostolic Exhortation *Reconciliatio et penitentia*, are rooted in personal sin, and thus always linked to the concrete acts of individuals who introduce these structures, consolidate them and make them difficult to remove.[45]

This is, I think, "where we are" in much of contemporary moral theology. Many of the quite personal problems that so engaged the manualists are, obviously, still problems. Indeed there is a pastoral wisdom there that remains somewhat undervalued, largely because it is unknown. Yet the focus has shifted. We are much more concerned about the rights of people that are denied by social structures. A symptom of this is the fact that the major problems in bioethics are perceived to be problems of access and distribution, problems of social organization and social responsibility. The same is true in other areas.

For example, the women's issue is seen to be a structural problem. Similarly, life issues (abortion, war, capital punishment, etc.) are increasingly approached as a whole in terms of a "consistent ethic of life."

4. THE AGE OF EXPERIENCE

Through many initiatives of Vatican II (and the theology that led to and formed it), we now are more aware than ever that one of the richest and most indispensable sources of moral knowledge is human experience and reflection. To be ignorant of it or to neglect it is to doom moral theology to irrelevance and triviality.

I am deeply aware of the traps of over-contrast. But that being acknowledged, there is a residue of truth in the general assertion that for some decades Catholic moral theology proceeded as if its responsibility was to form and shape experience, but hardly ever be shaped by it. The *over*-contrast in that generalization refers to the work of the theologians mentioned at the beginning of this overview. Anyone who reads "Notes on Moral Theology" from 1940 forward will see immediately that Ford, Kelly, Lynch, and Connery were intimately associated with psychiatrists, social ethicists, physicians, businesspersons and laypeople. My generalization does not refer to these eminent authors.

Rather it refers to official formulations. On the one hand, we honor key ideas in Vatican II. For instance:

> She [the Church] must rely on those who live in the world, are versed in different institutions and specialties, and grasp their innermost significance in the eyes of both believers and unbelievers. With the help of the Holy Spirit, it is the task of the entire People of God, especially pastors and theologians, to hear, distinguish, and interpret the many voices of our age, and to judge them in the light of the divine Word.[46]

For this reason the Council warned:

> Let the layperson not imagine that his/her pastors are always such experts, that to every problem which arises, however complicated, they can readily give him a concrete solution, or even that such is their mission . . . Let the layperson take on his/her own distinctive role.[47]

On the other hand, we seem not to know how to deal with this "take on his/her own distinctive role." There are repeated attempts by some *immobilisti* to marginalize it as "mere polls." And they have a point. But not the only point. When I include the "age of experience" as a dimension of where we are, I mean to underline the fact that both authoritative statements and current theology admit experience as a *locus theologicus* in principle. There remain tensions about how to use and interpret it in systematic moral reflection. This is particularly true of some so-called "authentic" utterances of the Holy See.

5. THE AGE OF CULTURAL DIVERSITY

In 1979 Karl Rahner published in these pages his "A Basic Interpretation of Vatican II." Rahner saw Vatican II as the inauguration of the Church as a world church. He saw three epochs in the history of Christianity: 1. The period of Jewish Christianity; 2. The period of Hellenism and European culture; 3. The period of the Church as a world church.

Up to Vatican II, Christianity was basically a Western export that attempted to proselytize by imposing the Latin language and rites, Roman law and the bourgeois morality of the West on various cultures. Our challenge now—and one with profound implications for moral theology—is to recognize essential cultural differences and with a Pauline boldness to draw the necessary consequences. For instance Rahner asks: "Must the marital morality of the Masais in East Africa simply reproduce the morality of Western Christianity, or could a chieftain there, even if he is a Christian, live in the style of the patriarch Abraham?" Simply to suppose that we have answers to questions like these is to fail to de-Europeanize Christianity and to "betray the meaning of Vatican II."

6. THE AGE OF TECHNOLOGY

Nearly every aspect of modern life in the Western world has been deeply affected by technology. The changes continue on an almost daily basis: travel, information flow, education, construction, cooking, business, medicine and so on. I have no precise idea how this relates to moral theology. But one cannot avoid the nagging suspicion that it may reinforce some deeply embedded Western and American value-priorities: efficiency and comfort. If these are indeed the values that shape the perspectives of many Americans, it should be fairly clear that we are knee-deep in the danger that they will corrosively affect our judgments of the morally right and wrong, and more generally of the priority of values.

7. THE AGE OF HOLINESS AND WITNESS

The past fifty years have led us to the point where we recognize the value *but limits* of rational argument and analysis. The very meaning of "in the Lord" is best gathered from the lives of the saints. Johannes Metz notes that "Christological knowledge is formed and handed on not primarily in the form of concepts but in accounts of following Christ."[50] That is why the history of Christian theological ethics is the history of the practice of following Christ, and must assume a primarily narrative form. We make Christ present in our world by embodying in our lives what the remarkable Joseph Sittler used to refer to as "the shape of the engendering deed."[51] The saints do that best.

What I am suggesting by inference is that moral theology today, in its self-concept, is much more sensitive to the central importance of witness, imagination, liturgy and emotions. There are many loose ends and incomplete agenda of course. But it is "where we are."

8. THE AGE OF THEOLOGICAL ANTHROPOLOGY

The *Institutiones Theologiae Moralis,* notwithstanding their compassion and practical pastoral wisdom, contained an image of the human person and of moral agency. That image: the agent as solitary decision-maker. That may be an overstatement, but I think not by much. It is the result of presenting the moral life largely in terms of obligations and sins—itself the precipitate of a confession-oriented moral theology.

Moral theologians today are much more aware of the need of a sound *theological* anthropology. By "theological anthropology" I mean a doctrine of the human person that views the human person in terms of the great Christian mysteries: creation-fall-redemption. It is a doctrine that would yield an appropriate emphasis on vision, perspectives, and character and the stories, metaphors and images that generate and nourish these elements. Vatican II summarized this very cryptically: "Faith throws a new light on everything, manifests God's design for man's total vocation, and thus directs the mind to solutions which are fully human."[53] The terms "God's design" and "total vocation" are shorthand for theological anthropology.

9. THE AGE OF ECUMENISM

Because of the ecclesiological moves of Vatican II (e.g., acknowledgement of the presence of the Spirit to non-Catholic Christians and the reality of church in their communions), it is simply accepted in contemporary moral theology that our non-Catholic Christian colleagues are an important *locus theologicus* in moral deliberations. This is in rather stark contrast to canon 1399,4 of the old code that forbade the reading of books of any non-Catholics who "*ex professo treated of religion*" unless it was absolutely clear (*constet*) that such treatments contained nothing against the Catholic faith. In other words, the very separation of a Christian from Catholicism contained a presumption that that person was not a source of religious and moral wisdom and knowledge.

A symbol of "where we are now" is the fact that not a few of our Catholic moral theologians have studied under fine theologians such as James Gustafson, Paul Ramsey, James Nelson, etc. Once again, I must advert to the fact that the discipline of moral theology has moved in this direction, yet it is far from clear that the sources of official statements have.

10. THE AGE OF WOMEN

I have already mentioned this above. Further comment, especially by a male, might easily support the accusation of self-contradiction.

The detailing of significant developments and descriptions of where we are implies directions for the future. But I want to go beyond implications. That brings us to Chapter Two.

CHAPTER 2

Moral Theology
in the Year 2000

Everyone has a dream these days. Cardinal Basil Hume reported one at the Synod of 1980.[1] Martin Luther King had one. Karl Rahner wrote his up in 1981.[2] The dream format is a remarkably useful vehicle. For one thing it brings the imagination into theology and that is not all bad. For another, it allows one to float what may appear to be unthinkable, unconventional and astonishing ideas without completely owning them. One can, as it were, be preposterous without being possessive. After all, "it was only a dream."

Yet, as we are all aware, today's reveries sometimes turn out to be tomorrow's realities. Thank God! Without dreamers where would we be? In this sense, it can be argued that it is our responsibility, an aspect of our share in providence,[3] to dream—that is, to foresee options and possibilities in order to burst the bonds of conventionality, and allow Christianity not only to remember the past but to create the future and thereby to meet the theological and pastoral needs of the believing community. It was in this spirit that Archbishop Rembert Weakland stated that "we are living at a time when we must re-imagine the Catholic Church. We must examine our own moral convictions, work through them in the light of the Gospel so that we hold them deeply for ourselves."[4]

I confess that I like the phrase "re-imagine the Catholic Church." It has a bouncy and daring optimism to it that ought to signalize believers in the Lord. It is a tacit acknowledgement that we can be and are corporately slovenly. Specifically, we tend to face new problems and challenges by leaning on ancient pillars. We are *landatores temporis acti*. Andrew Greeley had something like this in mind when he reported the defection of one out of ten Hispanic Catholics to Protestant denominations. Greeley likened the response of Catholic officialdom to this startling phenomenon to that of an average, overweight, slightly punch-drunk linebacker. "Despite its size and its strength it lacks the quickness and creativity to respond to challenges."[5]

"Re-Imagining the Catholic Church" sounds radical and revolutionary. Therefore it is important to understand what it does and does not mean. It does not refer to an aimless, destructive, change-for-the-sake-of-change dismantling. That is a road to nowhere. "Re-imagining" suggests rather a more creative and imaginative use of substantials already in place. In this sense it is radical—a recovery of roots (*radix*) long hidden by the barnacled accumulations of custom, habit, and cultural overlay.

Now if we must "re-imagine the Catholic Church" to keep it vital and vigorous in changing times, something similar must surely be said about moral theology within the Catholic Church. Moral theology is concerned with the behavioral implications of our "being in the Lord." If that very "being" can be twisted and deformed by human caprice, pride, blindness, passion, anthropomorphism and a host of other distortions, so can its behavioral implications, as John Mahoney, S.J., has recently pointed out in rich detail.[6]

In what follows, then, I want to outline and develop ten characteristics of moral theology as I would hope to find it in the year 2000. Such a re-imagining involves all sorts of human exercises: hoping, critiquing the past and present, regretting, aspiring, dreaming. None of this is immune from caricature. If it occurs all I can do is reemphasize that that is the way it is with dreams.

1. CHRISTOCENTRISM AND CHARITY

I dare say that the vast majority of Catholics, when they think of morality and the moral life, think of moral problems, of the rightness and wrongness of certain actions or omissions. Thus: Is premarital sex always wrong? Is it wrong to withhold or withdraw artificial nutrition and hydration from a patient in a persistent vegetative state? Is it wrong to threaten nuclear retaliation? Is it always wrong to speak falsehoods? And on and on. In this spirit a writer in the *New York Times* recently offered "four simple principles that can help analyze and resolve the ethical dilemmas that often characterize business competition."[7] These were presented as "practical guides" to "being ethical." "Being ethical," in other words, was conceived as a predicate of "business activities." In short, we identify ethics with dilemma or quandary ethics.

The reasons for such an identification are fairly clear. Cases are newsworthy eye-catchers. They get the headlines and arouse curiosity, and are amenable to legal wrangling and resolution. Furthermore, they provide a congenial meeting place for people who otherwise have very little in common and very little to share. Everybody has an opinion on abortion, on drugs, on first use of nuclear weapons, on apartheid, on *in vitro* fertilization. And why not? We are moral beings and this is the stuff of morality.

Well, not quite. An ethic that claims to be theological will root itself in God—God's actions and purposes. Its primary referents will be God's relation to us, and ours to God. The prime analogate—to use scholastic language—of the term "morality" will be this relationship. The most basic language—not the only—of theological ethics builds around goodness and badness, not rightness and wrongness of actions, since goodness-badness is basically vertical and has its aortal lifeline to the God-relationship.

In slightly different words, a Christian theological ethic is founded on the fact that something *has been done* to and for us, and that something is Jesus. There is a prior action of God at once revelatory and response-engendering. This prior action of God is reflected in the Pauline "therefore" which states the entire grounding and meaning of the Christian ethic. The Italian theologian Enrico Chiavacci puts it this way:

> In the New Testament the unique obligation of charity, which is the giving of self to God who is seen in one's neighbor, is grounded on the unique fact that God is Charity . . . "Walk in love *as* Christ has loved us and given himself" (Eph. 5:2). *"Therefore*, I exhort you brethren, through the mercy of God to offer yourselves . . ." (Romans 12:1). The fact that God—in his manifestation as philanthropy—is love does not refer to further justification; it is the ultimate fact. The obligation to love is based only on God's love for us . . . It is true . . . that in the "therefore" of Romans 12:1 we find the entire New Testament ethic.[8]

When I mention Christian theological ethics, I think primarily of those foundations that deserve the name theological. These foundations can be summarized in a systematic way with six assertions.

1. God's self-disclosure in Jesus Christ as self-giving love allows of no further justification. It is the absolutely ultimate fact. The

acceptance of this fact into one's life is an absolutely originating and grounding experience.

2. This belief in the God of Jesus Christ means that "Christ, perfect image of the Father, is already law and not only law-giver. He is already the categorical imperative and not just the font of ulterior and detailed imperatives."[9]

3. This ultimate fact reveals a new basis or context for understanding the world. It gives it a new (Christocentric) meaning. As a result of God's concrete act in the incarnation, "human life has available a new relation to God, a new light for seeing, a new fact and center for thinking, a new ground for giving and loving, a new context for acting in this world."[10]

4. This "new fact and center for thinking" that is Jesus Christ finds its deepest meaning in the absoluteness and ultimacy of the God-relationship. Outside the God-relationship efforts to know ourselves and be ourselves fully are doomed to falter.

5. This God-relationship is already shaped by God's prior act in Jesus (self-giving). "To believe in Jesus Christ, Son of God, is identical with believing that God—the absolute, the meaning—is total gift of self."[11] Therefore, the "active moment of faith takes place in the recognition that meaning is to give oneself, spend oneself, and live for others."[12] The Christian moral life is a recapitulation in the life of the believer of the "shape of the engendering deed," to use Sittler's language.

6. The empowered acceptance of this engendering deed (faith) totally transforms the human person. It creates new operative vitalities that constitute the very possibility and the heart of the Christian moral life.

I stress these points because there has been, and still is, a tendency to conceive of Christian ethics primarily in terms of norms and principles that may be derived from Jesus' pronouncements. There are such sayings recorded in the New Testament. But to reduce Christian ethics to such sayings is to trivialize it. When the Christian thinks of Christian ethics (or moral theology—I treat them as identical here), he/she thinks primarily of what Jesus has done to and for us, and therefore of *who we are*. As Sittler words it:

> He (Jesus) did not, after the manner proper to philosophers of the good, attempt to articulate general principles which, once stated, have then only to be beaten out in corollaries applicable to the variety of human life . . . His works and deeds belong together. Both are signs which seek to fasten our attention upon the single

vitality which was the ground and purpose of his life—his God relationship.[13]

In and through Jesus we know what that God-relationship is: total self-gift. For that is what God is and we are created in His image. To miss this is, I believe, to leave the realm of Christian ethics.

To see Jesus at the heart of moral theology is to say that charity is its heart and soul. For Jesus is the charity of the Father enfleshed. That is why I have always found Sittler's phrase—"the shape of the engendering deed"—so on target as a description of the structure of Christian ethics.

Yet it is so easy to forget this. There are four factors at work that can easily obscure this centrality of charity: casuistry, appeals to the natural law, emphasis on the magisterium, and the importance of philosophical ethics. Each of these factors plays an indispensable role in the full elaboration of Christian morality. Christian love must become "inprincipled," as the late Paul Ramsey used to say, and then be applied in a consistent and disciplined way to a host of intransigent and complex situations. Otherwise it remains at the level of pious fireside generalization. Similarly, the natural moral law is not a competitor with charity for jurisdictional primacy in Christian ethics. Natural law—we can deplore the word—has reference to those intelligible constants of the human person that delineate the minimal demands of charitable action.

As for the magisterium, Catholics treasure it as a privileged source of moral enlightenment. Something similar can be said of moral philosophy. It brings to moral reflection the analytic clarities and precision of reasoned discourse.

Yet, unless I am mistaken, the importance of each of these factors can be and has been overstated in such a way that it distorts Christian morality into unrecognizability. Casuistry can easily become legalistic minimalism. Respect for the magisterium easily converts into a fundamentalistic magisteriolatry that breeds conformism. Philosophy too often turns up as a poorly disguised and sterile rationalism. And the natural law is contaminated by the many caricatures once noted by John Courtney Murray.[14]

When these things happen the simplicity and splendor of a moral theology—and pastoral catechesis—anchored in and dominated by charity gets hopelessly blurred. Enamored of the parts, we grow blind to the whole. That is why it is still timely—indeed urgent—to dream of a moral theology in the year 2000 that can recover and reproduce the glorious and demanding simplicity of its founder.

2. UNIVERSALITY

As I dream of moral theology in the year 2000, I dream of a presentation of the moral life that will be appealing and make sense to Christians of many cultures. The Church is, as Rahner has noted, a world church.[15] I will refer to this characteristic of Christian morality as its "universalizing feature." I mean to underline the idea that Christian morality, while being theological to its core, must not be isolationist or sectarian. Isolating accounts of the Christian story would repudiate a constant of the Catholic tradition: that God's self-revelation in Jesus does not obliterate the human but illuminates it. As Vatican II worded it: "Faith throws a new light on everything, manifests God's design for man's total vocation, and thus directs the mind to solutions which are *fully human*."[16] It added: "Whoever follows after Christ, the perfect man, *becomes himself more of a man*."[17] Christian ethics, then, is the objectification in Jesus Christ of what every person experiences of her/himself in his subjectivity. In a sense we may say that the resources of scripture, dogma and Christian life are the fullest available "objectifications" of the common human experience. Fudging this runs afoul, at some point, of the Chalcedonian formulae about the true humanity of Jesus.

Catholic tradition has attempted, very clumsily at times, to capture this dimension of morality by reference to a natural moral law.

I mention this dimension of Christian morality because it has come under attack by several influential writers. For instance, my colleague at Notre Dame, John Howard Yoder, is associated with distrust of ethical approaches that appeal to commonly knowable and broadly shared values.[19] "Practical moral reasoning," he says "must always be expected to be at some point subversive. Any approach which trusts the common wisdom enough to make specifically subversive decisions unthinkable has thereby forfeited its claim to be adequate." I agree with that. But it does not directly address the point of the commonly knowable. Indeed, if subversive reasoning and conclusions were *totally* unsharable, they would be simply anarchical. Yoder argues that the search for a public moral language "is motivated . . . by embarrassment about particularity." When we focus on the generalizability of ethical demands, we forget that "we confess as Lord and Christ the man Jesus." To abstract from this particularity to get at the general is a denial of faith.

Stanley Hauerwas has continued Yoder's theme.[20] The renovation of moral theology called for by Vatican II has not occurred because of a lack of appreciation for the narrative character of Christian moral reflection. Rather the new "liberal" moral theologians continue to use the basic natural-law methodology of Neo-Scholasticism but with the language of human experience. This methodology of "universalistic laws," desires, tendencies fails to take as fundamental the community and thus its narrative context. This failure leads to a failure in pastoral practice.

Hauerwas then points out the direction of a true Christian ethic. Narratives are essential for our understanding of God, ourselves and the world. The central claim of Christian ethics is that we know ourselves truthfully only when we know ourselves in relation to God. Our participation in God's life is a participation in the history He creates, His story. And that story is particularistic, that is, it deals with Israel, Jesus and the ingathering of disciples we name the Church. "Christian ethics is, therefore, not an ethic based on universal presuppositions that can be known separate from these particular peoples' tradition." Rather, it is "the discipline that attempts to remind us of the kind of skills, linguistic, conceptual and practical that are necessary to be such a people." (I pause parenthetically to wonder how Christianity, in Hauerwas' reading, could ever have been preached to the Gentiles.)

How does this perspective affect practical problem-solving? Hauerwas insists that its effect should be to direct our attention away from "dilemma ethics." The first question in pastoral care is not "What should I do?" but "What should I be?" Furthermore, this perspective helps to make the Church's stance about marriage and divorce more intelligible in itself. This stand as absolute is not intelligible in itself. It must be seen as an aid to help us live more nearly faithful to the story that forms the Christian community. It functions as a reminder of what kind of "virtues are necessary to sustain a Christian people to carry on the story of God." Christian ethics, understood in this narrative way, is deeply antithetical to the natural-law method of Catholic moral theology. It does not pretend to be based on a universally valid stand applicable to all persons irrespective of their story. In this sense it may be called sectarian.

I agree with many of Hauerwas' emphases. But there is one that I cannot accept: Hauerwas' contrast between an ethic built on a particular narrative and one of "universalistic laws." This is also explicit in Yoder's work. That cuts reality too sharply. If one asserts that certain basic obligations or duties apply across the board to persons as persons, that is not an indication, as Hauerwas maintains, that one has failed to take community and its narrative context as fundamental.

Nor is it, as Yoder asserts, "motivated . . . by embarrassment about particularity." It is to argue something about the human condition that we think is generally knowable if our story is to include, for example, Romans 1.

The root of the dichotomy Hauerwas and Yoder assert between narrative and "universalizing" morality is the particularizing and exclusive character they give the story—as if the Incarnate Word of God had nothing to do with or to say about those persons who never lived that particular story. Thus I would guess—possibly erroneously—that Hauerwas' phrase "faithfulness to this man as a guide," which he correctly says is "morally central to Christian ethics," means that others simply cannot share *any* of the insights and judgments such faithfulness generates. Otherwise, why the overstated contrast between narrative and "universalizing" tendencies and the attack on the latter? I question that. There is no contradiction between being countercultural and yet culturally intelligible. Similarly, when Yoder sees a focus on generalizability as forgetting that "we confess as Lord and Christ the man Jesus," he is giving this confession a practical ethical content unavailable to those outside the confession.

Whatever the case, this exclusive dichotomizing is not the Catholic reading and living of the story; and Yoder's suspicions about dichotomies should have made him suspicious here. Roger Shinn makes this point very well. He notes that the ethical awareness given to Christians in Christ "meets some similar intimations or signs of confirmation in wider human experience." Christians believe, Shinn writes, that the Logos made flesh in Christ is the identical Logos through which the world was created. He concludes: "They [Christians] do not expect the Christian faith and insight to be confirmed by unanimous agreement of all people, even all decent and idealistic people. But they do expect the fundamental Christian motifs to have some persuasiveness in general experience."[21] It is this "some persuasiveness in general experience" that can found confidence in the possibility of public moral discourse, a possibility Hauerwas and Yoder distrust, and eventually disdain.

Therefore, when I dream of Christian ethics in the year 2000, I dream of one that will continue to maintain its confidence that it can communicate intelligibly to a broader (than the Church) society.

3. SUBSIDIARITY

The term "subsidiarity" was first used, to the best of my knowledge, by Pius XI in *Quadragesimo anno*. He stated:

> Just as it is gravely wrong to take from individuals what they can accomplish by their own initiative and industry and give it to the community, so also it is an injustice and at the same time a grave evil and disturbance of right order to assign to a greater and higher association what lesser and subordinate organizations can do.[22]

Clearly Pius XI was speaking of subsidiarity within the context of the legitimate but limited role of the state.

When I use the term of moral theology, I am obviously using it in an analogous sense. That sense refers above all to development of moral policy and decision-making. It suggests that higher, more centralized authority should not assume all responsibilities in these areas and thus relieve local authorities (e.g., national episcopal conferences) or individuals of their proper responsibilities.

This point can be made in any number of ways. I will use the distinction between principle and application to illumine it.

Some popes (Pius XI, Pius XII, John XXIII) spoke in rather sweeping terms about the Church's teaching competence, extending it quite indiscriminately to the whole moral law *including applications.*

A rather remarkably different approach begins to appear with Vatican II. The bishops provide guidelines for the interpretation of the *Pastoral Constitution on the Church in the Modern World.* They state that "in Part II (where special urgent moral problems are treated) the subject matter which is viewed in the light of doctrinal principles is made up of diverse elements. Some elements have a permanent value; others, only a transitory one . . . Interpreters must bear in mind—especially in Part II—the changeable circumstances which the subject matter, by its very nature, involves."[23]

The Council further noted that "it happens rather frequently, *and legitimately so,* that with equal sincerity some of the faithful will disagree with others on a given matter."[24] This legitimate pluralism is to be expected if even official teachers do not have all the answers, a point explicitly made by the Council where it stated:

> The Church, as guardian of the deposit of God's word, draws religious and moral principles from it, but it does not always have a ready answer to particular questions, wishing to combine the light of revelation with universal experiences so that illumination can be forthcoming on the direction which humanity has recently begun to take.[25]

This *nouvelle modestie* did not escape the notice of the American bishops. In *The Challenge of Peace* they explicitly stress the difference between universal moral principles and their applications.

> We stress here at the beginning that not every statement in this letter has the same moral authority. At times we reassert universally binding moral principles (e.g., noncombatant immunity and proportionality). At still other times we reaffirm statements of recent popes and the teaching of Vatican II. Again, at other times we apply moral principles to specific cases.[26]

The bishops note that where applications are concerned "prudential judgments are involved based on specific circumstances which can change or which can be interpreted differently by people of good will." They conclude that their judgments of application should be taken seriously but are "not binding in conscience."

Applications of moral principle demand special expertise and knowledge of circumstances, therefore they should be entrusted above all to those who have such knowledge and expertise. When a higher authority (whether it be the Congregation for the Doctrine of the Faith, a local bishop, a pastor) attempts to assume this role, we have a violation of subsidiarity. One of the results of this is that the Church is deprived of the richness of experience and thought some of its members can contribute. Another is the promotion of a kind of moral infantilism or dependency.

It was in this spirit that Vatican II issued the summons to lay people that I cited in Chapter One:

> Laymen should also know that it is generally the function of their well-formed Christian conscience to see that the divine law is inscribed in the life of the earthly city. From priests they may look for spiritual light and nourishment. Let the layman not imagine that his pastors are always such experts that to every problem which arises, however complicated, they can readily give him a concrete solution, or even that such is their mission. Rather, enlightened by Christian wisdom and giving close attention to the teaching authority of the Church, let the layman take on his own distinctive role.[27]

I confess that this is one of my favorite conciliar texts, not because it lightens the workload of moral theologians, but because it summarizes and symbolizes so many other things—theological things—the Council was striving to do. High on the list of these things was toppling the pyramidal notion of the Church wherein truth descends uniquely from above in a kind of mysterious paternalistic flow.

In this citation I believe we can legitimately read two assertions. First, conscience cannot be utterly preprogrammed. Second, laypeople have special competencies, and therefore special responsibilities. Physicians, for example, by virtue of their special expertise, should reflect on and pray over the moral and specifically Christian dimensions of their vocation and bring the fruits of their reflection to the entire Church. If they do not, where do we get such insights? This is the burden of the phrase "distinctive role." It is an example of what I mean by subsidiarity in moral theology.

4. PERSONALISM

I use this term in a specific sense and in a quite restrictive context. The context is the determination of the morally right and morally wrong of human actions. The specific sense is that it is the human person in all facets and dimensions that is the criterion of this moral rightfulness and wrongfulness. That formulation is meant to contrast with an approach that employs an isolated dimension of the human person as criterion, as I noted in Chapter One.

I do not think it is unfair to say that some earlier Catholic approaches fell into this trap. John Courtney Murray referred to this as the "biologist interpretation" and argued that it confused the "primordial," in a biological sense, with the natural.[28] Thus we find Franciscus Hürth, S.J., an influential advisor to Pius XI and Pius XII, laying heavy stress on biological facticity. "The will of nature" he says, "was inscribed in the organs and their functions." He concluded: "Man only has disposal of the use of his organs and faculties with respect to the end which the Creator, in His formation of them, has intended. This end for man, then, is both the biological law and the moral law, such that the latter obliges him to live according to the biological law."[29] For this reason, the late John C. Ford, S.J., and Gerald Kelly, S.J., wrote in 1963: "One cannot exaggerate the importance attached to the physical integrity of the act itself both in papal documents and in Catholic theology generally."[30]

I mention this personalism as a component of my dream because, while it is explicitly honored in some recent official documents (e.g., *Donum vitae*, the C.D.F.'s document on reproductive technologies), many of us believe that an older biologism reappears when (indeed, whenever) there is question of specific conclusions and applications.

5. MODESTY AND TENTATIVENESS

In Rahner's dream, the pope is imaged as saying:

> The ordinary magisterium of the pope in authentic doctrinal deci-
> sions at least in the past and up to very recent times was often
> involved in error and, on the other hand, Rome was accustomed
> to put forward and insist on such decisions as if there could be no
> doubt about their ultimate correctness and as if any further dis-
> cussion of them was unbecoming for a Catholic theologian.[31]

This is not just the *stylus curiae*. It seems to be a perennial
temptation of those to whom there attaches both jurisdictional and
teaching authority. There is the seemingly irresistible penchant to pre-
scribe and proscribe *urbi et orbi* with utter certainty and forever. It is
as if teaching would not be taken seriously unless it is proposed for all
ages.

Thus, for example, in the C.D.F.'s *Inter insigniores* (1976) the
norm of not ordaining women to the priesthood is said to be observed
"because it is considered to conform to God's plan for his church."[32]
That is a theological lock-in. It is quite possible, I believe, to oppose
ordination of women (I hasten to say that I do not) for reasons and
with analyses other than that.

We are all aware of the genuine complexity of many human
moral problems. My dream, therefore, is that acknowledgement of this
will take the form of appropriate modesty and tentativeness in authentic Church teaching as well as in theological reflection.

6. ECUMENICAL

As I noted in Chapter One, Vatican II acknowledged the ecclesial reality of other Christian churches, the presence of the Spirit to
their members, and the grace-inspired character of their lives. It en-
couraged ecumenical dialogue and work, and relaxed its discipline on
common worship. Pointedly it stated:

> Nor should we forget that whatever is wrought by the grace of
> the Holy Spirit in the hearts of our separated brethren can con-
> tribute to our own edification.[33]

The Council took this with utter seriousness and stated:

> In fidelity to conscience, Christians are joined with the rest of
> men in the search for truth, and for the genuine solution to the
> numerous problems which arise in the life of individuals and
> from social relationships. [34]

In these our times one would think that ecumenism in moral discourse would be a given. Yet let me share a sneaking suspicion. It is this: ecumenical procedure is honored *except where the Holy See has taken an authoritative position in the past.* In those areas—and we all know what they are—consultants are chosen only if and because they agree with past formulations. Others, even and especially Catholics, are positively excluded. That this is a threat to ecumenical dialogue is clear. It is also clear that threats to such dialogue are threats to the Church's credibility as well as its growth in understanding and witness.

That is why I dream of a moral theology by the year 2000 that is truly ecumenical.

7. INDUCTIVE IN METHOD

This follows from the personalism I noted in n. 4. Whether our actions or policies are supportive of persons or detrimental to them cannot be deduced from general principles. It takes time and experience. And the Church must have the patience to provide for this maturation process. In the decades prior to Vatican II a much more deductive approach was in evidence.

This is clear in the gradual transformation of social teaching in the Church. As the Jesuit editors of *Civiltà cattolica* point out, this teaching evolved through stages.[35] *Rerum novarum* represents the first stage. It was dominated by "Christian philosophy" and a "rigidly deductive" method. This had two shortcomings. First, it left no room for the relevance of the sciences (economics, sociology, political science). Second, and as a consequence, doctrinal elaboration was seen as an exclusively hierarchical task, lay persons being merely "faithful executors."

The second stage covers the pontificates of Pius XI and Pius XII and may be called the stage of "social doctrine." *Quadragesimo anno* used this term for the first time. It referred to an organic corpus of universal principles still rigidly deduced from social ethics. However there is greater emphasis on the historical moment and applications of principles to practice, hence the beginnings of a re-evaluation of the place of lay persons in the process.

The third stage began with John XXIII. John moved from the deductive to the inductive method, his point of departure being the "historical moment," to be viewed in light of the gospel. This led to a complete reevaluation of the place of lay persons vis-à-vis social teaching, a reevaluation completed by Vatican II. Lay persons do not simply apply the Church's social teaching; they must share in its very construction.

This is an interesting development. One thing seems clear: a similar development has not occurred in all areas of Catholic moral theology—for instance, familial and sexual morality. If a clearly deductive method, one that left little room for the sciences and lay experience, prevailed in the elaboration of social teaching, it is reasonable to think that the same thing occurred in familial and sexual morality. And if this social method has evolved since John XXIII, it is reasonable to think that the same thing ought to happen in all areas of Church teaching. But, as of now, it has not and therefore remains part of my dream.

8. PLURALISTIC

There is something in the Catholic spirit that seems to feel the need for absolute agreement and conformity, even to the most detailed applications of moral principles. I think I know what that "something" is. It is a past authoritative teaching and practice that thought it possible to dot every "i" and cross every "t" on very detailed matters and imposed such certainties in a quite forceful and vigorous way. Public questioning of such conclusions was simply out of the question. Such imposed uniformity created expectations about Catholic unity that were intolerant of pluralism. There is still a rather noisy but tiny minority that believes that we cannot disagree about, for example, *in vitro* fertilization between husband and wife, or about withdrawing artificial nutrition and hydration from persistently vegetative patients without forfeiting our basic Catholic unity.

In the United States these attitudes are concretely symbolized in the case of Charles Curran. Curran has repeatedly stated that his differences with authoritative pronouncements have three characteristics: 1. They concern matters remote from the core of the faith. 2. They are matters heavily dependent on support from human reason. 3. They are involved in such complexity and specificity that logically we cannot claim absolute certitude in their regard.[36]

I do not want to rehearse this issue here. Nor do I want to *promote* pluralism. Pluralism in these matters is a fact, not dominantly a value. But it is a fact that we should come to expect and peacefully accept, especially in a Church second to none in its reliance on the presence of the Spirit to its members.

In the decade ahead moral problems are only going to get more complicated and severe. That is why I dream of a moral theology that can live humbly, happily and holily amidst a degree of pluralism, indeed can welcome it as the *sine qua non* of growth in understanding.

9. ASPIRATIONAL

Moral theology will continue to be concerned with practical problems and problem-solving. And it should be. Rightfulness and wrongfulness of conduct, while secondary, remains important. But a too exclusive concern with it can diminish other extremely important aspects of morality.

To make this point let me distinguish between an ethics of minimal duty and an ethics of aspiration. The former is by and large minimalist, concerned with the negative, with uniform standards and legislative sanctions. Of it we may say what John Courtney Murray stated of the notion of natural law:

> It does not show the individual the way to sainthood, but only to manhood. It does not promise to transform society into the City of God on earth, but only to prescribe, for the purpose of law and social custom, that minimum of morality which must be observed by the members of a society, if the social environment is to be human and habitable.[37]

If I read the "signs of the times" correctly, there are very many people who, while by no means denying the importance of the "human and habitable," want more. They want an ethics of aspiration—one that is demanding, positive, aesthetic, centered on who they might become. We see this in medicine as physicians grow bored and restive with the commercialization of their profession. "Life must have more to offer than that," one said to me. We see it in business people who are sick and tired of a climate that makes profit not only a requirement but an obsession, that forgets that there are stakeholders other than stockholders. We see it in educators, attorneys, and even ministers who feel that a merely functional or sacramental description of their challenges diminishes them.

In a word, then, the moral theology of the year 2000 will, I hope, pay much more attention to "the 3 a.m. questions," the types of concerns we have as we hover between sleep and wakefulness. These are not the neon quandaries of ethics anthologies nor the details of tomorrow's schedule. They are questions of guilt, personal integrity, of what is my life becoming, of God in my life, of genuine love, of mortality. They are aspirational questions. They are much more invitational than obligational.

10. SPECIALIST

Here I can be mercifully brief. The day of the omnicompetent moral theologian is gone. Every aspect of life has its specialists. People spend professional lifetimes becoming experts in the oddest variety of specialties: snail darters, the duodenum, rocketry, river-bed composition, child-bearing in Tibet, computer software, etc. McNeil-Lehrer regularly parade them before us.

My single and unsensational point, already noted in Chapter 1, is that if moral theology in the year 2000 is to be truly influential and a leaven for contemporary life, it must have thoroughly trained specialists who can mingle as equals in a world of specialists. Our theology will not influence medicine unless our theologians are medically knowledgeable and sophisticated. Much the same is true of law, business and economics and other areas of human life.

In summary, then, I dream of a moral theology that is:

1. Christocentric and anchored in charity (vs. one onesidedly philosophical).

2. Universalizing in its appeal (vs. one narrowly sectarian).

3. With appropriate subsidiarity (vs. overcentralization).

4. Personalistic (vs. excessively biologistic).

5. Modest and tentative (vs. "infallibilistic").

6. Ecumenical (vs. exclusively parochial and Roman).

7. Inductive (vs. abstractly deductive in method).

8. Pluralistic (vs. a universal conformism).

9. Aspirational (vs. minimalistic).

10. Specialistic (vs. omnicompetent).

What will it take to get such a theology? The very question supposes that we are not there yet, indeed are far from it. I have no solutions-by-microwave. But one point returns persistently in my dream. It is the fact that in a world church where changes are so dramatic and frequent, an ecumenical council every one hundred years is, well, quite literally medieval. What councils meeting every ten years (I propose it here) might do to see that our structures truly reflect a world church is the matter of another dream. But I have no doubt that moral theology would be profoundly affected.

In the meantime, the best that our theologians can do is to toil humbly and courageously as if my reverie were a reality. In doing so they will hurry the day when it will be.

CHAPTER 3

Self-Assessment
and Self-Indictment

It is not altogether otiose to try to focus on one's own development. I say "not altogether" because if the focus is clear, it will reveal short-comings that others may avoid. In this spirit, this very brief chapter represents a kind of theological self-autopsy that aims at disclosing systemic shifts, major pathologies, and, so to speak, unaffected organs. Perspective is somewhat elusive here because the body is still warm and twitching.

That being said, I think it above all important to underline the idea that one's teaching and writing reflect inescapably the historical context in which one lived. That is true in my case, tangibly so. There are three discernible—at least to me—contexts that have framed my concerns, stamped my consciousness, limited my questions, and colored my analyses. To them in a moment.

I was trained in and for some years taught a moral theology with deep roots in what is now called a "classicist mentality." This mentality conceives culture normatively and abstractly and represents a certain disengagement from the forces shaping the contemporary world. It seeks and easily finds certainties and views departure from them as unfaithfulness, pluralism as bordering on anarchy. It is easy, and at some point terribly wrong and unfair, to caricature here. And no careful scholar will do so. Nonetheless it remains true that the ecclesiological and moral theological perspectives introduced by Vatican II have led to a consciousness that is much more historically oriented.

This has meant a new willingness to re-examine some traditional formulations that were authoritatively proposed to the Catholic community. The task of doing this is far from easy and, obviously, not always successful. There are some who have resisted such a re-examination and have remained personally, if not interpersonally and ecclesially, comfortable with a relatively traditional interpretative framework and vocabulary. There are others who have felt no need to do so because they have never been thoroughly trained in the "traditional Catholic categories." I fit somewhere in between. Trained in the classicist mentality, I have become conscious of both its strengths and its weaknesses—and the need to correct or modify the latter. This "in- betweenness" explains the three discernible contexts mentioned above: prior to Vatican II, Vatican II, the Encyclical *Humanae vitae* and after.

PRIOR TO VATICAN II

For many decades, even centuries, prior to Vatican II (1962-1965) Catholic moral theology conceived its chief task as being the training of priests to hear confessions. Within the sacramental perspectives of the times, the confessor was viewed as exercising a fourfold office: father, teacher, judge, physician. Specially necessary to effective ministry were charity (of a father), knowledge (of a teacher and judge), prudence (of a physician). I believe we did a very creditable job of preparing prudent and compassionate ministers.

The knowledge required of the confessor included many things, but above all knowledge of God's law *as proposed by the Church*, i.e., the Church's magisterium. At this period of time, for many understandable sociological reasons, the Church's magisterium was understood in a highly authoritarian and paternalistic way. One did not question ordinary noninfallible teaching. Dissent was virtually unknown and would certainly have been extremely risky.

Of this tendency, the great French historian of dogma, Yves Congar, noted that it reached its zenith under Pius XII (*Humani generis,* 1950). Pius stated: 1. The ordinary magisterium of the Pope requires total obedience. 2. The (or a) role of theologians is to justify the declarations of the magisterium.[1]

These were the perspectives, this the cultural context in which we worked. We saw no possibility that the Church would, or even could, change her position on moral matters where it had taken an authoritative stance (e.g., contraception). As I look over the texts I published for students at this time and the articles I wrote, they simply *supposed* the moral validity of the positions taken, *defended* them, and tried to *apply* them prudently and compassionately. Not questioning the conclusions, we would scarcely question the underlying principles. The best American proponents of Catholic moral theology in this era were John C. Ford and Gerald Kelly. They were rightly revered for their insights, charity, and common sense. It is understandable, then, why Daniel Callahan produced shock waves in 1964, as I noted in Chapter 1, when he described these two men as "loyal civil servants" and "faithful party workers" and their work as "years behind the (theological) revolution now in progress."[2] But that is the way things were in the American moral theological world. Moral theology had the following characteristics: casuistic, unecumenical, unbiblical, "domestic" in its concerns (social morality being relegated to the periphery), centrally controlled, natural law oriented, and sin-centered. I escaped such pervasive influences first not at all, then only gradually and more or less.

VATICAN II

What Vatican II did to and for moral theology is simply incalculable. It flip-flopped every one of the above characteristics. For instance, its ecumenical thrust opened the world of Catholic moral theology beyond the Catholic "club." It was about this time that Catholics began to join the Society of Christian Ethics. I date my friendship with prominent non-Catholic scholars to these years: Paul Ramsey, James Gustafson, Arthur Dyck, Edward LeRoy Long, Jr., Frederick Carney, Roger Shinn, William May, etc. Ecumenism of procedure, explicitly urged by the Council, was bound to influence methods and outcomes.

At this time, too, the broader themes of Christian aspiration and living, biblically inspired, began to replace an earlier emphasis on natural law, casuistry, one-sided sin-centeredness. The social encyclicals of John XXIII and Paul VI began to transform the moral consciousness of the Catholic moral theological community from an earlier overconcern with family and sexual concerns.

This was the period, then, when a great many things came unstuck. It is no coincidence that it was also the period of "The Great Debate" on contraception in the Catholic community. In September, 1963 a series of conferences began on the problem of population at the University of Notre Dame. They concluded in 1965. They brought together a host of well-known Catholics: John L. Thomas, Gregory Baum, Robert Johann, Andrew Greeley, Bernard Cooke, Philip Scharper, George N. Shuster, Bernard Häring, John A. O'Brien, Raymond

Potvin, William D'Antonio, David Burrell, Louis Dupré, Walter Imbiorski, James O'Gara, to name but a few. I was unaccountably included in the group. The Catholic teaching on contraception was the centerpiece. And its intellectual foundations did not fare well over the three-year period.

These meetings were symbolic of what I call "The Great Debate," great because it involved so much more than the single issue of contraception. It involved the meaning of authoritative teaching and the magisterium, the notion of the Church, the place of the lay voice in the formation of moral conviction in the Church, the understanding of moral norms, the relation of reason and morality, the significance of non-Catholic witness and conviction. Still, during these meetings I maintained my traditional position against any form of contraception.

During 1963-1966, the so-called Papal Birth Control Commission held its hearings. During that period I had extensive conversations with Josef Fuchs, a member of that commission. I had and have the greatest respect for Fuchs. He was my professor during doctoral studies in the mid-50s and is one of the finest theologians in the Church. Over a three-year period, Fuchs and I shared our difficulties on this question and I found myself gradually moving with him through a state of doubt to ultimate conviction that the Church's position could be and had to be reformulated. As I look back on this period it is clear to me that I needed someone of Fuchs' stature and undoubted loyalty to show me the possibility of change without unacceptable abandonment of essentials of "the Catholic idea." Without my explicitly adverting to it, what was really changing were basic notions of ecclesiology and eventually moral methodology. These notions had been set in motion by Vatican II, especially by its adoption of a concentric rather than pyramidal model of the Church and its heavy emphasis on the human person as central to moral reflection. This shift would clearly affect the notion and mode of exercise of authority in the Church, the articulation of moral conviction, the self-concept of the theologian, the types of sources thought relevant, etc.

THE ENCYCLICAL *HUMANAE VITAE* AND AFTER

It may be somewhat difficult for non-Catholics to realize what an enormous event this was in the Catholic Church. Catholic priests had been telling people for decades that contraception is seriously sinful and involved their eternal salvation. Could the Church, which claimed the guidance of the Holy Spirit in its teachings, be wrong on a thing like this? If so, would her directives be taken seriously in the future? Against the recommendation of a majority of advisors, Paul VI issued *Humanae vitae* in 1968. This put many of us on the spot, both on the moral issue itself, but above all on the ecclesiological implications. Was dissent from that type of affirmation tolerable, justifiable? On what grounds? What did Vatican II mean by "religious submission of mind and will" owed to the Supreme Pontiff when he issued statements like this? How should the Church go about facing moral problems of this type? *Humanae vitae* freed us to wrestle with questions like that. The issues were difficult and delicate and the stakes high. I forged my own response in the December (1968) issue of *Theological Studies* and ended up in Boston's Lahey Clinic for my efforts.

It was this happening more than any other that began to create divisions in the post-conciliar Church. *Humanae vitae* became the litmus test of Catholic loyalty, and dissenting scholars began to be described as "deviant," "disloyal" and a host of other almost repeatable things.

What at first appeared to many as a tragedy of huge proportions and a leapfrog backwards to preconciliar notions of the Church and ecclesial authority gradually took on a different look. The fact that we were forced to take personal positions on this single moral issue allowed us to see many other things in a much more explicit way, things that had remained in a kind of transitional haze since the Council.

It was at this time that I realized more clearly than ever the dependence of the magisterium on the theological work, and therefore the absolutely essential *critical* role of the theology. This opened many other doors. For instance, it became clear to me that the proper response to authoritative teaching is not precisely obedience (we obey orders, not teachers), but a docile personal attempt to assimilate the teaching. If that attempt fails—as it has for so many—then the personal reflections of those who have so failed must be seen as a source of new reflection on the matter. That leads to several interesting convictions: 1. that Church teaching is a processive dialogue, not a once for all *ipse dixit*; 2. that we all have a part to play in the ongoing reappropriation in changing times of the Good News; 3. that dissent, far from being viewed as a threat to authority, must be seen as an ordinary dimension of human learning and growth; 4. that we must be careful to distinguish, with Vatican II, the substance of the Church's concerns from its changing formulations; 5. that intelligent criticism of past authoritative formulations is a form of indispensable theological integrity and ecclesial loyalty, etc. These convictions are hard to come by in a historical religious community that so emphasizes the prerogatives of authority. They may be even harder to maintain and put into practice in contemporary circumstances. But I hope that a hard birth means a long life.

Humanae vitae opens, of course, on a much broader discussion: the very method of founding moral norms. In Catholic circles there were in place some fairly traditional concepts and vocabulary to deal with certain types of evils: "intrinsic evil" and the principle of double effect. This principle builds on the idea that certain effects (evils) cannot be directly done. This very neatly and astutely allows for certain exceptions but puts controls on them. But is this truly analytically satisfying? In 1972, at the Kennedy Institute of Ethics, I grappled with this problem in a paper that eventually was published as the Marquette Lecture "Ambiguity in Moral Choice." My indefatigable friend, Paul Ramsey, charged into my office one day and allowed that "this is a very significant and important book"—which meant that he disagreed with it radically! This led to *Doing Evil to Achieve Good,* an attempt by several commentators—above all Ramsey—to further clarify the discussion on moral norms. I remain convinced that the authors who follow along in this *Denkform* (Peter Knauer, Bruno Schüller, Josef Fuchs, Louis Janssens, Franz Scholz, Charles Curran, James Walter, Edward Vacek, and a host of others, myself included, commonly called "proportionalists") and in the process qualify some traditional Catholic categories are headed in the right direction and have the better of the argument. I also realize that some problems are outstanding.

While the notion of the moral magisterium and the understanding of moral norms have occupied a good deal of my time and effort during the past years, other matters more or less directly affected by these notions have also proved irresistible: the problem of divorce and re-marriage; the bioethical problems of experimentation, genetics, reproductive technology, life-preservation, abortion; the problem of nuclear deterrence; morality and public policy; the problem of homosexuality; the meaning of natural law. One problem overshadows them all: the relation of religious (Christian) belief to concrete areas of human behavior. I think my greatest failing as a moral theologian (others will certainly note many others) has been the failure to explore and make clearer and more persuasive Vatican II's statement: "Faith throws a new light on everything, manifests God's design for man's total vocation, and thus directs the mind to solutions that are fully human." But, as I stated at the outset, the body is still warm and twitching.

CHAPTER 4

How My Mind Has Changed

The title of this chapter will, I am sure, appear presumptuously inflated to a large number of people. It seems to assume that "my mind" is of some relevance and that any change in this mind might be of interest to someone, or even, heaven help us, of importance to anyone. Let me say from the outset that I disown such assumptions. Indeed, it is precisely because I do that I can write on lightheartedly and without accountability, knowing that nothing much stands or falls with the outcome.

Having registered this qualification, I want to suggest that change (implying a *terminus ad quem*) is intelligible only if we know the *terminus a quo* (the starting point). From the standpoint of an American Catholic theologian, that *terminus a quo* was the immigrant Catholic Church, the kind of church still nostalgically memorialized in some of Andrew Greeley's novels. I was raised in that church and some of my deepest religious and theological sensitivities—perhaps especially those I do not thematically recognize—took shape within it. Eugene Kennedy has described this church as follows:

> The unlettered Catholic who came to the United States in the last century fashioned a way of life within the host Protestant culture that was tight, intellectually narrow, and wrapped in an invisible and largely impermeable membrane that resisted social osmosis with the rest of the country. It was also the most successful era of development in the history of the Roman Catholic Church. This Catholic structure defended itself proudly against doctrinal and moral compromise; it was, above all, obedient to the authority which was exercised for generations without any serious challenge by its bishops and clergy and other religious teachers. Immigrant Catholicism .was, in fact, held together by the vigorous churchmen who retained their power over their flocks by exercising it regularly on an infinitely detailed category of behaviors,

ranging from what the faithful could eat on Fridays to what they could think or do in the innermost chambers of their personal lives.[1]

The moral theology that I was taught and that for some years I myself taught reflected the immigrant Catholic community described by Kennedy as well as the ecclesiology that nourished it. It was all too often one-sidedly confession-oriented, magisterium dominated, canon law-related, sin-centered and seminary-controlled, as I noted in Chapter 1.

This is where I started and represents my *terminus a quo.* I want to list ten general areas where I have experienced a change of mind or a shift of perspectives. Interestingly, nearly all these changes pertain to the area of ecclesiology; but they have very significant impacts on moral theology, both its method and its ultimate conclusions. Some of these perspective changes overlap significantly. That is not surprising since all of them, in one way or another, trace back to Vatican II and its ecclesiology. That Council shook up the Catholic Church in much the same radical and vigorous way that the stirrings of freedom and democracy rocked the Eastern Block countries in the last half of 1989. It was bound to affect the way I viewed myself, the Church, the world, and God and therefore the way I did theology.

1. NATURE OF THE CHURCH

It is easy to caricature here and I repent in advance my failures. Still I believe that my early view of the Church was dominantly pyramidal with authority and truth descending from above (pope and bishops) to rank and file believers (the rest of us). Such a model powerfully supports a kind of ecclesiastical gnosticism that exempts the hierarchy from standard forms of scholarly accountability and reduces the theological task to mediating authoritative documents. This ultramontanism peaked during the reign of Pius XII. Thus at that time few of us felt terribly threatened by the highly authoritarian and obediential motifs of *Humani generis.* That is, we thought, just the way things are. Many Catholics experienced little or no discomfort with the pyramidal model of the Church. It seemed natural to them, indeed *juris divini.* In those days triumphalism was not a reproach.

All of this came tumbling down with Vatican II. The theological and pastoral winds that blew freely from 1962 to 1965 led to a notion of church much more concentric than pyramidal. I noted the profound implications of this in Chapter 1.

That such ecclesiological themes have deeply affected my own thinking and theological work should be self-evident. Indeed, the following nine points are simply explications of these basic ecclesiological shifts.

2. IMPORTANCE OF LAY WITNESS

In the years prior to Vatican II, conscience formation by Catholics was one-sidedly paternalistic. The individual would approach a priest, usually in confession, as one prepared to give the answers. The person would detail the facts; the confessor would assess them with a *licet* or *non licet*. This reflected the neat, if artificial, subdivision of the Church into the teaching and learning Church.

Vatican II shattered this easy compartmentalization. It insisted that "it is for God's people as a whole with the help of the Holy Spirit, and especially for pastors and theologians, to listen to the various voices of our day, discerning and interpreting them, and to evaluate them in the light of the divine word . . ." It went on to issue that remarkable summons to lay people to take on their own distinctive role.[2]

I confess that in my early years as a theologian I thought it was my mission to have answers to most complicated problems. Where else would people get answers? The notion that lay people had a distinctive—and indispensable—role to play in the discovery of moral truth was hardly promoted by their designation as "the learning church." I have come to see and value lay experience and reflection and am richer for it.

3. THE LIMITATION OF PAPAL AND EPISCOPAL TEACHING COMPETENCE

Catholics accept the fact that Christ commissioned the Church to teach authoritatively in His name. Even though the manner of executing this commission has varied throughout history, still it is recognized that the duty falls in a special way on the pope and the bishops in union with the pope. The formula used since the Council of Trent to state the reach of this hierarchical competence is *de fide et moribus* (matters concerned with faith and morals). Thus Vatican II stated: "In matters of faith and morals, the bishops speak in the name of Christ and the faithful are to accept their teaching and adhere to it with a religious assent of soul."[3] The vague and sprawling nature of the phrase "faith and morals" fosters the idea that pope and bishops are equally and univocally competent on matters concerned with faith and morals. This would be particularly the case in a church conceived in a highly centralized and authoritarian way. Thus in the encyclical *Magnificate Dominum* Pius XII referred to the power of the Church over the natural law and saw it as covering "its foundation, its interpretation, its application."

It is somewhat difficult to say exactly how my mind has changed here because I think that we are still in the process of an ongoing development. Some years ago Karl Rahner argued that contemporary official formulations of the Church's ordinary teaching competence are unnuanced. Furthermore the American bishops in their pastoral letters on peace and the economy have distinguished between principles and their applications and stated of these latter that they are "not binding in conscience." That is an old-fashioned way of saying that episcopal competence is not the same when the bishops are dealing with applications as it is when they propose general principles. This is significant when we remember that most of the controversial moral questions (e.g., contraception) are matters of application of more general principles.

Just how we should state this hierarchical competence is not altogether clear. I think it is clear that Pius XII had an overexpansive notion of his competence built on the neoscholastic ecclesiology of his time. I do not mean that pastors of the Church should not offer guidance on the moral rightness or wrongness of human activity. Not at all. I mean two things. First, the pope and bishops simply must consult those who are truly competent. Authority is not competence. Second, even after such consultation they must show appropriate caution and modesty. For horizontal activity in this world does not belong to the Church's competence in the same way the deposit of faith does. Only with the ecclesiological moves made by Vatican II was I prepared to see this. Furthermore, I believe that a significant number of Roman curialists still do not share this view.

4. ECUMENISM IN THE SEARCH FOR MORAL TRUTH

Prior to Vatican II serious ecumenism was in the quite lonely hands of a small band of theological pioneers. Official attitudes and practices were structured by the conviction that non-Catholic Christians were the adversaries of our central religious and moral tenets. Canon 1399,4 of the old code was the symbol of this. It forbade the reading of books authored by Protestants that expressly treated of religious themes. The very separation of non-Catholics from the one true Church constituted a presumption against the reliability of their religious and moral thought. I think it accurate to describe my preconciliar attitude toward the work of my non-Catholic peers as one of condescending tolerance, a civil nod that said "Yes, but we have the last word."

Vatican II changed all that. Not only did it recognize the ecclesial reality of other Christian churches, but it stated explicitly that "whatever is wrought by the grace of the Holy Spirit in the hearts of our separated brethren can contribute to our own edification." In the field of moral theology it is no exaggeration to say that many of us learn more from our non-Catholic colleagues than we do from some Catholic theologians. The perspectives of the forties and fifties that shaped many of us strike us now as incredibly defensive and parochial. At that time to think of the Lambeth Conference as a possible source of enlightenment appeared theologically ridiculous. Now it appears required.

5. THE PLACE OF DISSENT

In preconciliar decades, disagreement with authoritatively proposed moral conclusions was virtually unheard of and would have been hugely dangerous for theologians. Yves Congar, O.P., has noted that the ordinary magisterium reached a kind of high watermark of one-sidedness in the pontificate of Pius XII as noted in Chapter 3. The pope went so far as to state that once he had expressed his judgment on a point previously controversial, "there can no longer be any question of free discussion among theologians." In that atmosphere a dissenting theologian was a doomed one.

At the practical level what changed many of us, and certainly me, was the encyclical *Humanae vitae* (1968) on birth regulation, as I noted in Chapter 3. Perhaps more important than the issue itself of birth regulation are the implications of this massive dissent. It suggested that the magisterium could be inaccurate even on an important moral question. It meant that "the light of the Holy Spirit, which is given in a particular way to the pastors of the Church" (*Humanae vitae*) does not guarantee lack of error or replace human analysis. It meant that the pope can choose the wrong advisors. It meant that a preoccupation with authority can itself lead to false steps. It meant that the Church must be willing to examine its past formulations in an open and critical way, for there can be deficiencies "even in the formulation of doctrine" as Vatican II put it. It meant that honest theological input is called for both before *and after* official statements. All this means, of course, that respectful dissent should be viewed not as a disloyal challenge to authority but as a necessary and valuable component of our growth in understanding. The *Humanae vitae* happening opened my eyes to my critical responsibilities as a theologian. I am comfortable with this even though the present policies of the Holy See are attempting—misguidedly, I believe—to dismantle the theological foundations of this comfort.

6. THE CHANGEABLE AND UNCHANGEABLE IN THE CHURCH

This is very closely connected to the previous point. Let me put it this way. The Catholic Church has endured for two millennia notwithstanding some quite gaping holes in the bark of Peter. It is Catholic belief that it will, because of God's provident presence to it, endure to the end of time. It is easy to promote the idea that because the Church will endure, so ought everything in and about it. This is particularly true in a community that sees itself uniquely commissioned to guard the deposit of faith, even to the point of infallibly proclaiming it. Thus it happens that we come to regard as unchangeable what is actually changeable. In doing so we provide powerful theological and emotional supports for institutional inertia.

There are many examples of this. One is the official teaching on contraception. The pope has connected this matter with abiding doctrinal truths in a way that is theologically unjustifiable. The Cologne Declaration of German theologians underscored this. Another example is the ordination of women. Official appeals to "God's plan" and "the will of Christ" try to transform the changeable into the unchangeable. I confess that prior to Vatican II I would have viewed the ordination of women as impossible, an unchangeable exclusion. Not so now. I see it as not only possible but desirable and inevitable. Two influences are largely responsible for this move. The first is the theology of Karl Rahner who showed so often and so convincingly that what we once viewed as unchangeable really is not. The second is the privilege of having experienced personally the ministry of women. This has had the effect of dissolving emotional obstacles that were far more formidable than any theological analysis anyway.

I would conclude, then, that by changing my attitudes on several deeply ingrained matters (e.g., contraception, ordination of women), I have uncovered a remarkably unthreatening attitude toward the changeable and unchangeable in the Church in general.

7. CERTAINTY AND UNCERTAINTY

There has existed in the Catholic Church, especially in the one hundred years prior to Vatican II, the belief that we could achieve clarity and certainty in most moral matters and that at a very detailed level. The pronouncements of the Holy See both generated and reinforced this belief. I suppose that a Church that sees itself commissioned to teach authoritatively on moral questions and that lays claim to a special guidance of the Holy Spirit in the process might find it uncomfortable (at least) to say "I don't know." When I look over the book-size notes I drew up for my students on justice, sexuality, cooperation, the sacraments, etc., I blush at the extent to which I shared this discomfort.

Call it wisdom, call it age, call it laziness—or a dash of all three–at any rate the old compulsion to be certain has yielded to an unembarrassed modesty about many details of human life. Unlike some of my cantankerous and crusading co-religionists on the right, I am now quite relaxed in admitting with Vatican II that "the Church guards the heritage of God's Word and draws from it religious and moral principles, without always having at hand the solution to particular problems." But, of course!

8. THE NATURE OF EFFECTIVE TEACHING IN THE CHURCH

There will always be a need for clarity of thought and expression as the Church guards and promotes its inheritance. I do not mean to suggest otherwise. But clarity of thought and expression does not exhaust the notion of effective teaching. There is the strong temptation to identify these two in a community where "jurisdictional and teaching authority reside in the same persons." Thus, if I have heard the following sentence once, I have heard it a thousand times: "The teaching of the Church is clear." Clear, yes. Effective? Persuasive? Compelling? Meaningful? Those are different questions and questions whose importance some church leaders minimize or fail even to recognize. Earlier in my theological life I did too.

When teaching is viewed from the perspective of the taught (rather than from the authority of the teacher), it is much more a matter of having one's eyes opened to dimensions of reality previously opaque. That is why I entitle this volume *Corrective Vision*. It is a personal and liberating appropriation, not dominantly submission to an authority. There are many ways of opening eyes other than throwing encyclicals at problems. Witness is surely one of them. We have been educated enormously in the faith by the Jesuit martyrs of El Salvador. Perhaps that is why the Church treasures its martyrs. It knows that they are irreplaceable teachers. They say things textbooks cannot say. In this respect John Paul II is most effective as a teacher through his symbolic acts and liturgies and least effective when he explicitly sets out to teach. For this reason it is paradoxically true to say that on his first visit to the United States John Paul II taught very much but really very little. Somewhat similarly, the Catholic Church will remain a muted prophet if the witness of its own internal life speaks louder than its words, for example, in the area of fairness and human rights.

9. THE IMPERATIVE OF HONESTY

The late distinguished exegete John L. McKenzie once noted that the Catholic Church is never further from Christlikeness and the Gospel than when it exercises its magisterium. Because McKenzie has not always conquered dyspepsia, it is easy and convenient to write off such a blast as the grousing and pouting of a habitual malcontent. That would be a mistake. McKenzie is on to something important. That something is but an extension of my previous point; but it is so important that it deserves to be signalized on its own.

McKenzie's immediate concern was what he regarded (rightly in my view) as the injustice of the procedures against Charles Curran. But the matter is much larger than that. It is a question of honesty in magisterial procedures. I do not believe it is the cynicism of advancing age that emboldens me to note this. I think it is genuine love of the Church.

The concern can be stated by a gathering of questions. Why is it that Rome generally consults only those who support its pretaken position? Why does Rome appoint as bishops only those who have never publicly questioned *Humanae vitae*, the celibacy of priests and the ordination of women? Why does a bishop speak on the ordination of women only after retirement? Why are Vatican documents composed in secrecy? Why does the Holy See not at least review its formulations on certain questions that it knows were met with massive dissent and non-reception? And on and on. Such questions spring from the coercive atmosphere established by the Holy See in the past decade. They have to do with basic honesty on the part of the teaching office, and ultimately its credibility. In my earlier years I would have thought that love of the Church translates into a benign silence on such issues. Now silence appears to me as betrayal.

10. THE DYNAMIC NATURE OF FAITH

Because God's great culminating intervention in Jesus must be passed from generation to generation, there is a great temptation to identify faith with adherence to the credal statements that aid such transmission. This is especially true in the Western world where reflection on the faith was for centuries eagerly hosted by universities. The Reformation understandably deepened the emphasis on propositional orthodoxy and thus contributed significantly to a one-sided view of faith that has endured even into the present, and especially in the coercive atmosphere of the present.

Actually faith is a response of the whole person. It is not something that one has once and for all—like a book on a shelf, a pearl in a drawer, a diploma on the wall, or a license in a wallet. It cannot be identified with a practice, a statement or a structure. It is mysteriously both God's gift and our responsibility. We must, as it were, recover and nourish it on a daily basis in spite of our personal sins and stupidities, and in the face of the world's arrogant self-sufficiency. Such a task is much more daunting and frightening than propositional purity. It is the continuing personal appropriation of God's self-communication.

I find it ironic that the most radical change of my mind over the years has been a keener grasp of its own inadequacy when dealing with ultimacy.

CHAPTER 5

Discernment in Ethics: What Does It Mean?

"Discernment" is a word not familiar to many non-Jesuits, at least as it is used in the Society of Jesus. People know in general what "discern" means. It refers to the act of perceiving, distinguishing, recognizing— as in the sentence "When you spoke I did not discern your true meaning and intention." In Jesuit history even up to the present, discernment is a much richer term. It refers to the art of seeing God's will in complex circumstances. It is an ongoing process of response to needs, people and events as these are encountered in changing circumstances. Many would argue that discernment is the distinguishing charism of the Society of Jesus. By that they would mean that men who are formed by the *Spiritual Exercises* of St. Ignatius to seek God's will in all things discover that will in a unique process called "discernment."

Is there any place in ethics or moral theology for discernment in its most general sense of "seeing into more deeply?" Obviously, I believe there is. But before entering this question in a more detailed way I want to say a few words about the notion of morality.

Try an experiment with me. May a person call long distance person-to-person to herself to let parents or friends know that she has arrived safely on a vacation trip?

A young man is invited to New York to interview with two companies, all expenses paid. He has both interviews on the same trip. May he accept money from both companies for the full air fare?

A second year medical student is deeply in love with a nursing student. They want to marry but cannot at present for financial reasons. They must wait two years but want to start living together.

Over the years a young Air Force reservist develops a deep conviction that war is totally unjustifiable in the Christian view of things. He is sent to the Persian Gulf and wonders what he is to do.

A young couple after seven years of marriage and no children wonder if they may try *in vitro* fertilization with embryo transfer in order to achieve a pregnancy, even though it has been rejected by a recent document of the Holy See (*Donum vitae*, 1987).

When people think of morality, these are the types of things they think of. They think of the thing done or omitted and its moral rightfulness or wrongfulness. Thus, when they think of decision-making and the discernment that ought to precede it, they think of discerning or determining right and wrong conduct and the sources of such a determination. For this reason we experience in moral tutelage a great attention given to the magisterium, to natural law, to moral arguments, etc.

Determination of what is concretely morally right and wrong is, of course, important. The second worst thing to not loving one's neighbors at all is to mistake what love calls for and end up hurting one's neighbor. In more traditional language we are accustomed to saying that we must have a rightly formed conscience. Furthermore, moral norms about what is right and wrong are associated with some moral concerns of the first magnitude: the magisterium and the use of authority in the Church; the theological weight of tradition; dissent; the meaning of the *sensus fidelium*; pluralism in theology; the duties of the individual conscience; pastoral guidance; the relevance of contemporary sciences to moral judgments and many other matters.

It must be noted, however, that excessive concern with rightfulness and wrongfulness obscures a very important distinction and subsequently a whole area of our moral lives. I refer to the distinction between right and wrong, good and bad. The right and wrong usage refers to what is objectively supportive and promotive of others or conversely what undermines their well-being and even their rights. The good/bad usage refers primarily to the person and to the person's dispositions. Specifically, it refers to the person's desire and intent to do what is supportive and promotive. For example, one who intends to, desires to do what is supportive of another or others performs a good act. That person may actually end up doing what is harmful and thus perform an act that is morally wrong; but it remains a morally good act. On the contrary, one who acts from motives of selfishness, hatred, or envy performs a bad act. Thus a surgeon acting out of the most despicable or selfish motives may perform brilliant life-saving surgery. His act is morally bad but morally right.

Moral-spiritual discernment concerns both right-wrong and good-bad. But this latter we have neglected. I want to concentrate on it here because our spiritual lives are not constituted by occasional hard decisions between right and wrong. Most of the time we know what is right and wrong. It is a question of doing it and even more radically of wanting to do it. Our spiritual lives do not lie asleep except for crises. They grow slowly and in small ways as the grass grows.

The moral-spiritual life is above all a growth process, the daily working out of our *adherere Deo,* the deepening and radicalizing of our love-option. Just as marriage is a thousand and one things a week, but above all beneath these things it is a growing two-in-oneness, so is our relationship with God a growth process in familiarity and friendship.

Many contemporary theologians believe that Christian faith and its sources provide no new concrete content in the moral life. Christian faith involves rather a modification of the decision-maker. Something profound has happened to us. Even better, something profound has been given to us in the charity poured forth into our beings. It is our task—and one with eternal stakes—to protect, nourish, support, extend, and deepen that great gift. That process is the most significant aspect of our moral-spiritual lives.

This process calls for discernment. Two facts of universal human experience make this obvious. The first is our lack of freedom. St. Paul stated: "For I do not do the good I want, but the evil I do not want is what I do" (Romans 7:10). Similar sentiments have been repeated thousands of times in the course of history: in poetry, on stages, in confessionals, on the lips of lovers seeking forgiveness and in the solitude of individual hearts. J. Robert Oppenheimer has been quoted as follows: "In some crude sense, which no vulgarity, no humor, no overstatement can quite extinguish, the physicists have known sin, and this is a knowledge which they cannot lose." Goethe regretted that God made only one person when there was in him room for two: the rogue and the gentleman. Disraeli moaned: "Youth is a blunder, manhood is a struggle, old age is a regret." *Simul justus et peccator* is a lapidary description of the human condition. In summary then, the first fact of our condition is a certain lack of freedom, an inconsistency in acting according to our basic option.

The second fact of our human condition is accurately described as lack of truth. We lie to ourselves and to one another. We turn away from the evil (and the good) in ourselves and in our actions. We prefer not to face it. It is uncomfortable, unflattering, unsettling. We are generous to a fault, especially our own. I have developed my own capacity to rationalize and to self-deceive to a remarkable refinement.

These two facts suggest that our lives are composed of both light and darkness. If we fail to perceive and acknowledge this we connive at the growth of darkness. Spiritual discernment is not targeted at the complexity of objective reality (right or wrong), but at our tendency to complicity in moral evil and our deepening and eager cooperation with the graceful presence and invitation of God our Father (goodness and badness). As Thomas Clarke, S.J. has noted, the enemies of such discernment are addictiveness and illusion.[1] Spiritual discernment is the art of dealing with these moral obstacles in our lives. Such moral obstacles do not show up only or primarily in the big classical moral dilemmas that occupy theologians and keep them off the streets— whether it is permissible to use nuclear weapons, whether sterilization is sometimes an option, whether capital punishment is morally tolerable, whether abortion laws ought to be relaxed, whether *in vitro* fertilization with embryo transfer is morally permissible.

The obstacles I have noted show up in our attitudes, habits and values that have become a part of our make-up and lead to patterns of action and reaction that reveal both light and darkness in our persons and introduce them into our world. Our attitudes, habits and values show up in small ways. They show up in the doctor at a dinner party who will see the patient tomorrow. They show up in the prayer delayed until I feel a little better. They appear in the comfortable but compromising half-truth that I speak and in the accurate but impatient words that were better left unspoken. These are the little badges of our illusion and addictiveness, our lack of freedom and our lack of truth. They are the vehicles of our attitudes, habits and values. Spiritual discernment is concerned above all with the imperfectly enlightened and liberated decision-maker, with our habits, attitudes and values.

What does our Catholic Christian tradition tell us about moral discernment, about getting at and making explicit these inner dynamics so that we can respond better to God's daily invitations and approaches to us? I believe that it tells us three things about discernment: 1) a basic notion about the moral-spiritual life; 2) a group of metaphors or models for interpreting our spiritual experience; 3) practical strategies in which our self-understanding can be enriched and deepened and can take concrete form.

1. A BASIC VIEW OF THE MORAL-SPIRITUAL LIFE

Many people, when they think of the term "morality," think of the moral character of a particular act, its rightfulness or wrongfulness. Since rightful and wrongful acts are kinds of moral acts, we tend to think of the moral life largely in terms of the thing done or omitted. Thus, certain "things" are mortal or venial sins.

This popular view understands our freedom too narrowly. It understands freedom as the freedom we experience in our object choices, for example, the freedom to attend Mass or not, to watch television or not, to go out to dinner or to stay at home. Obviously the freedom in our object choices is indeed true freedom. But there is another dimension to our freedom. It is not the freedom of choice to do a certain thing or not. It is the more basic choice with respect to the whole meaning and direction of my life. It is "yes" or "no" to the whole moral order. It is the free determination of one's self with regard to the totality of existence, a fundamental choice between love and selfishness, between ourselves and God our Savior. It is the fundamental acceptance or rejection of the grace that is the person of Jesus into my life as invitation of the Father. It is our acceptance or rejection deep in our persons of God's enabling love.

Theologians refer to this as basic or fundamental freedom. They sometimes use the term fundamental option, but this can be misleading because it suggests something close to freedom of choice. Actually basic freedom and its use is not an activity like the many daily and limited activities which occupy our lives. It underlies other choices; it inspires, animates and supports whatever I do or leave undone. Really it is not an act at all in the ordinary sense. It is rather *self-determination,* the direction I have given my life. Since it underlies other more superficial actions and choices and manifests itself in them, there is a continual interplay between this stance or basic position and particular acts. Acting according to this position or option, we deepen it. Acting at variance with it, we undermine and weaken it.

At this point let me turn to the theologian whose systematic writings brought the notion of fundamental freedom into the theological mainstream. That theologian is Karl Rahner. I want to let Rahner speak for himself, even if I realize that doing so is risky, the very risk being a nagging headache. Rahner notes:

> Man's freedom and responsibility belong to the existentials of human existence. Since freedom is situated at the subjective pole of human existence and its experience, and not within what is categorically given, the essential nature of this freedom does not con-

sist in a particular faculty of man alongside of others by means of which he can do or not do this or that through arbitrary choices. It is only too easy to interpret our freedom this way, an interpretation based on a pseudo-empirical understanding of freedom. But in reality freedom is first of all the subject's being responsible for himself, so that freedom in its fundamental nature has to do with the subject as such and as a whole. In real freedom the subject always intends himself, understands and posits himself. Ultimately he does not do *something*, but does *himself*.[2]

For Rahner, then, freedom is transcendental, "not an object of experience nor merely the quality of an action, but a basic mode of being." He immediately draws two conclusions from this. First, freedom, as the capacity to decide about oneself, does not stand behind the concrete physical, biological, historical dimension of the person, as if it were some unearthly power unrelated to historical life. That would be gnostic, dualistic. Rather it "actualizes itself" in and through the temporality that is our way of being. For this reason Rahner regards freedom as "much more nuanced, much more complex and much less unambiguous than the primitive, categorical conception of freedom as a capacity to do this or that arbitrarily."[3]

The second conclusion Rahner draws is that the actualization of this freedom "is not indeed an immediate, empirical, individual and categorically identifiable datum of our experience." It is "an element in the subject himself which the subject cannot make conscious and objectify directly in its own self."[4] Basic freedom is real in human experience, but is not "immediately and empirically observable in time and space." For this reason the "subject never has an absolute certainty about the subjective and therefore moral quality of these individual actions."[5]

The object, so to speak, of this core of transcendental freedom is God, absolute mystery, infinite horizon. Although we cannot know with certainty that a "yes" or "no" to God took place at a definite point in our lives, "we know that the entire life of a free subject is inevitably an answer to the question in which God offers himself to us as the source of transcendence."

Thus, for Rahner there are two levels or dimensions to our concrete (categorical) actions, the level of categorical freedom and the level of core or transcendental freedom. He puts it as follows:

> Since in every act of freedom which is concerned on the categorical level with a quite definite object, a quite definite person, there is always present, as the condition of possibility for such an act,

transcendence towards the absolute term and source of all of our intellectual and spiritual acts, and hence towards God, there can and must be present in every such act an unthematic "yes" or "no" to this God or original, transcendental experience. Subjectivity and freedom imply and entail that this freedom is not only freedom with respect to the object of categorical experience within the absolute horizon of God, but it is also and in truth, although always in only a mediated way, a freedom which decides about God and with respect to God himself. In this sense we encounter God in a radical way everywhere as a question to our freedom, we encounter him unexpressed, unthematic, unobjectified and unspoken in all of the things of the world, and therefore and especially in our neighbor. This does not preclude the necessity of making this thematic. But this latter does not give us our original relationship to God in our freedom, but rather it makes thematic and objectifies the relationship of our freedom to God which is given with and in the original and essential being of the subject as such.[6]

Thus the very constitutive core of the human person is a capacity, a freedom to accept or not the divine self-communication we call grace. Rahner emphasizes over and over again that this self-disposition before the absolute mystery of God is not a categorical, thematic datum of human experience that is immediately and empirically observable. As Ronald Modras summarizes:

This renders freedom not only difficult to define but a mystery which, both as a reality and a concept, escapes reflection into the sphere of incomprehensibility, where we dwell with our divine mystery. God is unthematically but really present in every act of freedom, both as its supporting ground and ultimate orientation.[7]

In summary, then, transcendental freedom is at the heart of Rahner's anthropology. But because human beings are a unity of materiality and spirit, this transcendental freedom can only exist and be actualized in time and history, or in Rahner's words, "I always act into an objective world." This is a world of conditioning, restrictions, necessities. Our transcendental freedom is, as it were, impacted in and inseparable from the categorical or object choices that make up our lives. For this reason, the human person is "a many-layered being . . . constructed as it were in layers starting at an interior core and becoming more and more external."[8]

Of this notion of freedom, Modras accurately states:

Here we find the basis in Rahner's anthropology for distinguishing between ordinary free decisions and those which constitute a fundamental option. It is out of the inmost core of our beings that we make those basic decisions of transcendental freedom (fundamental options) which lead to or away from God. But because freedom extends formally to the whole person, free actions can arise from outside the inmost core which do not affect us as acts of transcendental freedom do.[9]

This determination of ourselves is ourselves, what we are becoming. Of fundamental in the moral-spiritual life we could make the following observations:

1. *Free.* It may seem ridiculous to speak of transcendental freedom as being free. The point being made, however, needs to be made. Since our reflex awareness of freedom is of *freedom of choice* (object choice), there is the danger that we would limit the notion of freedom to such awareness. When we say that fundamental freedom is free, we mean to underline the fact that our fundamental posture or orientation toward the ultimate good of human life is in our power, is our responsibility. Thus freedom is clearly an analogous notion, being realized in both object choices and self-disposition.

2. *Supernatural.* In the economy of salvation, self-disposition occurs under the influence of the grace of the Spirit. It is self-disposition under divine empowerment, our acceptance (or rejection) of God's enabling love. Of course, there is mystery here in the coexistence of divine empowerment and human freedom.

3. *Obscure.* A person acting in basic freedom is totally present to him/herself, not as object but as subject, not as perceived, but as self-aware, not as seen from the outside, but as experienced in the self. Transcendental freedom is located at a level of consciousness which excludes adequate conceptual and propositional formulation, a level deeper than that of formulating consciousness. This accords well with several facts, as Josef Fuchs has repeatedly pointed out. For instance, St. Paul did not know whether he was worthy of love or hate. Or again, following Trent, theologians assert that we cannot have full certitude about the state of grace.

4. *Conscious.* Here again, we must be careful to avoid identifying consciousness with formulating consciousness. There is a form of self-awareness that does not lead to objective formulations.

5. *Variable as to time made.* That is, the capacity of self-disposition cannot be simply identified with the age of reason. It can

occur at a time when the person is, at least in the obscure depths, in possession of his/her total self. This will vary depending on many factors such as personal growth, parental influence, formal education.

6. *Stable.* The experience of that freedom that defines our personal center has the characteristic of totality and definitiveness. Because of its dimensions and intensity (in order to achieve totality and definitiveness), such a use of human freedom excludes the possibility of a series of quickly repeated transitions between life and death.

This anthropology is very compatible with the way scripture portrays the moral life. Scripture speaks about life-in-Christ as having a unity amidst diversity, a kind of compressed center. Charity is the epitome of the entire law (Galatians). It is more elevated than all charisms (1 Corinthians). Charity is the root of other virtues (Ephesians). It is the bond of perfection (Colossians).

If we turn the scripture coin, so to speak, we find a similar unity where sin is concerned. Biblical materials note that it is the heart that is sinful. Therefore, conversion of heart is necessary. The story of the prodigal son (Luke 15) is not the story of this or that action against God; it is the story of the son's self-sufficiency, of withdrawal of the son from the supremacy of the father. It is more Johannine to say "*qui tollit peccatum mundi*" than *peccata.* Individual sins manifest the internal situation (*anomia*) of the sinner, the self-sufficient rejection of God. Paul distinguishes sin-transgressions (*paraptomata*) from Sin (*hamartia*). This latter is a kind of power in human beings that is freely accepted and ratified and bursts forth in sin-transgressions.

In summary then, discernment must begin with a proper notion of the moral-spiritual life. We must see our moral life from the inside out. When we see it this way, we see it not above all as fragmented acts responding to do's and dont's; we see it not primarily as successes and failures, but as a precious gift entrusted to us—the friendship of God in His Son and through His Spirit. Like any friendship, this one must be nourished and fostered with mutual conversation, exchange of gifts, moments of quiet, strenuous acts of protection and resistance and glorious celebrations.

When we see our moral spiritual life in this way, we see it as a growth process, a gradual unfolding or drying up of our personal beings as Christians. This is what the Holy Spirit is operating within us. It is this life that we try to deepen with reflection on God's word, with nourishment in the Eucharist. It is this life that we try to protect and foster with constant but joyful conversion of heart in the sacrament of reconciliation. It is this life that we try to express in caring for the needs of others and in protecting their rights.

In this notion of our lives-in-Christ, freedom in its most fundamental sense is not a given quantity, but a task to be achieved through a lifetime. It is an acorn to be nourished into the oak. In cooperation with the Holy Spirit we extend our freedom, our liberation; we tighten our cling upon our God. That is the very meaning of constant conversion of heart; for even though we are converted in heart, we are not totally so.

2. THE METAPHORS OR MODELS FOR INTERPRETING OUR SPIRITUAL
   EXPERIENCE

The Christian tradition provides us with two helpful heuristic devices for understanding the dynamics of our lives. One of these devices looks at us as if it were from the inside, the other from the outside.

First a view from the inside. Salvation history is described in terms of creation-fall-redemption. This is not only temporal history but it is the shape of our own personal history. We bear the marks of this temporal history in ourselves, in our attitudes, habits and values. As Thomas Clarke has noted, our everyday lives in Christian perspective are simultaneously an act of continuing creation, a struggle with evil and a personal campaign for the victory and prospering of good.

Corresponding to the triad creation-fall-redemption are certain models and metaphors for viewing our experience and interpreting it. These models have their root in scripture, especially St. Paul and St. John. Some of them are the following:

Light	Darkness	Enlightenment
Freedom	Bondage	Liberation
Integrity	Brokenness	Reintegration
(wholeness)	(fragmentation)	
Health	Sickness	Healing
Peace	Estrangement	Reconciliation
	(alienation)	

It is part of the spiritual history of all of us to experience combinations of these models. Our lives are processes of enlightenment, liberation, reintegration, healing and reconciliation. These metaphors are ways of viewing what we are becoming, how we react to people and events and the kinds of decisions we make. They are, as it were, our "spiritual genetic constitution." There are secular variants of these models ("ship-shape," "down-and-out," "on-the-mend") but the advantage of the Christian models is that they have an ultimacy of reference—what God does for us in creation, what we do to ourselves in sinfulness, what God does for us in redemption.

Now let us turn to the second heuristic device, what I have called a view from the outside. Here I want to use Clarke's notion of climates. He points out that the human situation is made up not only of the characteristics of personhood (interiority, subjectivity) but also of climates (symbols, institutions, structures, manner of living, lifestyles, etc.). These "climates" refer not only to laws and structures of a formal kind, but to informal climates like accepted habits of speech, physical settings, the influence of tradition and custom, mind-sets, popular and public values, etc. Such climates have a profound influence on how we think, feel, and behave. They seep through our pores and become the shapers of our decisions and even our lives. The danger we daily face: that the values and priorities of a secular, material and unbelieving world will seep through and strengthen our lack of freedom and truth and run our lives in a kind of silent slavery. The opposite is also true. Personal attitudes and freely chosen relationships affect the climates in which we live and decide.

The notion of climates was not an invention of Christianity. Nevertheless, it is true to say that Christianity fostered a sharp awareness that the forces of sin and grace struggle outside of persons and personal relationships. Thus the biblical materials speak of "the prince of this world," "the power of darkness," "the elements of this world," "principalities and powers." These phrases are mentioned to convey the idea that sinfulness can get embodied in our very institutions and way of doing things, in the air we breathe.

It can be said that Christianity underlined the importance of climates by creating "climates of grace." Let the monastery be an example of this. All aspects of daily living (dress, bodily movement, work and rest, sharing of food, drink, possessions, humanizing and Christianizing of space and architecture by a daily rhythm of life) are part of a search for God, of liberation, enlightenment, healing, reconciliation, reintegration.

From this perspective the challenge of all of us—priests, doctors, lawyers, housewives, nurses, etc.—is to make our own life-structures, our daily way of living a "climate of grace," of search for an easy, joyful response to God's values and priorities. We can say that our challenge is to organize our life so that it is not an unreflected washing with the cultural tides.

If this is the climate we establish for ourselves, it will inevitably get into our habits, values and attitudes and thus into our decisions small and large. It will shape our priorities. And when this climate gets into our decisions and relationships, it will get into our world and have a transforming affect. It is no accident that the children of holy-loving people are so often stable, peaceful and unthreatened. It is no accident that we ourselves are more prayerful and sacrificial persons when we live close to prayerful, sacrificial people. Interiors become exteriors. Good people create good climates. And good climates support good people and their decisions.

The enemies of this process are illusion or ignorance and addictiveness or enslavement. Hence, from the perspective of discernment the most significant metaphors to describe our lives and experience are enlightenment and liberation. Enlightenment refers to enlightenment from illusion or blindness. Liberation refers to liberation from enslavement. Discernment is the ongoing process of recognizing these obstacles to our growth in the way of the Lord. There are two effects of discernment in the moral-spiritual life. One is negative: the disengagement from addictiveness, from absolutizing what is relative (idolatry). The other is positive: the experience of the attraction of the good, what St. Augustine called "victorious delight."

3. PRACTICAL STRATEGIES

This understanding of our moral-spiritual life must be embodied in viable strategies supportive of good habits, attitudes and values. I shall borrow these strategies from Thomas Clarke, S.J.

a. *Life-project.* Can I readily identify, at least for myself, what my life is all about? How would I formulate what I am seeking from day to day? Is such a life-project really related to the Gospel and to the central significance of Jesus Christ as the focus and meaning of my life?

b. *Self-knowledge.* How well do I know myself? Am I so well in touch with my personal story—its peak moments, crises, failures—that I can discern basic patterns of God speaking to me? How well am I acquainted with my inordinate affections as well as my ordinate ones? Does God's constant love and forgiveness really nourish me in my personal history?

c. *The neighbor.* What in me is especially a blessing for others? What is potentially damaging or bothersome? What are the obstacles of temperament and habit in me that make relating and deciding with others difficult? Do I evoke their best responses and contributions?

d. *Prayer.* Do I pray, really pray? In solitude or with others? Is my prayer enlightening, liberating, integrating, healing, reconciling? Does prayer provide the context within which I can cope with little hardships and disappointments? Or do I take flight into the sub-spiritual world of liquor, sex and drugs? Who is God for me? I for God?

e. *Scripture.* Does scripture really play an important part in my life and thought? Are there favorite verses or passages in time of crisis, doubt, joy, gratitude?

f. *Leisure and silence.* Is genuine leisure a reality in my life? Do I find it possible to be alone and still?

g. *Reflection.* Do I have some vehicle of daily or weekly reflection on what is happening in my life? Does it help me to be more reflective at other times without disengaging from the flow of life? Do I have some method for being quietly in touch with the movements of my heart, to sense its needs, to give it time to feel and reach out?

h. *Community.* Is there in my life at least one community which is truly a community of faith and worship, of witness and zeal? Or are all of my contacts merely business and social? In what way does this community aid me in self-understanding? Are there tensions in this community? What are the communities that constitute negative factors in my spiritual growth?

i. *Counsel.* Do I have one or more persons in my life with whom I can share my hopes and my fears, my decisions, my conscience?

As should be obvious, the strategies listed above constitute a kind of examination of consciousness. Moral-spiritual discernment is not primarily a matter of knowing philosophy and theology, norms and rules. It is primarily a matter of knowing deeply in faith Jesus Christ who is present to me in his Spirit. It is a matter of knowing the obstacles to and recognizing and heeding God's gracious invitations. It is a matter of knowing God's purposes for me on a daily basis. God's purposes are my growing enlightenment toward fuller freedom, a freedom that finds its meaning and fulfillment in an ever deepening "yes" to the God of my life.

Let me summarize. Discernment in the Christian tradition suggests three things: a correct notion of the moral-spiritual life; understanding the processes and influences of growth within and without us; adopting certain strategies to deal with these processes.

I was once told the story of a family whose house was on fire. The entire family had evacuated the house, except for the youngest son who went to the second floor and was trapped there. He panicked as the smoke enveloped him. On the ground outside the house the father called out "Jump, son." The little boy responded, "But I can't see you." The father yelled back, "That's all right, I can see you." Discernment is trust in and practical implementation of the truth that God sees us and has plans for us even if we don't see God; and that we can gradually overcome the smoke between us.

CHAPTER 6

The Search for Truth in the
Catholic Context

The Sept. 27, 1986, issue of *The New York Times* headlined an article, "The Vatican and Dissent in America." *The Chicago Sun Times* of Sept. 28 featured a long report with the title "Catholics in Conflict: Papal Crackdown Exposes Bitter Split in the U. S. Church." The Sept. 28 *Chicago Tribune* carried an article on Archbishop Rembert G. Weakland of Milwaukee entitled "Archbishop Asks Rome to Ease Up." The Sept. 28 *New York Times* presented this headline: "Two Bishops Weighing Vatican Trip to Tell of Turmoil in Seattle Area."

And so it goes across the country. Because the ink has flowed so freely in recent years, it is safe to say that most people are at least passingly aware of the dramatis personae and the storyline. The actors are chiefly three: the Vatican, the Catholic University theologian Charles E. Curran, and Seattle Archbishop Raymond G. Hunthausen. The bare facts of the storyline: Father Curran was stripped of his "canonical mission" (his juridical approval to teach as a Catholic theologian), and Archbishop Hunthausen's episcopal authority in five important areas (marriage tribunal, moral issues involving homosexuals and health care institutions, liturgy and worship, seminary and clergy formation, and the departure of priests) was transferred to recently-appointed Auxiliary Bishop Donald W. Wuerl.

What is going on here? Are we dealing with two isolated and unrelated incidents? The situations are certainly different. One involves the perceived deficiencies of episcopal leadership, the other perceived aberrations in the academic world of theology. In that sense, one could make the case that they are unrelated, as Vatican spokesman Archbishop John P. Foley has tried to do. Similarly, one could mount arguments that they are isolated interventions affecting only Catholic University and the Seattle archdiocese. Such incidents, it might be argued, are not likely to be repeated given the by-and-large negative furor they aroused. A symbol of this was the Rev. Andrew M. Greeley's bilious but basically on-target column headlined "Red Baron of Vatican at It Again."[1]

To view these incidents as isolated and unrelated because they concern individuals in distinct places and areas of concern would be tempting but shortsighted. I am not referring to an orchestrated brush-up of the American Church. I am referring to these interventions in terms of their implications and fallout. From this perspective they raise issues of the first magnitude for the American Church. The basic question they pose is: "How is the search for truth to be conducted in the Catholic context?" By "truth" I mean especially moral truths, because they are the chief concerns. The fact that Archbishop Hunthausen acts largely at the pastoral level and Father Curran at the theological should not distract us from the coincidence of concerns raised by their distinct searches. As Roberto Suro worded it: "The concern most often raised by Vatican officials involves the leadership of the Church in the United States, and both the Archbishop Hunthausen and Father Curran matters fall into this realm."[2] The questioned leadership is heavily in the moral sphere.

Both Father Curran and Archbishop Hunthausen have provided their own answers to this question in their respective spheres. Father Curran has said that public theological dissent is essential to that search. The matter is less clear in Archbishop Hunthausen's case because the indictments remain fuzzy. But unless I am badly mistaken, Archbishop Hunthausen has been saying by his pastoral procedures that some of the following are essential to the search: compassionate understanding of human weakness and failure, patient and attentive listening, trusting proportionate responsibility to others, playing it loose as things work out, and making bold, symbolic protest in some instances. The trouble is, or seems to be, that these responses are read by some as laxness on doctrine.

Most of us will have ready, even if unexamined, answers to the question raised above. Often enough such answers come packaged in aphoristic shorthand that displays a single dimension of the issue: local autonomy, authentic teachers, academic freedom, Roman centralization, confusion of the faithful, dual magisteria, personal responsibility, and so on. For instance, J. P. McFadden, editor of the ultra-right and muckraking *Catholic Eye*, summarizes the issue as follows: "The vast majority of Catholics are what they should be—sheep. The real intention of the Church is to guide those sheep."[2] End of analysis. Mr. McFadden did not describe his sheep as dumb because that would have been redundant.

Or again, Father Curran's dissenting writings have been likened to the disclaimers of a press officer who announces the policy of his company and immediately disagrees with it—as if such analogies accurately portray the notion of teaching and learning in the church.

In another attempt, Archbishop John R. Quinn of San Francisco summarized Father Curran's predicament in the light of obedience. "Through their [Congar, de Lubac, Murray, Gutiérrez, Boff] obedience to the church they grew in humility and holiness and ultimately had more influence in the church than they would have had otherwise."[4] This implied exhortation to supineness suggests two reflections.

First, the subsequent influence and holiness of those who suffer repression is simply not an issue. What should concern us is the repression, why these things happen, whether and when they are justified, how they can be prevented if not justified and what their effect is on believers as well as nonbelievers. Cardinal Joseph Frings of Cologne, Germany, raised the proper issue when he told Cardinal Alfredo Ottaviani (former Secretary of the Holy Office) at Vatican II that the methods and behavior of the Holy Office "are a source of scandal to the world."[5] He was, of course, referring to some of the very cases mentioned by Archbishop Quinn. Those creating scandal, however well-intentioned, are doing something objectively morally wrong. And if this is the case, someone has to say so. I am not implying that this is the case in the Curran-Hunthausen affairs, but only that it is the issue.

Second, to talk about suppression of dissent in terms of obedience and subsequent holiness (this latter a judgment beyond our making) is perilously close to sanctifying evil means by a good end. There comes a time when calling a spade something other than a shovel disguises and transforms it.

One thing becomes clear in such "answers." Very little is enlightened. That is the legacy of one-dimensional reductionism. Theological preferences—and often psychological discomforts and the unexamined institutional loyalties from which they spring—are promulgated without benefit of analysis.

Let me say at the outset that I agree in principle with Father Curran and Archbishop Hunthausen—"in principle" because both not only tolerate but encourage debate about details and particulars as part of their search. Because the issues are of such gravity for the American Church, and because they are dominantly theological, I want to list 10 points that structure my own agreement with Father Curran and Archbishop Hunthausen, as well as my profound disappointment at the silence of most bishops on these matters—notable exceptions are Archbishop Weakland, Bishop Matthew H. Clark of Rochester, N.Y., and Thomas J. Gumbleton, Auxiliary Bishop of Detroit. It would be highly imaginative to expect agreement on all of these points. But if they provoke more precise and enlightened disagreement, they will have served a useful purpose.

The search for truth does have a "Catholic context." This point might seem quaintly parochial. Truth is, after all, truth. There are well-accepted canons for its pursuit in the scientific community at all levels—historical, scientific, literary, philosophical, theological. Furthermore, earthly realities enjoy their own autonomy, as Vatican II expressly insisted. How, then, does the "Catholic context" make any difference in the search for truth?

The "Catholic context" makes a difference because theology is precisely theology. It is reflection on faith and its behavioral implications. In this sense, theology differs from other disciplines. The facts (truths) that found and energize the believing community and influence its moral behavior are not like data from other disciplines. They concern God's nature, intentions and actions as experienced and interpreted by a historical religious community.

Catholics believe that Christ established His Church with teaching authority as a protection against the opaqueness, weakness and other vulnerabilities of the human spirit. This authority roots in the conviction about the presence of the Spirit to the whole Church, but it is thought to be enjoyed in a special way by its pastors. One classic way of stating the claims of the hierarchy's ordinary use of this authority (and by "ordinary" I mean without the claim of infallibility, which is the way of most church teaching, certainly moral teaching) is to say that it enjoys the presumption of the truth. This presumption in turn generates a particular response from Catholics. It is a type of respect that most often translates factually into assent or acceptance. To deny this presumption is evidently to deny the authority itself. This authoritative teaching dimension is the chief reason for speaking of the "Catholic context" in the search for moral truth. To reject such a context is to misunderstand either theology and/or its Catholic specification.

But there the consensus ends and the face-off begins. My following nine points will touch dimensions of these disagreements. It must suffice here to underline the term "presumption" in the phrase "presumption of truth." Presumptions are not carved in granite. Presumptions can be and have been undermined by further consideration, changed facts, the presence of human folly and other factors. In a word, so-called official teaching enjoys this presumption to the extent that the undermining factors have been avoided insofar as is humanly possible. This is especially the case in the moral realm, where human experience and reflection are so vital in discerning the morally right and wrong. More specifically, the pastors of the Church enjoy this presumption only insofar as they have appropriately tapped the available sources of human understanding, as the late Karl Rahner, S.J., so often insisted. When they short-circuit these processes—whether by haste, hubris, pressure, political purpose or whatever—the presumption is correspondingly weakened. I say this for one simple reason: It is not often said. The terms "authentic" and "official" are often pressed on the noun "teaching" as if they were simply convertible with absolute certainty. When this happens we have corrupted a presumption of truth into presumptuousness.

There are limits to this teaching competence. This is a further specification of the point just made. The specification is necessary because, quite frankly, certain Catholic fundamentalists speak and act as if there were no distinctions or limits. This tendency was noted by the great French Dominican Yves Congar when he stated that the ordinary magisterium "has been almost assimilated, in current opinion, to the prerogatives of the extraordinary magisterium."[6] Thus we have what is known as "creeping infallibilism."

Human hankerings after simplicity and certainty have conscripted two theological supports for this creeping. One is the sprawling usage (by the Councils of Trent, Vatican I and II) of "faith and morals," sprawling because it fails to distinguish the deposit of faith from matters outside of it or not essential to it.

The Church's teaching competence is different when it deals with matters not of the deposit or not essential to it. Thus, traditional theology insists that the Church's teaching competence is analogous. That is, it means different things and makes different claims depending on the subject matter. Briefly, it can be infallibly competent or noninfallibly competent (which is not to be equated with "certainly true" and "probably erroneous"). The response of the believer is remarkably different in the two cases. In the first case it is an act of faith. In the second it is not, although "creeping infallibilists" would have us think so as they divide the world simplistically into orthodox and unorthodox, loyalists and dissenters (note the assumptions in that asymmetry). "Faith and morals" is often the vehicle of this simplicism, as if everything authoritatively proposed in the moral sphere pertained to the deposit of faith and is therefore "almost infallibly" taught. There is virtual theological unanimity that concrete moral norms do not pertain to the Church's infallible teaching competence.

The other support for "creeping infallibilism" is appeal to the "special assistance of the Holy Spirit", where ordinary moral teaching is involved. Pope Paul VI, in *Humanae vitae*, referred to this when he stated that "that respect [*obsequium*] . . . obliges not only because of the reasons adduced, but rather because of the light of the Holy Spirit which is given in a particular way to the pastors of the church in order that they may illustrate the truth."[7]

The distinction of the Church's teaching competence into infallible and noninfallible means, of course, that the assistance of the Holy Spirit is an analogous notion. That assistance can guarantee a teaching. If, however, the teaching is not presented in a final and definitive way, the assistance of the Spirit must be understood in a different (that is, analogous) way.

Further discussion of this point is unnecessary. The point I am making is that certain theological appeals ("faith and morals," "assistance of the Holy Spirit") can be and have been expanded uncritically in a way that removes any limits on the Church's teaching competence and caricatures the search for truth in the Catholic context.

Theology has a necessary but limited contribution to make. When people reflect on their faith and its behavioral implications, theology begins. And clearly, such reflection occurs at different historical times, with different circumstances and needs, different problems and challenges, different cultures. In other words, the faith must be appropriated over and over again. We must wrestle to own it and deepen it for ourselves in our times, as others in the past did. The past is instructive. It is not imprisoning. This means that new symbols and new formulations must be discovered. Theology attempts to lead and coordinate this effort. Without such exploratory struggles, we will be dealing with faith-in-formaldehyde, what the ecclesiastical historian Jaroslav Pelikan called the "dead faith of the living." Almost everyone admits this creative and innovative role to be among theology's most important. Therefore, not much more need be said.

I say "almost" because a tiny but noisy minority still stumps for an orthodoxy that is defined in terms of mere repetition of the past. *The Wanderer's* A. J. Matt, Jr. is the grand inquisitor of this movement. This minority is getting a hearing, a fact that fleshes out the Curran-Hunthausen story. As a senior Vatican official put it: "The conservatives in the United States organize letter-writing campaigns, and those letters get read even by the Pope."[8] Who is protesting this nonsense?

But important as it is, theology's role is limited. Certain limitations are obvious. We all see darkly, make false starts, succumb to our enthusiasms, construct wobbly analyses and resist criticism. I do not refer to such limitations here. Rather, I refer to the fact that theology is a scientific discipline in the service of the faith. Whether this service is an aid to the continuing daily reappropriation and deepening of the faith in our times is a heavy charge laid upon the pastors of the Church. In other words, theologians cannot speak for the whole Church. Only the Pope and the bishops with the Pope can do that.

Thus within the believing community, the magisterium and theology have two different but closely-related tasks that call for what the Most Rev. John S. Cummins, Bishop of Oakland, California, calls "respectful mutuality."[9] Bishop Cummins rightly states that both theology and the episcopate "exist within that community of believers and are meaningful only in relation to it." To treat theologians—and their analyses and conclusions—as if they were bishops is to mistreat them.

It seems to me that this is at the heart of the nervous worry about public dissent. Dissent quickly gets popularized, trickles down and comes to be viewed by the unwary as equally valid pastorally as official teaching. If that is the case, theologians are threatened by being taken for what they are not. But the answer lies in education, not execution.

Theology is a public enterprise. This might seem to have the bite of a harmless truism. But in the present circumstances it is crucial to emphasize this concept. Theology is not a closed society of arcane theory-spinners. It is a reflection *on the faith of the Church*, and therefore should flourish wherever that faith is found. Theological research examines, draws upon, challenges, deepens the faith of people—and therefore must interplay with, be available to, be tested by, make sense to those whose faith is involved. Briefly, since it is of the public, with the public and for the public, it must be done in public. Presumably Vatican II had something like this in mind when it stated that all the faithful possess "lawful freedom of inquiry and of thought, and the freedom to express their minds humbly and courageously about those matters in which they enjoy competence."[10]

Theology has an essential critical role. The Church is a pilgrim church. It is *in via* (on the way). That means that its formulations of its moral convictions are also *in via*, never finished and always in need of improvement, updating and adjustment to changing circumstances. Not only are moral and doctrinal formulations the product of limited minds, with limited insight, concepts and language; they are historically conditioned by the circumstances in which they were drafted. The Congregation for the Doctrine of the Faith acknowledged a fourfold historical conditioning (*Mysterium ecclesiae*, 1973). Statements of the faith are affected by the presuppositions, the concerns ("the intention of solving certain questions"), the thought categories ("the changeable conceptions of a given epoch") and the available vocabulary of the times.

Vatican II expressly adverted to this conditioning when it distinguished between the substance of the faith and its formulation. It stated: "The deposit of faith or revealed truths are one thing; the manner in which they are formulated without violence to their meaning and significance is another."[11]

This means that one of theology's most important roles is a critical one, a distancing from past formulations and the proposal of new ones more adequate to the circumstances and insights of the time. This distancing and reformation can be called critical evaluation or dissent. Without the fulfillment of this task—under whatever name— there is no doctrinal development. The Church's teaching gets frozen into the last official formulation. Critical evaluation is, then, only common sense. Gov. Mario M. Cuomo (D., N.Y.) noted this in a recent address in Brooklyn at St. James Cathedral. After stating that dissent itself is not harmful to the Church, Governor Cuomo asked: "How, after all, has the Church changed and developed through the centuries except through discussion and argument?"[12] How indeed?

The problem of the Church, then, is not precisely dissent. That we have always had. Indeed it is essential to the health of a living community, as the present Holy Father himself has persuasively argued (*The Acting Person*). He called it "opposition." But whatever its name—whether opposition, dissent, disagreement, critical evaluation— a community without it is a community in comfortable stagnation. It is a community ripe for the picking by any ideologues—fascists, Communists, left-wingers, right-wingers, nationalists and, let it be said softly, curialists.

The problem of the Church, then, is not dissent, but how to use it constructively, how to learn from it, how to profit by it. Every magazine editor knows this. Every public servant in a democracy knows it, too. Yes, yes, of course the Church is not a democracy. Left unsaid in that sweeping put-down is that the nondemocratic Church would have inflicted far fewer self-wounds had it made use of some democratic procedures in its teaching-learning processes. Americans know this down to their pulses. Vatican II learned it and asserted it in principle over and over again. The only remaining problem is to convince some Catholics that dissent is not a threat—unless they conceive the Church as an isolated fortress—but an invigorating contribution to continued life and growth. Dissent is an anathema only or especially to those who claim to have captured—really imprisoned—God and God's purposes in their own conceptual fortress.

In summary, since theology is both public and critical, public critical evaluation, or dissent, is part of its task. I am astonished at— and at some point deeply afraid of—those who question this or are threatened by it. Their agenda is showing.

To acknowledge the public and critical role of theology is not to espouse two magisteria. This statement is meant to meet head-on those who reject any public dissent as equivalent to espousing a second magisterium. That is, with all due respect, a red herring. Two different competences do not two magisteria make. Both competences—scholars and the magisterium—must relate healthily, even if not without tension, if the Church's teaching office is to be credible and effective.

So there is no question of the Pope vs. theologians, or bishops vs. theologians. Theologians will never be able to speak for the Church as the Pope can. That juridical point is not the issue. The issue is: What must the Church do to insure that its teaching is the soundest reflection of the Gospel at a particular time? Does the "certain charism of truth" traditionally and rightly attributed to the Pope and hierarchy exempt them from listening to the voice of experience and theological reflection? If the Church is intolerant of dissent, is it not excluding a possible source of correction and improvement, as well as of error? Is not public exchange the risk it must run if it is to be open to all sources of knowledge? What notion of Church and Church teaching is implied in the silencing of dissent? These are the true issues. To state them in terms of two competitive magisteria is utterly to juridicize such issues. If scholars present their views as if they were the last word ("authentic teaching"), then they are wrong, and that should be clearly pointed out. If, however, that "pointing out" takes the form of negating theology's essential critical role, then that error, too, must be identified for what it is—overkill.

The point can be made—how persuasively I leave to others—that the "confusion of the faithful" is not rooted exclusively or even primarily in theological dissent at all, but in the failure of authorities to listen in any meaningful way to the "sense of the faithful" and theological analyses that draw upon it. When traditional formulations are simply repeated in the face of competent challenges to them, teaching is reduced to ecclesiastical muscle-flexing. That *is* confusing, and it ought to be.

Dissent has its limits. Such limits are both pastoral and doctrinal. At the pastoral level, a prudent (I did not say pusillanimous) scholar will always view the value of his/her own opinions in the light of a larger whole—the good of the Church. This is but Christian realism. Sometimes the time is just not ripe for saying or doing what one thinks ought to be said or done. To act as if it were is to waft theology into an unreal world and exempt it from any accountability based in the messiness of reality.

As for doctrinal limits, Father Curran has argued that he dissents from no infallibly proposed teachings and follows the criteria for dissent established by the American bishops and therefore is within the limits of legitimate dissent. This has been rejected from two sources.

Cardinal Joseph Ratzinger's is the first rejection. "The Church," he said in a letter to Father Curran, dated July 25, 1986, "does not build its life upon the infallible magisterium alone but on the teaching of its authentic, ordinary magisterium as well."[13] True enough. But the implications of this statement are startling. The equivalent argument is that those teachings upon which the Church builds its life are removed from critical evaluation, or dissent. Even recent history would be harsh on that statement. Was not the rejection of common worship with other Christians a part of the Church's life prior to Vatican II? The same for rejection of religious liberty? The same for tolerance of slavery for so many centuries? Was not procreation as the primary end of marriage part of the Church's thought and life prior to Vatican II? And so on.

The second rejection is that of The Most Rev. James A. Hickey, Archbishop of Washington, D.C. He states that the norms for dissent established by the American bishops "are simply not workable." What does "not workable"[14] mean? What are the criteria for workability? Who is to blame and why if any public dissent is "not workable"?

And who decides these things? It may be comfortably left to the American bishops to decide whether a single member of the hierarchy can abrogate policies they have established for the entire U.S. Church.

Finally, it has been urged (by both Cardinal Ratzinger and Archbishop Hickey) that the Church has the right to have its doctrine taught faithfully and clearly, and to certify only those professors who will do so. That is certainly true, but it is certainly not all of the truth. Does it mean that after the official teaching is presented, no critical evaluation of it is ever called for, is ever permissible? Does that not imply that no criticism is *possible*? And if no criticism is possible, what has happened to the historically conditioned character of Church utterances clearly admitted by the Congregation for the Doctrine of the Faith? What has happened to doctrinal development? Indeed, what has happened to the distinction between infallible and noninfallible? And what has happened to our historical memories? The person who excludes dissent in principle from the role of the Catholic teacher, especially at the level of higher education, has confused teaching with indoctrination.

There are reasonable criteria for public dissent. This statement flows from the previous one. If there are limits to *what* may be the object of dissent, these limits themselves clearly act as criteria. Here I am underlining the quality of respect that ought to accompany dissent. This is one of three conditions (the others being absence of scandal and serious reasons) proposed by the American bishops for the legitimate expression of dissent. Such respect is not an assumed public politesse. It flows spontaneously from the conviction that the pastors of the Church have a unique, if not the only, voice in our moral guidance. Such respect will translate effortlessly into 1) respect for the office of the teacher; 2) critical reassessment of one's own conclusions; 3) a reluctance (and only that) to conclude to error because one knows that the wisdom of the entire Church (see above on the notion of presumption) has gone into the teaching in question, and 4) conduct in the public forum that fosters respect for the teaching office of the Church.

I would be dishonest if I omitted a gloss on No. 3 above. It is my unavoidable impression that much dissent in the Church is related to the suspicion that the wisdom resident in the entire Church has *not* gone into some teachings. More directly, bishops, theologians, priests and other competent Catholics have told me repeatedly that *in certain areas* Rome will say only what Rome has said. Why sexuality and authority are indissolubly wed in this way I shall leave to others.

To suppress dissent is counterproductive. One good reason for saying this is that disciplinary suppression is unnecessary. If Rome disagrees with the theology of Father Curran or the pastoral procedures of Archbishop Hunthausen, it could easily say so—*urbi et orbi*. But why remove a bishop's jurisdiction or a theologian's canonical mission to teach as a Catholic theologian? Why intimidate all bishops and all theologians in the process? Why undermine the very credibility of the magisterium in the process?

Another good reason for the counterproductivity of dissent-suppression is historical. Archbishop Weakland, in a refreshingly courageous analysis, reminded his diocese, and really all of us, that suppression of dissent leads to the comfort—and vitality—of the tomb. Roman interventions at the beginning of this century led to 50 years of theological ossification in the United States. Is that what we want when the world is being challenged as never before by scientific, technological and cultural sea-changes?

The solution lies in education of Catholics. Education to what? A host of things: history (yes, we need you desperately now, John Tracy Ellis, Gerald Fogarty, John O'Malley, James Hennesey, *et al.*); the role of bishops and theologians in the Church; the fact that God writes with crooked lines, and among those crooked lines are all of us; the real meaning of Catholic education, and so forth. The task is huge and the shortcuts tempting. But in the long haul there are no shortcuts.

How is the search for truth to be conducted in the Catholic context? The American bishops have provided us with a powerful example in the open and revisionary process used in the development of their recent pastoral letters on peace and on the economy. They have welcomed all points of view, even dissenting ones. A similar example can be provided by Catholic colleges and universities. The word "campus" is really the Latin word (*campus*) meaning field. It designates the arena where armies settled disputes with lance and sword. College campuses exist in part to render such incivility obsolete. The vigorous exchange of ideas by the open-minded in the university setting is the way to reconcile our differences. That is why colleges have campuses, open forums for the discussion and clash of ideas. The word "campus" should stand as a reminder that the clash of swords, the targeting of missiles and any use of force represent human failure, that vigorous but civil exchange is a form of loyalty to and protection of our humanity.

Suppression of dissent is a use of force. Can the Catholic Church learn a small lesson from the American bishops and its own universities on how the search for truth is to be conducted in the Catholic context? The question is far larger than the issues of Father Curran and Archbishop Hunthausen.

CHAPTER 7

Theologians and the Magisterium

"Oh no, not again" is likely to be the spontaneous reaction to the title of this chapter. In the past several decades the matter seems to have been talked to death. There is broad consensus among mainline Catholic scholars on many points. Yes, the pope and bishops are commissioned to protect the *depositum fidei*. Yes, they constitute the "authentic" magisterium. Yes, even their less than infallible utterances claim a special response from Catholics (*obsequium religiosum*). Yes, in discharging its teaching function, the magisterium has the right and duty to point out errors, even at times to discipline those responsible. As for theologians, they too are teachers, but do not speak in the name of the Church (in this sense, are not authentic or official). Their exploring and critical work is both public and indispensable. A modification of or distancing from past formulations (dissent) cannot be excluded in principle. When it occurs—relatively rarely, one would think, if the magisterium is operating in a healthy, open and nonideological way—it should be viewed constructively as a positive contribution to our growth in understanding and as a dimension of a theologian's loyalty. Points like these have been written about frequently, most recently in the document entitled "Doctrinal Responsibilities: Approaches to Promoting Cooperation and Resolving Misunderstandings Between Bishops and Theologians."[1] It can be said that they are in pacific possession. There is little need to repeat such matters in a book such as this.

However, even careful and balanced statements about the rights and responsibilities of bishops and theologians in the teaching function of the Church remain frustratingly abstract and sterile. There is the uneasy sense that such statements leave the real problem untouched and unfaced. The real problem lies in the fact that not a few—bishops and theologians—qualify *in practice* what nearly all would admit *in principle*. For instance, there are bishops who assert that theology is indispensable to their teaching role, and yet who totally disregard it when certain delicate and controversial moral issues are being discussed. Similarly, there are theologians who, while admitting the exploratory character of their work, present it as the basis for pastoral practice. This day-to-day or in-practice inconsistency constitutes the context or atmosphere in which theologians relate to the magisterium. Unless we deal straightforwardly with this atmosphere and some of its supportive—but often unexamined and implicit—assumptions, we will not have faced the problem of the relation of theologians and the magisterium realistically.

As a way of approaching this atmosphere or context, I want to propose a series of ten theses. I expect some of these theses to be controversial. Indeed, if they were not, we would very likely not have the inconsistency noted above between *in principle* and *in practice*. I cannot in a brief period fully explain or validate these theses. I can only lay them out in adumbrated form, recipe-like in the expectation that others will add seasonings and variations.

Before doing this, I must explain terms that I shall use in several places: "culture one," "culture two." These are borrowed from Eugene Kennedy's recent study (1988).[2] "Culture," as used by Kennedy, refers to an outlook on religion, Church and world and to the elements that shape these differing outlooks. The designation "one" refers to an outlook that "rises from and finds its concerns as well as its imaginative expression in the traditional institutional structures of the Church in the United States." "Culture two" is "far less absorbed with the inner and outer life of institutional Catholicism." Kennedy richly elaborates the differences between these two cultures throughout his book. But I believe it fair to say that the key differentiating feature of the two cultures is found in concern for and commitment to the institutional aspects of Catholicism. Kennedy finds this feature a much more accurate description of the differences among Catholics than liberal-conservative. It is Kennedy's thesis that culture one is dying, indeed that culture two is subtly transforming the American Catholic Church in its own image. Now to my theses.

1. Lumen gentium (n. 25) needs updating.

I refer specifically to the notion of "religious submission of mind and will" to the authentic but noninfallible teachings of the magisterium. As is well known, this phrase is brandished as a veritable weapon to exclude any public dissent. Karl Rahner argued that n. 25 of *Lumen gentium* is an inadequate portrayal of the appropriate theological response to authoritative noninfallible teaching. He stated (1980, p. 373):

> If, for example, the statements of *Lumen gentium* (n. 25) on this matter were valid without qualifications, then the world-wide dissent of Catholic moral theologians against *Humanae vitae* would be a massive and global assault on the authority of the magisterium. But the fact that the magisterium tolerates this assault shows that the norm of *Lumen gentium* (and many other similar assertions of the past one hundred years) does not express in sufficiently nuanced form a legitimate praxis of the relationship between the magisterium and theologians.[3]

In another study, Rahner touches on noninfallible teaching and asserts that "even the second Vatican Council did not speak clearly enough about such authentic but reformable Roman doctrinal decisions." Moreover, "Roman procedure after the Council left something to be desired by way of straightforward clarity and modesty."[4]

Rahner does not say positively and explicitly how he would modify n. 25; but it is not difficult to infer this. Repeatedly Rahner has insisted that the authentic magisterium has been in error. Therefore, the *obsequium religiosum* must be understood in such a way that the possibility of error is foreseen and provided for in the expected response.

When André Naud first discussed this matter[5] in 1980, he found *Lumen gentium* (n. 25, "adherence of mind and will") "extremely ambiguous" when taken together with the type of freedom asserted in 1967 by the German bishops in their famous *Königsteinerklärung*.[6] He argued that there is a need to clarify the sense of n. 25. Naud (1987) has recently returned to this subject and criticized the unique emphasis on assent. This has given rise to an absolutist (Naud calls it "rigid") reading of *obsequium religiosum*, when as a matter of fact a careful reading of the text, especially in light of its history, does not support such a rigid understanding. A recent article by Francis A. Sullivan, S.J., made the same point.[7]

How we word what is needed depends very much on the contemporary context. Naud, Sullivan and others are suggesting a more nuanced understanding of n. 25. I use the stronger "updating." Why? Because the present ambiguity of the text will continue to yield and nourish the more rigid reading. A symbol of this is, of course, Cardinal Ratzinger's indictment of dissent *in principle* through his absolutist reading of *obsequium religiosum* in the Curran case. He wrote:

> In any case, the faithful must accept not only the infallible magisterium. They are to give the religious submission of intellect and will to the teaching which the Supreme Pontiff or the college of bishops enunciate on faith or morals when they exercise the authentic magisterium, even if they do not intend to proclaim it with a definitive act. This you have continued to refuse to do.[8]

My first thesis calls for updating. The form this should take will be a synthesis and making explicit of the types of animadversions we find in Rahner, Naud, Sullivan, and others with regard to *obsequium religiosum* as applied to noninfallible teaching. In the past I have suggested a kind of shorthand for this synthesis. It reads: a docile personal attempt to assimilate the teaching, an attempt that can end in "inability to assimilate" (dissent).

2. The teaching of Humani generis about the impact of papal interventions in controversies is obsolete.

In *Humani generis* Pius XII wrote:

> But if the Supreme Pontiffs in their statements (*in actis suis*) deliberately state an opinion about a matter hitherto controverted, it is clear to all that that matter, according to the mind and will of the same Pontiffs, can no longer be held to be a question of free debate among theologians.[9]

This statement was repeated almost verbatim by John Paul II in 1987. At a meeting of natural family planning experts, he states: "What is taught by the Church on contraception does not belong to material freely debatable among theologians."[10]

I have treated this subject more at length in a recent book.[11] Suffice it here to say that it is now widely admitted by ecclesiologists that Pius XII was working out of a neoscholastic notion of the magisterium. Yves Congar, O.P., has cited *Humani generis*, and specifically the citation I have given above, as an example of this. Of the magisterium conceived in this neoscholastic way (with the ordinary papal magisterium demanding total obedience, and the task of theologians said to be strictly in the service and under the control of the magisterium), Congar asserts: Its pretensions seem excessive and unreal." He continues:

> Today, theologians are going beyond the ecclesiastical work-category formulated for them by Pius XII and Paul VI; they are living according to a common standard of scholarly research.[12]

Though Avery Dulles *senior* does not in some respects reflect Dulles *junior*, still seventeen years ago he wrote:

> As a result of the experience of the Council and the growth of critical theology, the neoscholastic theory of the magisterium is perceived as making insufficient allowance for distortion and possible error in the ordinary teaching of popes and bishops. Sophisticated Catholics of the 1970's are generally convinced that dissent and loyal opposition can play a positive role in the Church as well as in secular society. Any attempt by the hierarchy to settle disputed questions by unilateral decrees will inevitably be met by dissent or even protest on the part of some.[13]

Dulles is making two points here. First, the neoscholastic notion of magisterium is not theologically adequate. Indeed Pius XII's statement in *Humani generis* appeared in the original schema of Vatican II but was dropped in the revision. Second, it will not work. That is why I use the term "obsolete."

3. Competence (as in "teaching competence") is an analogous notion.

I mention this because the overall effect of an absolutist understanding of *obsequium religiosum* is that all teachings are viewed by ecclesiastical authorities as *practically* of equal binding force. As Naud remarks:

> Except on questions of politics and economics, the reader has the impression that the magisterium knows only the language of certitude. Everything is affirmed or condemned with such firmness and such apparent assurance that an ordinary reader has constantly the impression of being confronted by declarations of absolute certitude, irreformable in character, engaging the irreversible thought of the Church.[14]

Karl Rahner made the same point when, after noting that the ordinary magisterium had "often" been involved in error, he added: "On the other hand, Rome was accustomed to put forward and insist on such decisions as if there could be no doubt about their ultimate correctness and as if any further discussion of them was unbecoming for a Catholic theologian."[15]

Once we have accepted the distinction between infallible and noninfallible teaching, we have thereby stated a distinction between infallible competence and noninfallible competence.

Let me put the matter as follows. On the one hand, the Church claims teaching competence in the area of the natural moral law, even its applications. On the other hand, Vatican II states that the charism of infallibility is coextensive with the "treasure of divine revelation" (what Vatican I called the *depositum fidei*). This would exclude from infallibility those moral questions that are not revealed. "Competence," therefore, is a very analogous concept. One can be competent without being infallibly competent. As we shall see, that is the case in concrete moral questions.

There are those who try to avoid this problem by including concrete moral questions under title of "truths of salvation."[16] The argument is: whatever affects our salvation is an object of infallibility; for that is the very purpose of the charism.

Here a very important distinction must be made, the distinction between moral goodness and moral rightness. Moral goodness refers to the person as such, to the person's being open to and decided for the self-giving love of God. It is the vertical dimension of our being. It is salvation. Therefore what we can say about the moral goodness of the person is a "truth of salvation."

Another level is the horizontal. This refers to the proper disposition of the realities of this world, the realization in concrete behavior of what is promotive for human persons. We refer to this as the rightness (or wrongness) of human conduct. We sometimes call this inner-worldly activity "moral" rightness or wrongness. But it is moral only in an analogous sense. That is, moral goodness contains an inclination, an intention, a good will, a readiness to do what is right. It is because of this relationship between personal moral goodness and material rightness that this rightness is called "moral." But this rightness is not *directly* and *in itself* concerned with personal moral goodness. Salvation (as in "truths of salvation"), therefore, does not have a *direct* relationship to right behavior, but to personal goodness. Concrete moral norms, therefore, are truths of salvation only in an analogous sense.

It is the failure to distinguish the pairs good-bad, right-wrong that leads to an uncritical notion that the Church is *equally* competent on all moral questions, a notion that does not make a great deal of sense in our time.

What is the right way of acting in different areas of human life is determined by human experience, human evaluation, human judgment. St. Thomas says: "We do not offend God unless we harm our own good." What is harmful to us is a human determination. Joseph Fuchs adds: "The Catholic lay people as Catholics, the priests as priests, the bishops and the pope as such do not have a specific Christian or ecclesiastical competence in regard to these matters."[17]

Earlier, Karl Rahner approaching this matter from the point of view of infallible teaching, stated:

> Apart from wholly universal moral norms of an abstract kind, and apart from a radical orientation of human life towards God as the outcome of a supernatural and grace-given self-commitment, there are hardly any particular or individual norms of Christian morality which could be proclaimed by the ordinary or extraordinary teaching authorities of the Church in such a way that they could be unequivocally and certainly declared to have the force of dogmas.[18]

What Rahner is saying is that "particular or individual norms" (about rightness or wrongness) are not "truths of salvation" as this phrase is understood by certain "infallibilists."

These statements of Rahner, Fuchs, and others do not mean that the pastors of the Church should not offer guidance on right-wrong activity such as peace, economics, sexuality, abortion, etc. It merely suggests appropriate caution and tentativeness; for horizontal activity in this world does not belong to the Church's competence in the same way as the *depositum fidei*. In this sense we may say that the Church enjoys the assistance of the Spirit in offering concrete moral guidance, "but this assistance does not necessarily mean the specific assistance that, according to Vatican I and Vatican II, is promised to her, and guarantees infallibility under certain conditions."[19]

I believe that a discerning reader might easily detect a difference between the rather sweeping statements of, for example, Pius XII in *Magnificate Dominum* and those of Vatican II. There is a certain modesty in Vatican II on natural law. The Council applies the notion to universal principles. Only very egregious actions are listed and it is stated that the human conscience gives voice to these principles.

The point I am making—and in doing so I am following the lead of Rahner and Fuchs—leads to the conclusion that the term "competence" when applied to the teaching office of the Church is an analogous term—which means that it must be understood differently when applied to different realities, specifically the deposit of faith and the concrete applications of this. The Church has a definite mission to provide concrete moral guidance. For "faith throws a new light on everything, manifests God's design for man's total vocation, and thus directs the mind to solutions which are fully human."[20] But this mission with regard to concrete moral guidance (rightness-wrongness) is not precisely and *directly* concerned with "truths of salvation," and hence is not buttressed by the certainty and stability such truths can rightly claim. This is clear from the history of moral teaching in the Church. We cannot be accused of washing dirty linen in public when we candidly acknowledge that our tradition is not free of moral distortion and error.

It is also clear from the Pauline corpus. For instance, in Galatians, Paul refers to the good news that he has directly from the Lord. It is not "human knowledge." There are other matters that are indeed human knowledge (e.g., in 1 Cor 7, whether to live in virginity or not). The moral rightness-wrongness of concrete actions is in this latter category. And so are matters like capital punishment, abortion, business ethics, social ethics, contraception, and sexual ethics in general.

I mention this here because there is still a deep-seated hankering in the Church to "infallibilize" the ordinary activity of the magisterium, as Yves Congar has often noted. For instance, K. D. Whitehead, writing in the *New Oxford Review*, stated of past controversies: "What was better understood in the past, however, that is not so well understood today, is that where the teaching authority of the Church stepped into these controversies to *decide* some aspect of them, any further 'dissent' from the points decided meant that one was henceforth placing oneself in the ranks of the heretics."[21] To this the proper response is: What is better understood today is that Whitehead has fallen into serious theological error by lumping any dissent from a decision of Church authority with heresy. Such expansiveness only heaps ridicule on the teaching office of the Church. What is also better understood today is that the solution to complex moral questions cannot simply be "decided" by Church authority—if "decided" means resolved independently of evidence about the personally promotive or destructive character of the actions in question.

4. The notion of the assistance of the Spirit is analogous.

Above, Josef Fuchs was cited as stating that the assistance of the Spirit to the ordinary, noninfallible magisterium "does not necessarily mean the specific assistance that, according to Vatican I and Vatican II, is promised to her and guarantees infallibility under certain conditions." Clearly, then, this assistance is analogous—different when applied to different realities. Yet it is often presented in an univocal way, a way that makes any questioning of authentic noninfallible teaching out of order.

André Naud adverts to this while discussing the differences between the rigid and supple approaches to *obsequium religiosum*. Typically the more rigid approach invites assent not in virtue of the quality of the arguments invoked by the magisterium, but in terms of its authority. Thus, following *Humanae vitae* itself, the Spanish bishops wrote:

> The Pope speaks as supreme pastor of the Church, and not as a private doctor. His authority does not derive from the scientific value of the arguments that he invokes, but from the mission he has received from Christ and from the assistance of the Holy Spirit promised to him.[22]

The less rigid approach refuses to allow this radical break between arguments and conclusion. If the Spirit is assisting the magisterium, we should expect this assistance to show up in the quality of the arguments. For this reason, too, the less rigid approach allows more influence to theological opinion and the personal assessment of the competent person.

I have the distinct impression that the analogous character of the assistance of the Holy Spirit to the magisterium is neglected both in official statements and more popular exchanges.

5. The notion of the assistance of the Holy Spirit needs careful theological analysis.

I believe it is correct to say that the notion of the assistance of the Holy Spirit needs a good deal of theological attention. If it remains as opaque as it actually is in the documents of the magisterium, it is likely that the voice of the hierarchical magisterium will continue to be loudest and clearest when it says "authority and special assistance" and that of others loudest when it says "evidence and reasons." Both emphases are important, of course, but if they are left unrelated, are we not still vulnerable to the dangers of a simplistic notion of assistance?

What, then, is the meaning of "the assistance of the Spirit" where the authoritative noninfallible magisterium is concerned? Any who undertake to speak about the action of the Spirit, especially if they try to explain how the Spirit works, realizes in advance that they are more than ever likely to end up with a theological foot in their mouth and make an utter fool of themselves; for the operations of the Spirit are above all ineffable. Yet the possibility of gaining some understanding and the anticipation of charitable correction by others minimizes the arrogance of the attempt. With this in mind I should like to offer a possible approach.

In facing this question two extremes must be avoided. The first would explain the assistance of the Spirit to the magisterium in a way which dispenses with human processes. The second would simply reduce this assistance to human processes. The first is the notion of a special assistance by the Spirit which represents a new source of hierarchical knowledge, arcane and impervious to any criticism developed out of Christian experience, evidence, and reasoning. Such a notion of assistance results in a form of fideism which makes it difficult, if not impossible, to see how any authoritative utterance is not thereby practically infallible. Furthermore, this notion of assistance is a summary edict of dissolution for the scholarly and theological fraternity.

The second extreme is such an emphasis on analysis and reasons that the action of the Spirit is simply identified with the shrewdest thinkers in the community and ultimately imprisoned in the best reasons they can unravel. This is an extreme for many reasons, not the least of which is that it is a form of neorationalism which overlooks the complexity and developmental character of moral cognition, especially by bypassing the real significance of the communitarian aspect of moral knowledge, and especially of the *sensus fidelium*. If the action of the Spirit is primarily directed to the Church as a whole, and secondarily and in subordination to the needs of the Church, to its pastors as pastors, then surely this fact must influence the emergence of moral knowledge, the operations of the magisterium, and the notion of the special assistance of the Holy Spirit to the magisterium.

It would seem that any explanation of the assistance of the Holy Spirit to the magisterium (noninfallible) must be adequate to four factors: (1) the judgmental competence of the hierarchy within the whole teaching process, (2) the activity of the Spirit in the formation of such judgment, (3) the possibility and fact of error in these judgments, and

(4) the relevance of the experience and reflection of the whole Church in forming these judgments.

I should like to suggest that the middle course we seek is one which would associate the activity of the Spirit with human processes without identifying it with them. The nature of this association can perhaps be illumined by a reflection on error. When error occurs in human judgments, it would seem to occur in either of two ways: in the gathering of evidence or in the assessment of the evidence. Obviously there can be many reasons why either of these processes would function inadequately, but it is the breakdown of one of them to which judgmental error can be traced. If this is true, then is it not reasonable to think that at least the proper implementation of these processes is generally required to avoid error in complex decisions?

When this is applied to the magisterium, we might say that error could occur either through evidence-gathering or evidence-assessing. Hence at least adequate evidence-gathering or evidence-assessing are required if error is to be avoided. Evidence-gathering is inadequate when consultation is not broad enough to allow the full wisdom stimulated by the Spirit's activity in the whole Church to emerge. Evidence-assessing breaks down when consideration of the evidence is insufficient to allow the Spirit to aid in the emergence of its meaning. In the contemporary world these inadequacies would seem to be traceable to a failure in the fullness of the collegial process at all levels.

Now the magisterium of the Church has special advantages to overcome these handicaps in arriving at moral truth. First of all, bishops *as pastors* are in a unique position to be in contact with the convictions, problems, beliefs, joys, sufferings, and reflections of all groups in the local Church. That is, they are positioned to consult the experience and convictions (the wisdom) of their flock. As *collegial pastors* they are in a position to pool this wisdom and weigh it through a process of dialogue and debate. In this sense the episcopal and papal magisterium have sources of information which exceed those available to anyone else. Summarily: negatively, the magisterium is in a wonderful position to reduce the barriers which bind the Spirit; positively, it is positioned to engage the total resources of the community and thus give the Spirit the fullest possible scope.

Therefore, though we cannot capture in human categories the operations and assistance of the Holy Spirit, can we not identify the human processes within which the Spirit must be supposed to operate? And since the hierarchy is uniquely situated to implement these processes, is it not open to the assistance of the Spirit in a special way when it does so? That is, the ability of bishop-pastors (and through them the pope) to range beyond the isolation of their own reflections or those of restricted groups is the foundation for the confidence that in doing so they will be specially open to the Spirit, and that their authentic pronouncements will show this.

Therefore who would doubt that when the magisterium actually draws upon the wisdom resident in the entire Church, and actually submits itself to an adequate evaluative process, it is better positioned than any individual or group of individuals to relate this to Christian conduct? A prudent and sensitive Catholic would be willing to accept such conclusions precisely because (and providing that) he or she had the assurance that they proceeded from a store of wisdom far beyond the solipsism of his/her own insights. And for this reason one would find it quite acceptable to say with *Humanae vitae* that acceptance of these judgments is owed "not only because of the reasons adduced, but rather because of the light of the Holy Spirit which is given in a particular way to the pastors of the Church in order that they may illustrate the truth." On the other hand, one may legitimately expect that this "light of the Holy Spirit" will manifest itself concretely in the "way the question itself is handled. That means in the solid presentation of proofs from human experience and with good arguments."[23]

6. A coercive ecclesial atmosphere is counterproductive in every way.

By "coercive ecclesial atmosphere" I refer to a gathering of symptoms familiar to all. Bishops are appointed by ideological conformity. Theologians and bishops are disciplined. Obedience is demanded to all teachings. Judicial processes fail the criteria of due process. Consultation is secret and highly selective, only those qualifying who agree with a pretaken position. I believe I am describing an actual situation. The wounds inflicted by a coercive atmosphere I see as the following:

A. THE WEAKENING OF THE EPISCOPAL MAGISTERIUM

Here we should recall the theological force of episcopal agreement described in *Lumen gentium*, no. 25. If the bishops around the world are united with the pope in their teaching, then that teaching can achieve a greater level of stability and certainty, and indeed achieve infallible status if the teaching is a proper object of infallibility and is presented as something to be held definitely. But the unity must be genuine and clear.

In a coercive atmosphere both the genuinity and clarity are put in serious doubt. First, the genuinity. Here we would recall one of the arguments made during the deliberations of the so-called Birth Control Commission. It was contended that the Church could not modify its teaching on birth regulation because that teaching had been proposed unanimously as certain by the bishops around the world with the pope over a long period of time. To this point Cardinal Suenens replied: "We have heard arguments based on 'what the bishops all taught for decades.' Well, the bishops did defend the classical position. But it was one imposed on them by authority. The bishops didn't study the pros and cons. They received directives, they bowed to them, and they tried to explain them to their congregations."[24] In a coercive atmosphere people will repeat things because they are told to and threatened with punishment if they say anything else. Episcopal unity is revealed as enforced, not genuine.

As for clarity, the more likely scenario in a coercive atmosphere is that the bishops (some at least) will say nothing if they disagree. In such circumstances, to read episcopal silence as unanimity is self-deceptive.

When the genuinity and clarity of episcopal agreement have been cast into grave doubt by a coercive atmosphere, the episcopal magisterium itself has been undermined. The meaning of consensus has been eviscerated. The bishops should be the first ones to protest this diminishment of their magisterium, and the atmosphere that grounds it.

B. THE WEAKENING OF THE PAPAL MAGISTERIUM

This follows from the first point. If bishops are not speaking their true sentiments, then clearly the pope is not able to draw on the wisdom and reflection of the bishops in the exercise of his ordinary magisterium. When this happens, the presumption of truth in papal teaching is weakened, because such a presumption assumes that the ordinary sources of human understanding have been consulted, as the late Karl Rahner so repeatedly argued. That is why what is called the "enforcement of doctrine" is literally counterproductive. It weakens the very vehicle (papal magisterium) that proposes to be the agent of strength and certainty.

C. THE MARGINALIZATION OF THEOLOGIANS

Coercive measures will almost certainly have the effect of quieting theologians, at least on certain issues. This further erodes both the episcopal and papal magisterium by silencing yet another source of understanding and growth. Many bishops, most recently James Malone, have noted the absolute necessity of theology for their work. In Malone's words, "As a bishop in an episcopal conference which had devoted substantial time and energy to the place of the Church in the world, I can testify to the irreplaceable role of the theological enterprise."[25] If reputable theologians are marginalized, the magisterium is proportionately weakened. And it is no response to exclude from the "reputable" category those with whom one disagrees. That begs the (or any) question.

D. THE DEMORALIZATION OF PRIESTS

When juridical coercion (which is not altogether out of place) too easily dominates the Church's teaching-learning process, priests (and other ministers) become demoralized because they are expected to be official spokespersons for positions they cannot always and in every detail support. Thus they become torn by their official loyalties and their better judgment and compassion. Archbishop John Quinn adverted to this in the Synod of 1980.[26]

E. THE REDUCTION OF THE LAITY

Coercive insistence on official formulations tells the laity in no uncertain terms that their experience and reflection make little difference. This in spite of Vatican II's contrary assertion: Let it be recognized that all of the faithful—clerical and lay—possess a lawful freedom of enquiry and of thought, and the freedom to express their minds humbly and courageously about those matters in which they enjoy competence."[27] If such humble and courageous expression counts for nothing, we experience yet another wound to the authority of the ordinary magisterium. The search for truth falls victim to ideology.

F. THE COMPROMISE OF FUTURE MINISTRY

When a rigid orthodoxy is imposed on seminarians in the name of unity and order, the very ability of these future priests to minister to post-Vatican II Catholics is seriously jeopardized. I have seen this happen. Many thousands of Catholics have studied and struggled to assimilate the Council's perspectives. They do not understand and will not accept a new paternalism in moral pedagogy. This means frustration and crisis for the minister trained to practice such a pedagogy.

G. THE LOSS OF THE CATHOLIC LEAVEN

Coercive insistence that the term "official teaching" is simply synonymous with right, certain, sound and unchangeable (an identification powerfully supported by the suppression of any public dissent) will lead to the public perception that the role of Catholic scholars is an "intellectual form of 'public relations,' " to borrow from Clifford Longley.[28] That means the serious loss of theological credibility in precisely those areas of modern development (e.g., science and technology) where the Church should desire to exercise a formative influence. The present pontiff wants both to unite the Church and to shape the world, both utterly laudable apostolic objectives. The means to the former could doom the latter.

7. There are significant indicia that many officials view the magisterium and their positions in a narrowly culture one way.

I shall mention but a few. During November 1988, Archbishop Alberto Bovone, secretary of the Congregation for the Doctrine of the Faith, expressed concern to the American bishops about a draft of the document "Doctrinal Responsibilities" on relationships between bishops and theologians. He referred to "an attitude which tends to equate bishops and theologians appears to inspire the whole orientation of the document."[29] Why this nervous fear that the two (bishops and theologians) are "on an equal footing"? Does this not point to the primacy of position as a dominant concern?

Another example. There appeared on January 23, 1989, in L'Osservatore Romano an article on Donum vitae, the 1987 instruction of the CDF on reproductive technology.[30] It was concerned with the doctrinal authority of Donum vitae. The article argues strenuously that Donum vitae is authoritative and demands "obedience of judgment and practice." It refers to the contrary practice of four European Catholic universities as a "most serious rebellion." Whether a document is absolutely accurate cannot be collapsed and identified with whether it is authoritative. The two are different notions. An overriding concern with the authority of a teaching is too easily associated with diminished concern for its validity and persuasiveness. The demand of obedience to a teaching is too often transparent of its analytic fragility.

A third example is the new oath being required of theologians and others at the beginning of their tenure in certain positions. The imagination is not stretched dangerously when it is stated that loyalty oaths suppose and reflect an attitude of suspicion. Behind such suspicion is an intense preoccupation with authority and conformity to its prescriptions and proscriptions.

Finally, when a group of Italian theologians expressed concerns similar to those made public in the so-called "Cologne Declaration," the pope himself responded, reminding the bishops that they are the *veri dottori* of their dioceses.[31] Since theologians are certainly true teachers in their own right—even if by different title—*veri* can only mean official (or authentic). Once again the preoccupation with officialness.

8. Modern Catholics, especially of the culture two description, want a magisterium that is truly effective in the world.

"True effectiveness" is associated with a teaching office that attempts to inspire, enlighten, lead, invite, encourage. It does this above all by its own priorities, processes and personnel. Contemporary men and women want a magisterium that truly educates, i.e., opens eyes to unsuspected beauty and challenge in our lives. They want teachers who truly teach and maximize the potential of those taught. They will continue to reject a teaching office that is more concerned with control. The symptoms of control and the controlled group are well known. In "teaching" there is dominance of the negative, the condemnatory and the intolerance of pluralism. In administering there is oppressive centralization. There is avoidance of risk, conformism, "don't-rock-the-boatism." In policy planning there is waffling, fear of the fresh issue, enslavement to traditional phrases, anger at uncertainty. The use of power is secretive. Discussion is closed and draws on limited competence. The controlled are told what they may and may not do, not what they can achieve. They are reminded of the importance of a structure, not their own importance. They are constrained, not challenged; forbidden, not stimulated. The personality traits of the controlled are equally clear: fear, anxiety, joyless security, rejection of creative risk, growing apathy. In Catholicism there is a suffocating and cloying ultramontanism.

If the above describes anything in the reality of the contemporary Church, it substantiates my thesis that Catholics—as well as many others—want a truly effective magisterium. They will no longer tolerate one that identifies teaching with controlling.

9. Theologians must be pastorally sensitive.

"Pastorally sensitive" means many things, one of which is not "theologically supine." Theologians must present their analyses with due modesty. Their claims to prophecy should be reluctant and rare. Furthermore, they should help the public understand that it is sometimes necessary for the magisterium to take an authoritative position, even if it is tentative. Theologians must write, speak and act in a way that fosters respect for the magisterium. Finally, they should be ready, willing and able humbly to admit mistakes.

10. The public needs much more effective education than we have so far achieved.

The concrete needs are the following:

a. The Catholic public must have a much more accurate notion of the place of the magisterium and scholarship in the Church. The gigantic character of the educational task becomes apparent when we recall that many priests have not achieved this accuracy.

b. The public must be educated to understand that the Church does not have all the answers, or an immediate one to a new question. Vatican II acknowledged this openly.

c. The Catholic public—and most especially competent professionals—must be educated to the responsibilities inseparable from their own competence.

d. The Catholic public must be educated much more than they are to two facts: i) priests do not always speak accurately and critically on religious and moral issues; ii) moral theologians, in their public statements, do not always speak for the Church, or even for all other moral theologians. Sometimes their views are strictly personal, and we have to find a way of clarifying this.

e. Finally the Catholic public should know that the media thrive on confrontation. Many issues are not nearly as confrontational as they are made to appear.

These ten theses do not describe the relationship—codependent and cooperative—of theologians and the magisterium. Rather, they point up aspects of the contemporary scene that constitute the atmosphere or context in which this relationship must be lived out. The ultimate aim, I would think, is the delightful *conspiratio* that prevailed during Vatican II.

CHAPTER 8

Theology as a Public Responsibility

In an address to the National Federation of Priests' Councils on April 30, 1991, Bishop Kenneth Untener discussed three characteristics of the true prophet.[1] One was freedom, the freedom to speak the hard message for the right reasons and the freedom not to speak it for the wrong reasons or at the wrong time. Untener then noted, "I believe that there is a lack of this freedom among bishops today," not on all issues, but certainly on issues within the Church. In his words: "But on issues within the Church, I am embarrassed. We have seemed fearful to speak on Church issues that are right before our eyes, but which are unmentionable. We are like a dysfunctional family, unwilling to talk openly about things that are on everyone's mind, even when we are together at an NCCB meeting."

Being "unwilling to talk openly" is not an innate episcopal reluctance. It is a response to, and reflection of, an atmosphere of coercion resulting from a policy of intimidation. Its impact goes far beyond episcopal silence on certain issues. When applied to theology, this policy seeks the privatization of theological reflection. Because I regard this as a noxious development and inconsistent with the very notion of theology, I want to (1) describe this development and (2) underline the public nature of the discipline of theology. I hope that this will encourage others to fulfill courageously the public dimensions of their theological responsibility.

By "privatization" of theology I mean the removal of its critical and creative functions from public scrutiny and their confinement to a narrow few in the church (the hierarchical magisterium and theologians). It is as if the rest of the believers had no interest and stake in theological inquiry. Privatization has the practical effect of excluding from theological deliberation the very people whose faith and lives are being discussed and whose reflection and input are utterly essential if the magisterial process of the Church is to avoid the accusation of presumptuousness and magic.

Vatican II rejected the privatization of theology in any number of places, but perhaps nowhere more clearly than in the Pastoral Constitution on the Church in the Modern World (n. 62). After stating its hope that lay people would be well formed in the sacred sciences, the Council continued: "In order that such persons may fulfill their proper function, let it be recognized that all of the faithful, clerical and lay, possess a lawful freedom of inquiry and of thought, and the freedom to express their minds humbly and courageously about those matters in which they enjoy competence."[2] The council pointedly did not say that clergy and lay people should speak up only if they agreed with magisterial statements. They are to speak because presumably the Church can and must learn from them. There is no talk here about taking one's problems quietly to magisterial authorities, about writing only in professional journals, about not speaking to the media, about suffering in silence. Such caveats flow from a rather remarkably different ecclesiology.

The open and unthreatened perspectives I find in the Council contrast quite notably with those in the June 26, 1990 document of the Congregation for the Doctrine of the Faith entitled, "Instruction on the Ecclesial Vocation of the Theologian."[3] I believe that document to be a veritable charter for the privatization of theology and all that it involves.

The CDF Instruction, signed by Cardinal Joseph Ratzinger and Archbishop Alberto Bovone, distinguishes between dissent and the personal difficulties a theologian might have with a particular teaching. The document describes dissent as "attitudes of general opposition to Church teaching which even come to expression in organized groups." Or again, it is said to be "public opposition to the magisterium of the Church." It is further depicted as an attitude toward noninfallible teachings that sees them as having "no obligatory character about them leaving the individual completely at liberty to adhere to them or not. The theologian would accordingly be totally free to raise doubts or reject the noninfallible teaching of the magisterium particularly in the case of specific moral norms." In brief, dissent involves disrespect for, and even rejection of, the authoritative magisterium.

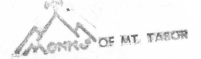

This idiosyncratic description of dissent leaves us with two unrealistic alternatives. Either there is *no* dissent in the Church according to the document's description (for I know of no theologian who believes he/she is totally free to reject noninfallible teachings) or *any* dissent is unacceptable because it inevitably involves disrespect. I view this as idiosyncratic because most people understand dissent as disagreement with a particular teaching, not overall rejection of the teacher or of teaching authority as such.

That leads to what the document refers to as the "personal difficulties" of a theologian with a particular teaching. I shall cite the document fully here because it is at the heart of our accusation of privatization. The case concerns "non-irreformable magisterial teaching." The document states:

> If despite a loyal effort on the theologian's part the difficulties persist, the theologian has the duty to make known to the magisterial authorities the problems raised by the teaching in itself, in the arguments proposed to justify it or even in the manner in which it is presented. He [sic] should do this in an evangelical spirit and with a profound desire to resolve the difficulties. His objections could then contribute to real progress and provide a stimulus to the magisterium to propose the teaching of the church in greater depth and with a clearer presentation of the arguments.
>
> In cases like these, the theologian should avoid turning to the "mass media" but have recourse to the responsible authority, for it is not by seeking to exert the pressure of public opinion that one contributes to the clarification of doctrinal issues and renders service to the truth.
>
> It can also happen that at the conclusion of a serious study, undertaken with the desire to heed the magisterium's teaching without hesitation, the theologian's difficulty remains because the arguments to the contrary seem more persuasive to him. Faced with a proposition to which he feels he cannot give his intellectual assent, the theologian nevertheless has the duty to remain open to a deeper examination of the question.
>
> For a loyal spirit, animated by love for the church, such a situation can certainly prove a difficult trial. It can be a call to suffer for the truth, in silence and prayer but with the certainty that if the truth really is at stake it will ultimately prevail.[4]

These interesting paragraphs give rise to a host of tantalizing questions. For instance, what confidence would an individual theologian have that his "recourse to the responsible authority" would do any good if even public statements by whole groups of theologians (e.g., the so-called Cologne Statement) are ignored? Does not the hierarchical magisterium also have a "duty to remain open to a deeper examination of the question," especially when it knows that large numbers of theologians worldwide disagree with certain of its teachings? What are theologians to do when their theological representations are met with intransigence? Or when genuinely debatable issues are prematurely closed or said to be no longer a matter of free theological debate? Is every statement to the mass media an attempt "to exert the pressure of public opinion"? Why can it not be viewed as an attempt to inform the public or air one's own view "humbly and courageously," as Vatican II worded it? It is my belief that the Holy See is not concerned about theologians using the media, but their using the media to voice disagreement. In this sense the Holy See is not opposed to publicity, but only to bad publicity. But it cannot defend such inconsistency. If Rome wants support for its good statements from its theologians in the media, it must expect a similar honesty when its deliverances are less than compelling.

But my concern with such questions is peripheral. The single feature in the CDF document that I wish to underline is that when the theologian finds her/himself unable to assent—I would call this dissent—that person is to (1) represent the dissent to magisterial authorities; (2) not state it to the media; and (3) indeed, remain silent. Some commentators have stated that the Ratzinger document does not mean to exclude publication in scholarly journals. Perhaps that is so, but I find no basis for that reading in the Instruction. The Instruction regards a dissenting opinion as a "call to suffer for the truth, *in silence* . . ." (my emphasis). At one point Cardinal Ratzinger refers to "*untimely* public expression" of an opinion divergent from that of the magisterium (my emphasis). But the CDF's statements and actions, for example in the Curran case (Cf. Chapter 9), indicate that *any* public expression of dissent is regarded as untimely. In sum, the CDF removes any disagreement with authoritative noninfallible teaching from the public realm. I call that the privatization of theology.

This privatization of theology has its roots in a very definite ecclesiology, one I believe was abandoned by Vatican II. The key element in this ecclesiology is the pyramidal structure of the Church and, as a result, the heavily obediential character given to the teaching-learning process of the Church. It is basically an authority problem. Bishop Raymond Lucker words our point as follows: "For those in power in Rome, the Church is not 'the people of God' that Vatican II talked about. It is an imperial monarchy that must maintain absolute control."[5]   The teaching-learning process of the Church is viewed within the dominance of the superior-subject relationship.   For this reason Lucker accurately notes that "in such a system, those in charge can exercise raw power, because their judgment is automatically correct and they need not worry about the consequences. They have to be right; that is the highest aim, good, object. And conversely, error has no rights. So if you are deemed to be in error, Rome feels that it has the duty to punish you."

The glaring symbol of all this is the Instruction's unqualified assertion that "the pastoral task of the magisterium is one of vigilance" (n. 20, p. 122). Once that foot is forward, it becomes clear why open discussion amounts to "confusion of the faithful" and why confusion at any level is seen as an unmitigated disaster. It also becomes clear why unity is confused with uniformity on all matters. It becomes clear why consultation is limited, why authorship is secret, why disagreement is not tolerated—in brief, why theology *must be* privatized. If vigilance is the self-description of the pastoral task of the magisterium, then theologians are above all those who are watched, scrutinized and eventually controlled.

The working out of this ecclesiology is inexorable and predictable. Only a privatized theology is a safe theology, and only an atmosphere of coercion will keep theology safely privatized. Thus it is that bishops are "unwilling to talk openly." Thus it is that theologians avoid subjects where disagreement is not tolerated, or seek employment in non-Catholic institutions where disagreement is no occupational threat. Thus it is that seminarians are directed to "safe" seminaries where teaching and scholarship are second-rate at best.

But coercion can be extremely harmful. Avery Dulles, S.J., once noted that the effort to stamp out dissent "inhibits good theology from performing its critical task, and is detrimental to the atmosphere of freedom in the Church."[6] Just how detrimental was made clear by Archbishop Rembert Weakland in a column he wrote for his archdiocesan newspaper in 1986.[7] He noted that the suppressions associated with the Modernist crisis "resulted in a total lack of theological creativity in the U.S.A. for half a century."

In the previous chapter I listed the impacts of a coercive ecclesial atmosphere that attempts to privatize theology.

In summary, the exclusion of public theological questioning and critique will deprive the People of God of the fruits of open and honest reflection on the practical implications of their faith. They have a right to this, as I shall develop below. For this reason I agree with a recent statement of the distinguished theologian and homilist Walter Burghardt, S.J.[8] Speaking of controversial issues and preaching he noted: "On such issues, in a short span of time, I dare not speak in dogmatic fashion, as if I alone am the trumpet of the Lord. But if I dare not dogmatize, I may still raise the issues, lay them out, even say where I stand and why. Not to impose my convictions as gospel, but as a spur to personal and communal reflection." If this is true of the homilist, it is, I believe, *a fortiori* true of the theologian.

This brings me to my second major point, the public nature of theology. Theology is public in nature, first, because *faith* is public in nature; secondly, because it is done always in the service of the *Church*, which is the whole People of God; thirdly, because it serves the *pastoral* needs of the Church; and, fourthly, because theologians are true *teachers*.

Theology is public in nature, first, because *faith* is public in nature. St. Anselm of Canterbury's definition of theology is "faith seeking understanding." If theology is private, then so, too, is faith.

But such a conclusion would be absurd on its face. Faith has always been understood as a gift of God to be shared with others. God communicated and made a covenant in Christ with a people, a community. This self-communication and covenant are public in character. Therefore, deepening Christian faith by critical reflection upon it is an inherently public undertaking. Consequently, this faith is to be proclaimed, witnessed to, and even died for. "'The word is near you, in your mouth and in your heart' (that is, the word of faith that we preach), for if you confess with your mouth that Jesus is Lord and believe in your heart that God raised him from the dead, you will be saved" (Rom 10:8-9).

Thus, it is impossible (because radically illogical) for a faith which is inherently public to be critically reflected upon and articulated only in private. To be sure, those who argue for the private nature of theology are not consistent. When a particular theologian's conclusions are consonant with, or supportive of, official teachings, no objection is raised against making those conclusions public.

Theology is public in nature, secondly, because it is done always in the service of the *Church*. But, as the Second Vatican Council reminded us, the Church is the whole People of God, not just the hierarchy. This is to say that theology is not done primarily, much less exclusively, in the service of the hierarchy, but primarily for the sake of the whole community of faith and, beyond that, for the wider human community.

To propose, even by implication, that the theologian is only a behind-the-scenes adviser to the hierarchy (the pope, the other bishops, and the Curia), serving always and only under their mandate and at their pleasure, is to suggest that the other members of the Church (the vast majority) have no direct personal or communal interest in the process by which their own faith is examined and explained, nor in the practical outcomes of those deliberations.

Such a proposal, even if only implicit, suggests that those outside the hierarchy have no capacity—intellectual, moral, or spiritual—to grasp the theological process or its outcomes. Accordingly, the attempt to privatize theology and the faith which theology seeks to understand insults the intelligence, good will, and powers of spiritual discernment of educated lay persons, religious, and clergy, and deprives them of what is theirs by baptismal right: an understanding of their faith commensurate with their intellectual, psychological, moral, and spiritual development.

Even the Revised Code of Canon Law, following the lead of the Second Vatican Council, acknowledges this as a right. The Christian faithful "have become sharers in Christ's priestly, prophetic and royal office [and] are called to exercise the mission which God has entrusted to the Church to fulfill in the world, in accord with the condition proper to each one" (Can. 204, n. 1).

As such, they have "the right to a Christian education by which they will be properly instructed so as to develop the maturity of a human person and at the same time come to know and live the mystery of salvation" (Can. 217). More specifically, "Lay persons are bound by the obligation and possess the right to acquire a knowledge of Christian doctrine adapted to their capacity and condition so that they can live in accord with that doctrine, announce it, defend it when necessary, and be enabled to assume their role in exercising the apostolate" (Can. 229, n. 1). They also "possess the right to acquire that deeper knowledge of the sacred sciences" (n. 2).

Theology is public in nature, thirdly, because it serves the *pastoral* needs of the Church. Religious educators, catechists, and preachers of the word depend upon theology because they have the ministerial responsibility of "echoing" (the literal meaning of catechesis), handing on, and proclaiming the faith—a responsibility that is simply impossible to fulfill without theology. Indeed, faith itself cannot be apprehended except theologically. To be self-conscious of one's faith is already to be engaged in a theological interpretation of it, no matter how rudimentary, inchoate, or unscientific that interpretation may be.

The question, therefore, is not *whether* the faith will be echoed, handed on, and proclaimed theologically, but rather *what kind* of theology will be employed in the process. As suggested above, the privatization of theology is not really the privatization of *all* theology, but only of the theology done by scientifically competent theologians who will inevitably disagree from time to time with one aspect or another of certain official teachings. There is no attempt to privatize the "safe" theology of many bishops, of many members of the Curia, and of "approved" theologians. But the public—both inside and outside the Church—is less and less interested in that "safe" theology because it seems to them incapable of illuminating and strengthening their faith or of drawing out its implications in an increasingly complex world. It is widely met with apathy.

Unfortunately, the Vatican's view of today's laity seems to be captured in the odious term "simple faithful." In a well-publicized paper given at St. Michael's College, Toronto, on April 15, 1986, Cardinal Ratzinger put it straightforwardly: "The Church's main job is the care of the faith of the simple. A truly reverential awe should arise from this which becomes an internal rule of thumb for every theologian." Moreover, Cardinal Ratzinger has made this the governing rule for ecclesiastical authorities as well. Their primary responsibility is to protect the simple faithful against theologians who criticize in any way whatever an official teaching of the church. "The care of the faith of the 'little ones,' " he insisted, "must always be more important than the fear of some conflict with the powerful" (p. 770).

Theology is public in nature, fourthly, because theologians are true *teachers*. As Avery Dulles has persuasively argued, the term "magisterium" itself applies to theologians as well as to bishops, and this has been the case since the Middle Ages.[10]

He has characterized as "reductionist" the view which collapses theology into the hierarchical magisterium. "On the ground that the ecclesiastical magisterium has a higher access to the truth (*charisma veritatis*), it is argued that the pope and bishops, by virtue of their grace of office, can do better everything that the theologian as such can do. The idea that the theologian might also have a grace of office seems not to be considered."[11] That idea is conspicuously absent from the Vatican's "Instruction on the Ecclesial Vocation of the Theologian."

My argument is that the theologian's grace of office necessarily involves him/her in public discourse and indeed the kind of discourse that cannot exclude some tension and disagreement. The theologian engages in this public discourse at a variety of levels and through a variety of means: the media, the academy, publications, and conferences.

First, in the electronic and print media. If theology has no place in the media, then a critically examined faith has no place in the media. And if that is the case, then society itself is effectively closed off from a critically examined faith. The result is that religion, and Christianity in particular, will remain for society a naive belief at best, a dangerous superstition at worst.

Nevertheless, the Vatican Instruction looks upon the media only in negative terms, as the place to which dissident theologians repair in order to "exert the pressure of public opinion" on the formulation of doctrine (n. 30).

Other groups take a broader and more positive view of the media. For instance, one does not hear the American Medical Association complaining when almost every month on network television news a tentative scientific finding in the latest issue of *The New England Journal of Medicine* is broadcast to millions of viewers. Professionals know that if their journals are not cited or if society takes no interest in their research, they are simply irrelevant. Therefore, they see the media as extensions of their work, not as its enemies.

More to the point, if theologians are not engaged with the media, they lose an extraordinary opportunity for education and at the same time a vacuum is created. Religious issues *are* of profound interest to the wider public. But if competent theologians are not available (or willing) to discuss them, others will be sought out for comment and interpretation in their stead. Vacuums have a way of attracting amateurs. The real concern of the Church should not be to restrict or stifle such public reflection, but to educate the public to both its need and limits.

The theologian engages in public discourse, secondly, in academic settings, especially the university. Several aspects of this engagement highlight the public character of theology. Universities and colleges, even those which are private, are public institutions in the sense that they are subject to law and open to public scrutiny. Next, while there are a few theologians who engage only in research (the so-called "ivory tower" scholar), almost all professionally active theologians have teaching positions, a public function. Furthermore, all active theologians, in turn, are members of professional organizations, e.g., the Catholic Theological Society of America and the American

Academy of Religion, whose meetings and publications are also public in nature.

The theologian engages in public discourse, thirdly, through his or her own scholarly writings in professional journals, collections, monographs, encyclopedias, and journals like *America* and *Commonweal*. It is important to note that even scholarly journals, such as *Theological Studies*, are public in nature. Anyone can subscribe to them; anyone can go to a library and read them. It is utterly naive, therefore, to think that the general public can be insulated from theological controversy if theologians were to confine their "speculations" to professional journals, any more than the general public can be insulated from medical controversy by medical scientists' confining *their* writing to *The New England Journal of Medicine.*

The theologian engages in public discourse, fourthly, through lectures and addresses given at national, regional, and local conferences of religious educators and other pastoral ministers. Theologians do not invite themselves to these meetings. They are asked to speak because religious educators, catechists, and other pastoral ministers perceive the need for up-to-date, academically and pastorally credible theological interpretation, and recognize, at the same time, the limited usefulness of approved theology, which is little more than a "party line."

Because faith is a public possession and theology is a public reflection, the real and abiding challenge to the Church today is first-class education at all levels. Public theological discourse, whether through the media, academic institutions, publications, or conferences, is an essential vehicle of this education. Theology has a responsibility to the Church, the intellectual and professional communities, and society at large to provide a critical explanation and interpretation of the faith and to clarify its personal and social (economic, cultural, and political) implications in an increasingly complex world. The attempt to privatize theology is a flight from this responsibility.

CHAPTER 9

L'Affaire Curran II

Charles E. Curran, for many years professor of moral theology at the Catholic University of America, is now teaching at Southern Methodist University as the Scurlock University Professor of Human Values. In itself this is not surprising. For a number of years Curran has done teaching stints at secular institutions such as Cornell University, the University of Southern California, and Auburn University. Curran's presence at such universities as Southern Methodist, however, reflects the fact that he is not welcome at Catholic institutions of higher learning. Indeed, in every case where efforts have been made at departmental levels to settle Curran in a Catholic institution, he has been positively excluded by upper administration. I regard this exclusion as a continuing complicity in the original injustice done to Curran and as harmful not only to him, but also to Catholic higher education in this country and to the Church.

First, the injustice. In a letter dated July 25, 1986 (but presented to Curran on August 18) the Congregation for the Doctrine of the Faith (CDF) informed Curran that he could "no longer be considered suitable nor eligible to exercise the function of a professor of Catholic theology."[1] At this same time Archbishop (now Cardinal) James A. Hickey, Chancellor of the Catholic University of America, informed Curran that he was initiating proceedings for the withdrawal of Curran's canonical mission, an official approval required of those teaching theology at a so-called pontifical university. At the time Curran was a full professor with tenure at Catholic University.

The removal of the canonical mission was the sad conclusion of a series of exchanges begun in 1979. It is this process and its outcome that I have called unjust. Continuing exclusion of Curran from Catholic college and university theology faculties represents complicity in the original injustice. These are serious charges and deserve very careful documentation.

Before explaining my judgment, I want to anticipate an objection. Does not the Church, through its pastoral leaders, have the right to protect its God-given message from serious error? Of course. Does it not have the right publicly to identify those judged to be undermining or distorting this message? Of course. Does not the Church have the "freedom to maintain her own academic institutions in which her doctrine is reflected upon, taught and interpreted in complete fidelity?" (Ratzinger). Once again, yes, but with an important qualifier. Catholic colleges and universities, unlike seminaries, are not "her own academic institutions." Positions on the theological faculty were not created by Church authorities and appointees are not controlled by them. Professors in these positions do not hold ecclesiastical offices and hence do not function in the name of the Church. Does not this freedom imply "the right to choose for her theological faculties those and only those professors who, in complete intellectual honesty and integrity, recognize themselves capable of meeting these requirements?" (Ratzinger). Yes, but once again we are dealing with an ecclesiastical appointment (as, for example, in a seminary or German university), not with college or university positions as they exist in this country. These latter are institutionally autonomous and must honor the principle of academic freedom.

Such juridical questions—really assertions—do not properly pose the issue. At stake is not the right of the Church to teach and to defend its teaching against error, but the proper scope and use of that right. We can envision situations when a public censure of a scholar could conceivably be appropriate, even mandatory, but such public censure would never mean expulsion from a theological faculty at a university or college. Only the theologian's academic peers can take that action in accordance with the statutes of the institution.

Even if it is conceded that the Vatican has the right to intervene in the case of a pontifical university, I believe that the protective prerogatives of the Church were improperly and unjustly exercised in the Curran case for two reasons: the process and its outcome.

.The process. It is all but universally acknowledged that the judicial process that prevails in the Congregation for the Doctrine of the Faith is woefully inadequate in the contemporary world. The French Dominican Bernard Quelquejeu has noted the following Roman practices as flouting rights recognized by modern societies:

- lack of separation of the prosecuting and judicial authorities;
- the author being investigated is informed of the investigation only at stage thirteen (of eighteen);
- the author under investigation cannot choose his defender; indeed he will not even know his identity;
- the accused has no access to documents touching on the charges;
- there is no publicity to the proceeding;
- there is no right of appeal.[2]

In 1984 Ratzinger admitted that the Congregation had decided to revise its procedures. However, he stated that workload and time constraints have prevented this. Given the offensive and downright unfair character of the procedures in place, the proper conclusion should have been and still is: no revision, no investigations. The CDF's recent (May 24, 1990) statement on dissent does not alter this conclusion.[3] In that document Ratzinger wrote: "The fact that these procedures can be improved does not mean that they are contrary to justice and right." To that I reply: it all depends on the nature of the required improvements. As the procedures now stand I believe they are "contrary to justice and right." Ratzinger continues: "To speak in this instance of a violation of human rights is out of place for it indicates a failure to recognize the proper hierarchy of these rights as well as the nature of the ecclesial community and her common good." This last sentence is far from clear. But if Ratzinger means that due process rights are of lesser importance in the Church or that they cannot be violated by Church authorities because of the very nature of the Church, I have no choice but to disagree, and resoundingly. There are objective standards for due process widely recognized throughout the world. They are not identical with what Rome thinks due.

Paul Sieghart, the international jurist, adverted to these matters in his Cardinal Heenan Memorial Lecture (December, 1988). "Within its internal structures," he said, "my own church . . . has not yet even begun to practice what it has so forcefully preached for 25 years and more in the matter of human rights."[4] With regard to due process he asked whether all parties "have the right to be tried in their presence, to be represented, to know as much of what is alleged against them as the tribunal itself knows, to hear and test all evidence given against them, to have their own witnesses heard, to equality of arms with their opponents, to publicity if they wish it, to a fully reasoned judgment, and to have the proceedings reviewed on appeal by an independent superior tribunal?" His answer was no and he referred among others to the case of Charles Curran. In brief, the institutional structures and procedures are unfair to start with. Investigations conducted within them are bound to be unfair. In Curran's case there was no formal process at all. This is all the more reason for seeing injustice in the way the matter was handled.

Now to the outcome. We refer to the ultimate judgment and its rationale. Curran was judged to be neither "suitable nor eligible" to teach Catholic theology. For a professional theologian to be so stigmatized by the Church's highest authorities translates as a judgment issued to the believing community that the person in question cannot be trusted in the very profession to which he has devoted his life: reflection on the faith and its moral implications. Indeed it asserts that the person's work is harming the Church. That is extremely serious business. It unavoidably connotes disloyalty to the magisterium by obstinate adherence to one's own opinion. For unnumbered thousands of people and into an indefinite future Curran's past, present and future work will be under a cloud, his theological—and to some extent his personal—reputation sullied.

What reason is given for the CDF's judgment? From the very beginning there has been a single issue: public dissent. (By "public dissent" we mean nothing more than disagreement with an officially formulated position, such as the intrinsic moral evil of every contraceptive act. We do not mean Ratzinger's rather idiosyncratic understanding of dissent as "general opposition to Church teaching," "seeking to exert the pressure of public opinion," "public opposition to the magisterium.") All along Curran tried to find out from the CDF its attitude toward dissent. Only at the end of the process (July 25, 1986) did Ratzinger clarify the CDF's position on dissent. As three astute Franciscan theologians (Regis A. Duffy, William E. McConville, and Kenneth R. Himes) noted in these pages, fruitful dialogue "is exactly what has not taken place" between the CDF and Curran.[5] Ratzinger finally made two points. First, he stated that:

> one must remember the teaching of the Second Vatican Council which clearly does not confine the infallible Magisterium purely to matters of faith nor to solemn definitions. *Lumen gentium* 25 states: ". . . when, however, they (the bishops) even though spread throughout the world, but still maintaining the bond of communion between themselves and with the successor of Peter, and authentically teaching on matters of faith or morals, are in

agreement that a particular position ought to be held as definitive, then they are teaching the doctrine of Christ in an infallible manner."[6]

Fair enough. But Curran's dissenting positions do not touch infallible teachings. Ratzinger adduces as an example the Church's teaching at Trent on the indissolubility of sacramental and consummated marriage. But theologians have admitted for decades that Trent's teaching does not exclude the practice of "economia" in the Greek Church, that is, the permission of a second marriage in certain cases after a sacramental and consummated first marriage. If one argues that Curran's dissent on contraception involves infallible teaching, the vast majority of theologians would deny that, and indeed would share Curran's position. They would further insist that in a coercive atmosphere apparent unity is specious since bishops are not free to say what they really think. Here it is helpful to recall what the Canadian bishops wrote in 1968 about Catholics who cannot accept *Humanae vitae*. "Since they are not denying any point of divine and Catholic faith, nor rejecting the teaching authority of the Church, these Catholics should not be considered, or consider themselves, shut off from the body of the faithful."[7] Ratzinger, therefore, can adduce no writing of Curran that denies infallible teaching.

Ratzinger's second assertion is more ominous. He adds: "Besides this, the Church does not build its life upon its infallible magisterium alone but on the teaching of its authentic, ordinary magisterium as well."[8] The implication of this statement is that whatever the Church builds its life upon is not a proper matter for critical evaluation and possibly public dissent. Even recent history would not support this. Was not the rejection of common worship with other Christians a part of the Church's life prior to Vatican II? The same for rejection of religious liberty? The same for the tolerance of slavery for many centuries? Was not procreation as the primary end of marriage part of the Church's thought and life prior to Vatican II?

Actually Ratzinger's position represents a denial of the legitimacy of public dissent *in principle*. This has led ecclesiologist Francis Sullivan, S.J., of the Pontifical Gregorian University in Rome, to remark: "The idea that Catholic theologians, at any level of education, can only teach the official Church position and present only those positions in their writings is new and disturbing."[9]

Rejection of public dissent in principle would stifle theology's critical role. This was implicitly acknowledged by the American bishops in their pastoral letter of 1968 "Human Life in Our Day," when they stated the conditions for licit public dissent. "The expression of theological dissent from the magisterium is in order only if the reasons are serious and well-founded, if the manner of the dissent does not question or impugn the teaching authority of the Church, and is such as not to give scandal."[10] Curran has consistently argued—rightly in my judgment and in that of his students and most peers—that his positions have satisfied these conditions.

Cardinal Hickey stated several years ago that the norms for dissent noted by the American bishops "are simply not workable." With all due respect I must remark that a bishop or the bishops cannot take away what they have not given in the first place. The legitimacy of dissent from noninfallible teaching is not an episcopal grant or concession. Only a very juridical mind could think so. Rather such legitimacy is rooted in the imperfection and contingency of human knowledge when that knowledge is concerned with quite specific human actions. Thus Curran has always argued that his dissent touches matters that are remote from the core of faith, heavily dependent on support from human reason and involved in such complexity and specificity that one really cannot lay claim to unchangeable certitude. In this he is being loyally Thomistic. For St. Thomas observed that the more the mind descends to particulars, the more it encounters contingency and change—and uncertainty.

In summary, then, serious harm was done to Curran through a flawed process and on the basis of a rationale (rejection of any public dissent) that is "new and disturbing" and that will not survive historical and theological scrutiny. That is why, prior to Curran's censure (March 12, 1986) a group of Catholic theologians (all past presidents of the Catholic Theological Society of America and The College Theology Society) issued a statement putting the following questions to the CDF:

> 1) Which noninfallible teachings are serious enough to provoke such a result, and how are these teachings determined? 2) How many noninfallible teachings would one have to disagree with before this result would follow, and how is that number determined? 3) If disagreement with any noninfallible teaching of the Church is sufficient to provoke this result, *on what theological, doctrinal or historical basis is that principle deduced?* (emphasis added).[11]

Unless these questions are consistently and satisfactorily answered—and they have not been—punitive actions based on the premise of settled answers is unjust.

In summary, then, when investigatory procedures are structurally unjust, and when the theological rationale for punitive action against an individual is not accepted by many bishops (we state this as a fact we know via private conversations), most theologians (this is documentable), and very many (not all) laity, we are staring face-to-face at an injustice.

Since it is my conviction that this is an accurate analysis, I believe that continued exclusion of Curran from Catholic colleges and universities is a form of self-censorship by college and university administrators that amounts to continuing complicity in an injustice. Recall some facts here. 1) The Catholic University board of trustees was willing to offer Curran employment at CUA, even if not in the theology department. Indeed, after the June 16, 1990, censure of Catholic University by the American Association of University Professors, William J. Byron, S.J., president of Catholic University, stated that the offer to let Curran teach social ethics outside the theology department "remains on the table." 2) As Ladislas Orsy, S.J., has recently shown, one does not need a canonical mission at non-pontifical colleges and universities.[12] Therefore, the removal of such a mission should not affect Curran's eligibility for other Catholic colleges and universities. 3) Over 750 theologians in North America have signed a statement of support for Curran attesting to his excellent reputation in his field. 4) Curran is the only theologian to have been president of the following three societies: Catholic Theological Society of America, Society of Christian Ethics, American Theology Society. This is a clear indication of the academic esteem he enjoys. 5) He was the first recipient of the prestigious John Courtney Murray Award from the CTSA. 6) Curran is a diocesan priest in good standing who is supported by his bishop, Matthew H. Clark, of Rochester, New York, as "a moral theologian of notable competence whose work locates him very much at the center of that community and not at all on the fringe."[13]

I conclude from the above that the exclusion of Curran from Catholic colleges and universities has no sustainable basis in law, academics or theology. Certainly the Right would be livid and vociferous were some Catholic university to hire Curran. But that is an unworthy basis for continuing the self-censorship that now prevails, especially if one concurs with my analysis of the original injustice.

But Curran's personal fate is not my only concern. The outcome and the process by which that outcome was reached have inflicted grave harm on the academic reputation of The Catholic University of

America, and its School of Religious Studies in particular, on Catholic higher education generally, and on the Catholic Church itself.

The harm to the academic reputation of The Catholic University of America is painfully self-evident. In the minds of many scholars and potential graduate students outside that university, CUA is no longer a place where the fundamental principles of academic freedom and institutional autonomy are securely established. I mean this in no way as a critique of the many excellent professors at CUA. My concern is institutional policy. As the Investigating Committee of the American Association of University Professors observed in its report last year: "Ultimately Professor Curran lost his position in Catholic University's Department of Theology because of opinions expressed in his published works."[14] And according to District of Columbia Superior Court Judge Frederick Weisberg's decision of February 28, 1989, what happened to Father Curran could also happen, for the very same reasons, to any other member of the CUA faculty: "On some issues— and this case certainly presents one of them—the conflict between the University's commitment to academic freedom and its unwavering fealty to the Holy See is direct and unavoidable. On such issues, the University may choose for itself on which side of that conflict it wants to come down, and nothing in its contract with Professor Curran *or any other faculty member* promises that it will always come down on the side of academic freedom" (emphasis mine).[15]

What did happen to Curran was in violation of the 1940 Statement of Principles on Academic Freedom and Tenure, a joint statement of the Association of American Colleges and the American Association of University Professors endorsed by some 130 educational and professional organizations. That statement declared: "The teacher is entitled to full freedom in research and in the publication of the results. . . . Limitations of academic freedom because of religious or other aims of the institution should be clearly stated in writing at the time of the appointment."[16]

The Catholic University of America has no statement labeled "Limitations," although two items in the faculty handbook suggest limitations related to the institution's religious aims. However, a former dean of the School of Religious Studies who had "a main role in preparing this statement" informed the AAUP Investigating Committee that "the statement was not intended to preclude dissent from noninfallible teaching."

The Investigating Committee of the AAUP continued: "The president, chancellor, and board of trustees seemed all too ready, nonetheless, to conclude that the Sacred Congregation's declaration was controlling and that withdrawal of Professor Curran's canonical mission had to follow as a matter of course. . . . In contrast to the administration and the board, the *ad hoc* committee of the Academic Senate perceived the need to protect both Professor Curran's academic freedom and the university's autonomy, which it saw being eroded by their actions. . . ."[17]

The AAUP committee then concluded straightforwardly: "In forcing Professor Curran to relinquish all teaching of Catholic theology at Catholic University, the administration and board of trustees violated his academic freedom; for they were moved to their decision by a declaration of the Sacred Congregation for the Doctrine of the Faith based upon publications that were protected by academic freedom under the 1940 Statement of Principles and the policies of Catholic University itself."

The report continued: "The university's autonomy and the academic freedom of its faculty may not have been important to the Sacred Congregation, but they should have been of first importance to the board of trustees," which, according to the Joint Statement on Government of Colleges and Universities formulated by the American Council on Education, the Association of Boards of Universities and Colleges, and the AAUP in 1966, is "expected to serve as a champion" of academic freedom and institutional autonomy in times of "grave crises."

I noted that the harm is not restricted to CUA but affects Catholic higher education. Once again note the remarks of the AAUP Investigating Committee. "Although initially the inquiry of the Sacred Congregation affected only Professor Curran, its repercussions have been felt throughout the university and far beyond its bounds."

It used to be said that anti-Catholicism is the anti-Semitism of intellectuals. Whatever the case, many secular liberals (and many secular conservatives, for that matter) have always doubted the capacity of Catholics to engage in serious intellectual inquiry, at whatever levels. Accordingly, Catholic colleges and universities have remained suspect in their eyes, occupying a notch only marginally higher than Bob Jones University, Oral Roberts University, or Jerry Falwell's Liberty Baptist University. A body of dogmas, not a dispassionate commitment to the pursuit of truth wherever that pursuit might lead, is the controlling force in such institutions—at least in the minds of their critics.

The Curran case has handed these critics, not all of whom can be dismissed simply as bigots, a powerful piece of evidence in support of their thesis. This is exceedingly unfortunate because Catholic educators generally are firmly committed to the twin principles of institutional autonomy and academic freedom.

In 1972, for example, the International Federation of Catholic Universities declared that a Catholic university "must be a university in the full sense of the word, with a strong commitment to and concern for academic excellence. To perform its teaching and research functions effectively a Catholic university must have true autonomy and academic freedom."[18] The document made no distinction between so-called secular and Catholic models of academic freedom.

In 1976 the College and University Department of the National Catholic Educational Association insisted that "freedom from outside constraints is the very breath of life for a college and university."[19] The NCEA document recognizes no internal role for the hierarchy in the academic process.

Indeed, that same paper anticipated the kinds of negative reactions from outside the Catholic educational world that the Curran case has evoked: "If the integrity and freedom of the academy is attacked . . . the Church will be the first to suffer. Its enemies will contend derisively that truth cannot be upheld or defended without resort to penalties and outside sanctions, confirming for some the suspicion that Catholic institutions cannot be true universities."

Even the U.S. Catholic bishops implicitly accepted the principles of academic freedom and institutional autonomy in their 1980 pastoral letter on Catholic higher education.[20] "Policies, standards, curricula, governance and administration," the bishops said, "should accord, therefore, with the norms of quality accepted in the wider academic community." The "norms of quality accepted in the wider academic community" are not consistent with the norms to which the Vatican, Cardinal Hickey, and the administration and board of trustees at Catholic University appealed in moving the Curran case to its final outcome.

How to repair the damage that has been done to CUA, to Catholic higher education, and to the Church itself? The only way in which Catholic University can regain its deserved reputation as a leading center of theological and biblical scholarship would be by offering Father Curran an opportunity to teach in the field in which he is tenured, namely, Catholic moral theology, in one of the non-ecclesiastical faculties of the University: the Department of Religion and Religious Education or even the Department of Sociology. But it must be as a Catholic moral theologian, and not as a social scientist. In this way, Catholic University could honor the special relationship with the Holy See in the ecclesiastical degree program while at the same time honoring its oft-stated institutional commitment to academic freedom and institutional autonomy.

Catholic higher education can repair the more indirect, but no less serious, damage done to itself by the Curran case if a prestigious Catholic university like Notre Dame, Boston College, or Georgetown were to offer him a tenured professorship in theology. It is not that Father Curran's theological colleagues do not want him in their institutions. Most would give their proverbial right arms to get him. The resistance is coming not from the theology departments in these institutions, but from upper administrations which are afraid of what might happen to their reputations and capacity for fundraising if they did hire Father Curran. They are intimidated by the actual or potential opposition of the local bishop, of religiously and politically conservative members of their boards of trustees, of some members of their own religious congregation, of angry right-wing alumni, and of similar constituencies. So much for "freedom from outside constraints" in the academy.

But as I have indicated above, the original action against Charles Curran and the process by which it was taken were unjust. What is worse, the action and the process also *appear* to be unjust to those outside not only of CUA but of Catholic higher education and of the Catholic Church generally. I can understand why an unenlightened individual bishop may not want to have Father Curran speak at one of his diocesan events, or why the Vatican may not now be eagerly disposed to making Father Curran a bishop, or even a monsignor. But it is at once unintelligible and inexcusable that Catholic educators who know better should now have assumed the disturbing role of accomplices to the original injustice—an injustice not only to Father Curran but to Catholic higher education and to the Church he continues to serve so faithfully.

This is no longer the time, therefore, to shake a fist of indignation at Cardinal Ratzinger, or at Cardinal Hickey, or at the president and board of trustees of the Catholic University. They have, for all practical purposes, passed the baton along to others; namely, the presidents and chief academic officers of our major Catholic colleges and universities. The present and future reputation of Catholic higher education is in their hands. The Curran affair offers them an extraordinary opportunity to show what they can do with it.

CHAPTER 10

The Shape of Moral Evasion in Catholicism

Every large organization does it. By "it" I refer to the attempt to display the organization's policies and practices in the best possible light to sidestep messy and unfinished issues. During times of crisis, it is known as "damage control." We have seen this in government over and over again, from Watergate to the Iran-Contra affair, to the downing of Iran Air 655. We have seen it in the corporate world, from giants like General Motors and McDonnell Douglas to the corner grocery store whose meat proved tainted. The medical profession has been notorious for years for the "closing-ranks-syndrome," its corporate reluctance to deal publicly with incompetence.

This nearly instinctive structural reflex of self-defense is understandable. Organizations either succeed or fail, grow or wither, in terms of public perception. That is why public relations is such a high priority on an organization's flow chart, whether it be a hospital, a university, a law firm, a Boeing, a Ford, an I.B.M., or Johnson and Johnson. A hostile shot in *Forbes Magazine* creates corporate panic at I.B.M. And that is also why organizations have such a difficult time owning up to shortcomings or mistakes. It is much easier to closet them or gloss over them.

A whole new vocabulary has sprouted up around the best-foot-forward tactic. We hear of "limited hangouts," "stonewalling," "blue-ribbon committees," "inoperative statements," "bureaucratic clogs," "communication gaps," "classified knowledge," "not for attribution," and so on. Lately, however, the corporate world has learned that the best way to deal with a fumble is to call it that, admit it, try to trace its source and rectify it. The symbol: Chrysler's Lee Iacocca's response to the scam involving used cars sold as new: "We made a damn dumb mistake and it will not happen again."

That something analogous to the self-protective reflex could happen in the Church should come as no surprise. The Church is, among the many other glorious things that it is, also an organization, and as organization it is human to its chromosomes. That "something analogous" I will call "moral evasion." By "evasion" I refer to the resistance to facing squarely a challenging, unpleasant, erroneous, anguishing fact or problem by redescribing it and calling it by a different name that elicits different responses, analyses and loyalties. The qualifier "moral" is used for several reasons: 1. Such evasion often concerns moral problems; 2. It is an exercise of moral agency and involves moral responsibility; 3. It has moral repercussions.

The structure of moral evasion is quite simple. It begins by stating what is unquestionably true, and often laudably so, and thus achieves prima facie plausibility. But such statements most often polish down, minimize or omit what is controversial, inaccurate, unestablished, unpleasant, or erroneous. Thus they "face" a problem by skirting it, delaying it, hiding it, supposing its easy answer, or diverting attention from it.

There are many reasons why Church leaders would be especially vulnerable to the enticements of moral evasion. For instance, the institutional Church (the Vatican, remember, is *also* a sovereign state) is an important player on the international stage. Its effectiveness in this role depends to a great extent on its credibility, which is obviously very intimately linked to public perception. But there are two reasons in the moral sphere why moral evasion could be a particularly powerful allure. First, the pope and bishops are said by traditional theology to enjoy a special guidance of the Holy Spirit as they go about the business of providing moral guidance. Second, this guidance is authoritatively proposed. That is, it is often presented as an authentic interpretation of God's will and carries with it the implication of eternal sanctions.

Within this framework it is easy to understand the almost irresistible pull of moral evasion. To admit a mistake, to acknowledge doubt, to reverse a policy, to face a hard problem—these and similar things inevitably look to church leaders dangerously close to a distancing of the Spirit and therefore to forfeiting the authority itself. This is all the more the case if there is little historical precedent for this and therefore no pastoral preparation for it. Thus it was that Paul VI was persuaded by a minority of the so-called Birth Control Commission that any modification of *Casti connubii* would compromise his authority. Who would trust authoritative teaching in the future if what previous popes had rejected as serious violations of the natural law were now modified? If the Spirit truly guides the pastors of the Church, how is such change conceivable? When the stakes are escalated in this way, the attractiveness of moral evasion (as over against repeated excruciating agonies every time a moral problem arises) becomes enormous.

In what follows I will, in a sacramental spirit, propose seven examples of at least possible moral evasion. Then I will briefly point out their repercussions. Unless I am mistaken, many of these examples have become so commonplace that they are no longer recognized as evasions at all. That could render them all the more seductively dangerous to the health of ecclesial life. Unrecognized threats are doubly threatening. Because evasion occurs in different situations and in different ways, it has many shapes, but always there is the familiar face: the lacquering of a hard fact, problem, truth, situation.

1. "THE PRESENCE OF CONFUSION" SYNDROME

Before the arrival of John Paul II in the United States in September (1987), several bishops noted that there was a large amount of confusion within rank-and-file Catholicism. They undoubtedly had in mind confusion about the Church's moral teaching on matters such as birth regulation, homosexuality, the status of the irregularly remarried, reproductive technologies, and abortion. Confusion is defined as a state of perplexity and bewildered uncertainty, the posture of one at a crossroad who doubts whether right or left is the proper turn. There are some, of course, who for years have been eagerly reporting to anyone who will listen the source of this confusion: permissive and spineless bishops, deviant ("modernist") theologians, disaffected and media-hungry ex-priests, activist nuns and liberal Catholic magazines (have I omitted anyone, Mr. Matt [*The Wanderer*]?). The Pope would set matters straight.

There can be no doubt that there is some confusion in the Church. But there ought to be. Many contemporary problems are so complex and specific that they ought to generate confusion, as Vatican II readily admitted. Thus the uncontestable fact is out front. But what this scenario conveniently overlooks is the quite chasmic difference between confusion and—let us avoid the dread buzz word "dissent"—respectful disagreement. A *Time* poll taken in the fall of 1987 revealed that a huge 93% of American Catholics believe that it is possible to disagree with the papal judgment on individual moral points such as those mentioned above and yet remain good Catholics. The Pope disagrees with this, as he made clear in his speech to the American bishops in Los Angeles. But since the *Time* poll was taken after the papal speech, we may say, in a sense, that 93% of Catholics disagree with the papal disagreement with them, on the assumption that they were aware of his statements.

Whatever the case—and I do not want to explore the theological implications of all of this here—one thing seems clear: there is much more disagreement than confusion. Certain Catholic reactionaries will insist that *any* disagreement with papal judgments is really a form of confusion. While I think that to be historically and theologically unfounded, it is not to the point here. What is to be underlined is that by center-staging confusion among Catholics, whatever its amount, one evades the need to face head-on the fact of dissent and its perhaps uncomfortable implications.

The term "confusion" suggests a great deal. For instance, it suggests that Catholics do not know what the official teaching is. It further suggests that all that is needed is a repetition of clear Church teaching to dispel it. Within the Catholic ethos confusion can be handled. A timely edict will do. In this spirit a recent article in *Crisis* (June, 1988) asserted that Paul VI in *Humanae vitae* did not intend to present argumentation for his teaching, but only to *clarify* it.[1] (It would be interesting to explore what notion of teaching and learning is implied when clarification is severed from justification and reduced to repetition).

As against confusion, dissent is much messier, the more so when it is respectful. It raises all kinds of problems. Very few of us welcome problems, especially those to which we have no immediate answers. Intellectual suspended animation is a kind of spiritual torture. There is a quick fix: rather than deal with dissent, call the situation one of "confusion." Physicians are familiar with this: "Take an aspirin." Notice the subtle transfer of onus here. Confusion is a kind of mental disorientation in the ranks. Respectful disagreement, far from being disorientation, is aggressively saying to the leader: "It is *you* who are inaccurate or premature. The burden is on *you* to reconsider."

2. "THE EMPHASIZE THE GENERAL" SYNDROME

When the instruction of the Congregation for the Doctrine of the Faith (C.D.F.) on reproductive technology (*Donum vitae*) appeared in March (1987), *America* headlined an essay by Archbishop Daniel

Pilarcyzk "Taking it on the chin—for Life" (4/11/87).[2] The instruction, in other words, was presented as being chiefly about the dignity of human life. That this was an overarching concern was uncontestably true. It was no less true of *Humanae vitae* in 1968. Paul VI had wonderfully inspiring things to say about marriage and those who have not read his encyclical are the poorer for it. I believe the same is true of the C.D.F.'s instruction on reproductive technologies.

Both documents drew remarkably concrete conclusions that grabbed public attention and fired controversy. They cut where the cake was. And authority was holding the knife. *Humanae vitae* proscribed all contraception and the C.D.F.'s instruction did the same for any reproductive technology that replaces sexual intercourse.

Both documents appealed to the inseparability ("by divine design") of the unitive and procreative dimensions of sexual intimacy. In non-theological shorthand: No lovemaking without being open to the possibility of procreation. No procreation without lovemaking. Babies must be begotten, not made. There is here a remarkably profound insight into the wonderful enmeshment of human love and human life. Sunder that and what do we have? Foreseeably, intimacy turned narcissistically and destructively in on itself, or procreation by fabrication where loving support is iffy and adventitious. The basic insight is absolutely sound.

But in all situations, in every act? Where the fruit of love must be limited to assure the fruits of marriage? Where an otherwise sterile marriage strives for its "ultimate crown" and "supreme gift" (Vatican II), the child?[3] Many have been unable to accept the absolutism of these conclusions. But that is not the point here. It is rather that by reading these documents as if they were above all and only "ringing affirmations of life" (or as "prophetic") one walks away from (evades) the very concrete problems they were trying to face in the first place: the limited and conflictual character of the human situation. One walks, as it were, the high road. The price of this is sometimes steep. Those who must live on the low road may no longer look up.

3. "THE CHURCH HAS ALWAYS TAUGHT" SYNDROME

Historians of theology are now long accustomed to the fact that Catholic officialdom never admits to error or previous inadequacies. When change occurs, it is invariably couched in terms of "development" and "continuity." Thus: "This is what the official teaching was *substantially* saying all along."

Fair enough. Indeed, here is the uncontestable truth out front. There are very legitimate distinctions between, for example, the substance of the Church's teachings, and its formulation at a particular moment of history, as both John XXIII and Vatican II insisted. Furthermore, there are modifications that merit description as "development" (of something seminally but inexplicitly present). When such things occur there is a genuine sense in which it is true to say "the Church has always taught."

However, there also may be simple reversals, takebacks traceable to a reassessment of the human scene, things previously proposed that we would no longer propose. In the judgment of many theologians, we saw this in the Church's conclusions about religious liberty at Vatican II. This was the most controversial single issue at the Council, according to John Courtney Murray, because, as he softly worded it, it raised concretely the problem of doctrinal development. "Development," of course, suggests continuity, a further unfolding of a constant core. If the teaching on religious liberty were only development in that sense, one must wonder at the furor it created. Development can also mean simple change. When simple change occurs, the earlier positions often disappear in a haze of historical amnesia—as they did, for instance, in the case of the decrees of the Biblical Commission and the teaching of Leo XIII on Church and State. The less said, the better.

"Development," then, in the ecclesial context, is an ambiguous term. Its more explicit sense (suggesting basic continuity) supports the description of modification and change under the rubric "the Church has always taught." But because it is ambiguous, it can be used as a comfortable screen hiding (evading) the fact that a simple change or reversal has occurred. When "development" is used, then, to describe notably different situations, it functions as an anesthetic numbing us to the painful implications that the Church has changed its outlooks and conclusions on some rather important practical matters. To continue to use "the Church has always taught" and "development" to describe remarkably different phenomena is to run from (evade) the problem of change.

The Church, quite bluntly, ought to be able to change because times change. It ought to be able to recognize and repudiate past incompletions and inaccuracies and to see that previous policies and formulations were the product of cultural variables. The Church is a pilgrim church. Catholics must be prepared pastorally for this possibility. If we adopt a vocabulary that makes it seem that real change is not occurring or cannot occur, we evade the issue.

4. "THE CHURCH IS NOT A DEMOCRACY" SYNDROME

One usually hears this statement in reaction to polls of Catholics on some controversial moral problems, or as a comment about the widespread nature of dissent in certain sensitive areas.

There is in the assertion uncontestable truth, or rather truths. The pope, and the bishops with the pope, enjoy both a jurisdictional and teaching role that is not restricted or controlled by plebiscite, or subject to its vagaries. Furthermore, what is morally right or wrong is not determined by headcounting. To think so would be a radical negation of the very need and meaning of a moral magisterium. Finally, the believing community is not reducible to a nation-state. It has dimensions (sacramental, mysterious, eschatological, etc.) that simply do not coincide with secular societies. "The Church is not a democracy" says all of that.

But this sweeping aphorism says a lot more, and in doing so leaves untouched (evades) some key problems. Indeed, unless I am mistaken, the sweeping character is meant to *imply* one particular answer to these problems, but in reality evades them. For instance, the fact that the pope enjoys a unique moral teaching role within the Catholic idea does not tell us what resources he must use in fulfilling this role, what theological expertise he must draw upon, how the experience of competent lay people must play a role in forging Church convictions and conclusions, what place there is for corrective critical response to papal formulations, how moral arguments and analysis affect the value and validity of papal conclusions. These are the truly interesting and heavy issues.

Or again, the uncontestable fact that the Church is not just a secular society like other nation-states, but is a mysterious spiritual, sacramental and eschatological reality says nothing about the existence and extension of rights in the Church or about due process in conflicted relationships.

"The Church is not a democracy" *seems* to and, in argumentative contexts, intends to answer these questions. Actually it only evades them by folding them into the embrace of a broader jurisdictional aphorism. Within this embrace, due process, for example, can turn out to mean what Rome thinks is due.

5. "THEOLOGIANS SPECULATE" SYNDROME

This is very close to the previous evasion. In some sense, it is but a specification of it. But in a Church divided on a number of moral issues it deserves explicit treatment.

One of the major tasks of theology is to reformulate for our time and culture the "great deeds of God" (*magnalia Dei*). For theology is faith reflecting on itself. Faith is far more than intellectual assent to credal statements. It is acceptance of and total commitment to God's self-revelation in Jesus. Moral theology attempts to discover and enlighten the behavioral implications of such acceptance and commitment.

Since acceptance of God's self-revelation occurs in different times and cultures, its meaning must be examined and reexamined as times, circumstances, cultures change. That is why it is true to say that we must wrestle with our faith on a daily basis to repossess it. The theologian exists to aid in that process.

In this light, one of theology's roles is that of explorer. It tests past formulations, proposes new ones, probes the interconnections of mysteries and in general tries to plumb human experience of the divine in a way that illuminates it, reveals its splendor and depth. This involves speculation (looking into things) and possibly even more false starts than we care to admit.

Theological exploration does not always succeed. It can distort, falsify, impoverish. Human effort will always bear the imprint of human handling. But without it, the Church is crippled because its faith stagnates in conceptual frameworks and symbols of a different era.

So while theologians do speculate—that is the truth up front—the sense of "theologians speculate" is that they *only* speculate. The implication is that their work is airy irrelevance that should have very little to do with the ultimate outcome of the Church's moral discernment process. Theologians may present analyses and arguments rooted in evidence from human experience, but "real truth" comes from elsewhere. This total severance of theology from authentic teaching represents the canonization of jurisdictional muscle.

I call "theologians speculate" an evasion because its apologetic use supposes an answer to a serious question that has not been approached, much less analyzed: the relation of theological arguments and analyses to concrete moral conclusions in the life of the Church. Toward the end of *Humanae vitae* Paul VI asked of priests a loyal acceptance of his teaching because appropriate deference (*obsequium*) "obliges not only because of the reasons adduced, but rather because of the light of the Holy Spirit, which is given in a particular way to the pastors of the Church." Clearly he implied that the reasons adduced or adducible have *something* to do with the conclusion (thus the language "not only because of the reasons"). How much? Paul VI only raised the problem. "Theologians speculate," while stating a truth, evades that knotty problem with an implied answer that Paul VI himself could not in consistency accept. In this way a truth becomes a half-truth.

6. "IF YOU ONLY HAD MY EXPERIENCE" SYNDROME

Often enough we hear the White House press secretary respond: "I am not at liberty to say." Sometimes, in translation, that means: "There are things going on here, sensitive international involvements, future implications that should stay unstated. And if you knew these things, you would agree with us." Briefly, "we have the facts, you do not. So unless you are in our position, you are in no position to criticize or disagree." The blanket that wraps it all up: national security.

The analogue to this in Church life is the appeal to pastoral experience, the assertion of the bishop (or pope, pastor, superior or teacher) that he has the overall picture, has access to sources of information, has dealt with the problems of people (etc.) in such a way that it overwhelms any contrary argument or point. Here we have a blanket, too: the good of the faithful. I blush to say that I have done this as a priest and teacher. And the approach has its validity; otherwise, intelligent people could not get away with it. It is literally true. People with position and experience should be expected to have a broader focus than others. The trouble is that too often we use such appeals at the very time our arguments and responses to challenges are weakest. That is the telltale giveaway.

In summary, such appeals can easily become crutches that stand in for reasoned responses. Thus the evasion. A truth is stated, but the real issue is not engaged.

7. THE "FAILURE OF TONE" SYNDROME

Presently I am told that there is in Rome a great concern about "tone." Alan Jay Lerner and Frederick Lowe, in frivolous moments, might easily have lyricized this as "the moan of Rome falls mainly on the tone." I take this concern to refer to respect for authority, specifically the magisterium. That is an absolutely legitimate concern. Dissent that turns to disdain is disagreement become disorder. It simply misses the point by shooting far beyond it. It targets the teacher and his office, not the message.

That being said, however, not all has been said. Emphasis on tone can foster a dialogue-by-indirectness that nurtures evasion. Let an example suffice. Suppose that the American bishops, and Catholics in general, resent the secretive financial policies of the Holy See (as it is clear that they do). This is the group that constitutes one of the major financial resources of the Vatican. Americans, being terribly pragmatic, are likely to show their pique by voting with their wallets.

There are several ways open to the bishops of hammering home to Rome this particular nail. One is the forthright "Shape up or . . ." That is unacceptable. It is a failure in tone. Why? Because it embarrasses the Holy See. Why? Because others are allowed to see that the presence of money talks at the Vatican. That is a bit unseemly for the world's foremost spiritual authority.

So what happens? The American bishops inform the Holy See that it has been a poor year for Americans, that prices are up, the dollar is weak. There has been a draught. The American Church has had other extraordinary expenses, etc. Thus Peter's Pence is off.

The Vatican understands exactly what this *means* ("Shape up or . . ."). But it has not been *said*. The symbols are at one level, the actual communication at another. It is a form of *politesse* that makes its point but not too pointedly. By that I do not mean cynically that it satisfies the ALH test (acceptable level of hypocrisy). By no means. It is a cultural thing common to other levels of social contact.

There is a single problem with it. Tone can become so dominant a concern that it fudges—and therefore evades—the issue. Problems remain unconfronted, larded over in a way that leaves everyone comfortable when they should be uncomfortable. Indeed we can get to the point where any public disagreement with official policies or instruction is viewed as a failure in tone. When that happens, hard questions get fogged by institutional *delicatesse*. In a word, they are evaded. At that point, it is paradoxically true to say that the more we hide, the less we hide.

These are but seven instances of moral evasion. There are many more institutional practices and policies, as well as theological dicta that carry with them the potential for evasion. For instance: the annulment process, appeals to academic freedom, the selection of bishops, the indulgent, "hide-the-offender" approach to the problems of clerical abuse of minors, "the end does not justify the means," to cite but a few.

Moral evasion has many identifiable repercussions. For example, it can easily foster cynicism, a particularly virulent cancer in a community whose health depends upon mutual trust. Another offshoot is corporate inertia, the collapse of creativity in the face of new problems and challenges.

But in my judgment the single most significant effect of moral evasion in ecclesial life could be in the personal spiritual realm. One of the remnants of our sinful but restored condition is our blindness. The biblical triad creation-fall-redemption is repeated in our personal histories in the Johannine themes of light-darkness-enlightenment. We must struggle to see into ourselves. Our growing enlightenment is a fragile and vulnerable undertaking. We resist it because it can be painful and demanding. Before we can deal with the forces of good and evil in ourselves, we must be able to recognize them. In spiritual literature this is known as "the discernment of spirits."

Throughout the centuries Christianity has been convinced that, besides grace, there are robust forces at work ("the powers of darkness") as obstacles to this discernment—for it is the beginning of conversion. These forces powerfully support self-deception, rationalization, the comforts of complacency, all kinds of denials and repressions—anything to insure that we are, as it were, generous to a fault, especially our own. Thus the Church's liturgy, in one way or another, so often prays: "Lord, that I may see!"

When moral evasion exists in our policies, practices, ways of speaking and analyzing, it operates as a strong institutional or atmospheric reinforcement for our own noxious tendency toward the type of personal spiritual evasion that is our own worst enemy.

For this reason alone—but for many others, too—the Church should be the most transparent of communities, and as such, an exemplar and invitation to others. Its well-placed trust in the Spirit should make it preeminent in going, tranquilly and joyfully, eyeball to eyeball with problems, threats, embarrassments, doubts, evils, controversies, and difficulties of all sorts, including this chapter.

If it does not, it is guilty of its greatest evasion: the assurance that "I am with you always until the end of the world" (Mt 28:20).

CHAPTER 11

Theology and Bioethics

As we enter neighborhood homes, many of us have been quickened with the peculiar hospitality of a sign that reads: "Beware of dog." There are doubtless many people around who believe that an analogous hospitable sign is in place when a theologian is present with those who gather to discuss the ethical dimensions of biomedicine. Theologians just may bite. Or perhaps worse, they may not. At their worst they are seen as extremely dangerous. At their best, they are harmless, that is, useless. For these reasons they should preferably be out of sight, or at least on a short leash. Perhaps Alisdair MacIntyre had something like this in mind when he concluded one of his essays on medical ethics as follows: "Theologians still owe it to the rest of us to explain why we should not treat their discipline as we do astrology or phrenology. The distinctiveness and importance of what they have to say, if it is true, make this an urgent responsibility."[1]

I confess to being terrorized when my task is described as an "urgent responsibility" (and my terror is not diminished when I read what I have done). Clearly implied in MacIntyre's ultimatum is the conviction that theologians have not successfully articulated the "distinctiveness and importance of what they have to say." Faintly implied—unless I misread him—is the assertion that they really cannot because they do not have that much to say. An urgent task is thus transformed into an impossible one—and under threat of relabeling as *disciplina astrologica*. I like neither the odds nor the possible outcome. But to avoid the latter I must risk the former.

Both terms in my title ("theology," "bioethics") need explication and narrowing if I hope to avoid unthreatening generalizations and verbal incontinence. First, then, *theology*. Theology starts when faith begins reflecting on itself. This pirates the definition of theology of

Anselm of Canterbury: *fides quaerens intellectum* (faith seeking understanding). Two things should be stated at the outset. First, there are different faiths (e.g., the Catholic faith, the Jewish faith, the Muslim faith). Second, the communities in which these faiths originate exist in history and therefore must continually reappropriate their inheritance in changing times and diverse circumstances—and often with different purposes in view. On the first count it is clear that there can be radically different theologies, and on the second it is clear that there can be many theologies within an individual faith community, a fact reflected in the varying theologies of the New Testament authors. This means, of course, that how theology is said to relate to bioethics can vary from community to community, and within the same community at varying times.

Let me narrow the proportions of my "urgent responsibility" (i.e., impossible task) by saying: 1) that I will speak as an adherent of the Catholic faith (it is the only one I know from experience) and therefore will understand theology as reflection on *that* faith only; 2) that I will make no claims that my reflections are *the* theology or the *only* theology of that faith. Such claims are blasphemous in their pretensions that God can be adequately caught (really straight-jacketed) in human concepts. Rather my reflections should be seen as one possible way of approaching the subject. Clearly such a narrowing is meant in no way to detract from the validity or beauty of any other faith or theology.

But such narrowing is not enough. I must make explicit the implications of the statement that theology is reflection on *faith*. There is the danger in our time that the term "faith" will be collapsed into a bloodless, intellectualistic acceptance of credal statements. When "I believe" is sterilized into mere affirmation of propositions, faith has lost its heart and soul. In this sense Johannes B. Metz states: "Christ must always be thought of in such a way that he is never merely thought of."[2] Merely to "think of" Christ is to trivialize Him, to reduce Him to one more (among many) observable historical event, to an example of humane benevolence. For the person of Christian faith, Jesus Christ is God's immanent presence, His love in the flesh.

Let me borrow from the late Joseph Sittler at this point.[3] Sittler has noted that the theme of the biblical narratives is God's "going out from Himself in creative and redemptive action toward men." He refers to "God's relentless gift of Himself," "the undeviating self-giving God," "the total self-giving God," "God's undeviating will to restoration," the "history-involved assault of God upon man's sin," "the gracious assault of his deed in Christ." Jesus Christ is no less than God's self-giving deed.

The response of the believer to this person-revelation is the total commitment of the person known as faith. Once again Sittler:

> It is not possible to state too strongly that the life of the believer is for Paul the actual invasion of the total personality by the Christ-life. So pervasive and revolutionary is this displacement and bestowal that terms like influence, example, command, value are utterly incapable of even suggesting its power and its vitally recreating force.[4]

The believer's response to this specific, momentous and supreme event of God's love is total and radical commitment. For the believer, Jesus Christ, the concrete enfleshment of God's love, becomes the meaning and *telos* of the world and of the self. God's self-disclosure in Jesus is at once the self-disclosure of ourselves and our world. "All things are made through him, and without him was not anything made that was made."[5] The response to this personal divine outpouring is not a dead and outside observer "amen." It is a faith-response empowered by the very God who did the redemptive and restorative deed in Jesus Christ and is utterly and totally transforming—so much so that St. Paul must craft a new metaphor to articulate it. We are "new creatures," plain and simple. Faith is the empowered reception of God's stunning and aggressive love in Jesus.

Theologian Walter Kasper summarizes it as follows:

> Faith is not simply an intellectual act or an act of the will. It includes the whole man [sic] and every aspect of the human reality. . . It embraces the whole of Christian existence, including hope and love, which can be seen as two ways in which faith is realized.[6]

Faith, then, is the proper term "to point to the total commitment of the whole person which is required by the character of the revelation."[7] When I speak of theology (as relating to bioethics), it is theology as reflection on *that sense of faith* that I speak. I go out of my way to emphasize this because there are many influences tempting us to treat theology primarily as reflection on credal statements hammered out as communicative and protective vehicles of a more profound and original happening (God's self-communication and our response to it). For one thing, it is much easier to deal with credal statements, since faith itself, being a *response to God*, exceeds the reach of human language. For another, the historical religious communities that provide the context of the faith-response have myths and symbols that differentiate them and there is the temptation to confuse these with faith itself. Finally, the temptation becomes almost irresistible when these myths and symbols lead to distinct ethical codes.

My second introductory qualifier concerns the term "bioethics." Bioethics is a subspecies of ethics. There has been a tendency to equate ethics with "quandary ethics."[8] Symbols of this abound. We are fascinated and fixed by the tangled casuistry of plug-pulling, palliation decisions, proxy determinations. Cases are newsworthy eye-catchers and amenable to legal resolution. Thus courses in bioethics are loaded with Quinlan, Jobes, Fox, Storar, Chad Green, Conroy, Baby M, Jehovah's Witnesses, pregnancy reduction, testing for seropositivity, triage decisions, dilemmas about confidentiality. Test me by picking up any issue of *The Hastings Report*. It is no diminishment of casuistry to say that it does not all of ethics make, especially an ethics that calls itself Christian, most especially one that claims to be *theological*.

An ethic that claims to be theological will root itself in God— God's actions and purposes. Its primary referents will be God's relation to us, and ours to God. The prime analogate—to use scholastic language—of the term "morality" will be this relationship. The most basic language—not the only—of theological ethics builds around goodness and badness, not rightness and wrongness of actions, since goodness-badness is basically vertical and has its aortal lifeline to the God-relationship.

In slightly different words, a Christian theological ethic is founded on the fact that something *has been done* to and for us, and that something is Jesus. There is a prior action of God at once revelatory and response-engendering. This prior action of God is reflected in the Pauline "therefore" which states the entire grounding and meaning of the Christian ethic.

As I noted earlier, in and through Jesus we know what that God-relationship is: total self-gift. For that is what God is and we are created in His image. To miss this is, I believe, to leave the realm of Christian ethics.

There is another aspect to the notion of "ethics" (and therefore bioethics) that needs mention here. There are four levels at which the term can be understood where rightness or wrongness of conduct is concerned.[9] These distinctions are not often made but I think them essential if we are to gain precision in speaking of the relation of theology to bioethics.

First, there is what we might call an *essential* ethic. By this term we mean those norms that are regarded as applicable to all persons, where one's behavior is but an instance of a general, essential moral norm. Here we could use as example the rightness or wrongness of killing actions, of contracts, or promises and all those actions whose demands are rooted in the dignity of the persons.

Second, there is an *existential* ethic. This refers to the choice of a good that the individual as individual should realize, the experience of an absolute ethical demand addressed to the individual. For instance, an individual might conclude that his/her own moral-spiritual life cannot grow and thrive in the health care environment, hence that this work ought to be abandoned. Or, because of background, inclination, talent, etc., an individual might choose to concentrate time and energy on a particular aspect of health care.

Third, there is *essential Christian* ethics. By this we refer to those ethical decisions a Christian must make precisely because he/she belongs to a community to which the non-Christian does not belong. These are moral demands made upon the Christian *as Christian*. For instance, to regard fellow workers as brothers and sisters in Christ (not just as autonomous, to-be-respected persons), to provide a Christian education for one's children, to belong to a particular worshipping community. These are important ethical decisions that emerge only within the context of a Christian community's understanding of itself in relation to other people.

Fourth, there is an existential Christian ethics—those ethical decisions that the Christian *as individual* must make, e.g., to undertake the ministry of the priesthood.

I introduce these distinctions because the relation of theology to bioethics is but an instance of a larger theological discussion that has been occurring for a number of years—the dispute about whether Christian ethics is a *Glaubensethik* or is, to use shorthand, autonomous.[10] The discussion has been lively, even heated at times, especially in Germany. But I have the distinct impression that, while the discussants seem to disagree, they are often in reality not discussing the same question. They are often talking past each other. The distinctions I have noted would prevent much of this confusion. More concretely, it should readily be granted that revelation and our personal faith do influence ethical decisions at the latter three levels (existential, essential Christian, existential Christian). One's choice of issues, and the dispositions and motivations he/she brings to these issues can be profoundly affected by one's personal appropriation of revealed truth (faith in the sense explained), by one's prayer life and by the community in which these develop. But these are not the levels discussed by the proponents of an autonomous ethic. Rather, it is the level of essential ethics only, a point that is fudged unless the distinctions noted above are kept in mind.

With these introductory notes on faith and ethics as a background, let me now turn to theology and bioethics.

Let me begin my attempt by citing James Gustafson:

> For theological ethics . . . the first task in order of importance is to establish convictions about God and God's relations to the world. To make a case for how some things really and ultimately are is the first task of theological ethics.[11]

I agree with Gustafson's description of the first task of theological ethics, though it is clear we would disagree significantly about "how some things really and ultimately are." How, then, are they, "really and ultimately"? In its *Declaration on Euthanasia* the Congregation for the Doctrine of the Faith made reference to "Christ, who through his life, death and resurrection, has given a *new meaning to existence.*"[12] If that is true (and Christians believe it is), then to neglect that meaning is to neglect the most important thing about ourselves, to cut ourselves off from the fullness of our own reality.

"A new meaning to existence." Those are powerful words. If Christ has given "a new meaning to existence," then presumably that new meaning will have some relevance for key notions and decisions in the field of bioethics. At this point it is a fair question to ask: what is this new meaning?

Theological work in the past decade or so has rejected the notion that the sources of faith are a thesaurus of answers. Rather they should be viewed above all as narratives, as a story. From a story come perspectives, themes, insights, not always or chiefly direct action guides. The story is the source from which the Christian construes the world theologically. In other words, it is the vehicle for discovering and communicating this new meaning.

At this point let me attempt to disengage some key elements of the Christian story, and from a Catholic reading and living of it. One might not be too far off with the following summary.

- God is the author and preserver of life. We are "made in His image."
- Thus life is a gift, a trust. It has great worth because of the value He is placing in it (Thielicke's "alien dignity").

- God places great value in it because He is also (besides being author) the end, purpose of life.

- We are on a pilgrimage, having here no lasting home.

- God has dealt with us in many ways. But his supreme epiphany of Himself (and our potential selves) is His Son, Jesus Christ.

- In Jesus' life, death and resurrection we have been totally transformed into "new creatures," into a community of the transformed. Sin and death have met their victor.

- The ultimate significance of our lives consists in developing this new life.

- The Spirit is given to us to guide and inspire us on this journey.

- The ultimate destiny of our combined journeys is the "coming of the Kingdom," the return of the glorified Christ to claim the redeemed world.

- Thus we are offered in and through Jesus Christ eternal life. Just as Jesus has overcome death (and now lives), so will we who cling to Him, place our faith and hope in Him, and take Him as our law and model.

- This good news, this covenant with us has been entrusted to a people, a people to be nourished and instructed by shepherds.

- This people should continuously remember and thereby make present Christ in His death and resurrection at the Eucharistic meal.

- The chief and central manifestation of this new life in Christ is love for each other (not a flaccid "niceness," but a love that shapes itself in the concrete forms of justice, gratitude, forbearance,* chastity, etc.). Especially for poor, marginal, sinners. These were Jesus' constant companions.

For the Catholic Christian, this is "how some things really and ultimately are." In Jesus we have been totally transformed. This new life or empowerment is a hidden but nonetheless real dimension of our persons, indeed the most profoundly real thing about us.[13] The biblical materials present the history of the world in terms of creation—fall—redemption. As Thomas Clarke, S.J., has noted, this triad also describes our personal history and is mirrored in Johannine and Pauline imagery; light-blindness-enlightenment; freedom-bondage-liberation; integrity-brokenness-reintegration; health-sickness-healing; peace-estrangement-reconciliation. From the perspective of faith, we are in the process of being redeemed, and that process takes the form of enlightenment, liberation, reintegration, healing, reconciliation.[14] I have already suggested thè integrating shape of our lives from this faith-perspective: the self-gift of agape. We must be progressively healed, enlightened, liberated, reconciled, reintegrated into the fullness of this original empowerment. In the concise words of Thomas, charity is the form of the virtues. Our lives are the struggles of pilgrims to render this central vitality ever more dominant, facile, spontaneous. As exegete L. Cerfaux puts it, "Charity is the normal occupation of the Christian."[15]

Now, what does all of this have to do with bioethics? I want to reject two possible extremes from the outset. The first extreme is that faith gives us concrete answers to the problems of *essential* ethics. Josef Fuchs, S.J., is surely correct when he writes:

> Medical ethics is theological, and hence Catholic-theological, ethics if it proceeds from faith, i.e., from the Catholic faith. This faith is ultimately not the assertion of the truth of certain faith propositions, but an act, in the depth of the person, of giving and entrusting oneself to the God who reveals and imparts himself to us. Naturally, no concrete ethics—and therefore no medical ethics—can be developed out of faith understood in this way.[16]

By "concrete ethics" I understand Fuchs to be referring to what I have called *essential* ethics.

The second extreme is that faith has no influence whatsoever on bioethics. It would seem passing strange indeed if what Sittler calls "the invasion of the total personality by the Christ-life" had no repercussions on one's dispositions, imagination and values.

How, then, does faith exercise its influence? I will take my lead from Vatican II. In an interesting sentence, "The Constitution on the Church in the Modern World" states: "Faith throws a new light on everything, manifests God's design for man's total vocation, and thus directs the mind to solutions which are fully human."[17]

Here we have reference to a "new light." The nature of this "new light" is that it reveals human existence in its fullest and most profound dimensions ("God's design . . . total vocation"). The effect of this new light is to "direct the mind." To what? "Solutions which are fully human." The usage "fully human" I take to mean a rejection of any understanding of "a new meaning to existence" that sees it as foreign to the human, and radically discontinuous with it.

The Catholic tradition has encapsulated the way faith "directs the mind to solutions" in the phrase "reason informed by faith." Reason informed by faith is neither reason *replaced* by faith, nor reason *without* faith. It is reason shaped by faith. Vincent MacNamara renders this as follows: "Faith and reason compenetrate one another and form a unity of consciousness which affects the whole of the Christian's thought and action." What is the effect of such a Christian consciousness? MacNamara uses several phrases: "people who see things in a particular way, because they are particular sorts of people." "It [faith] determines, to some extent, one's meanings, what one sees in the world, what are the facts of life, and what among them are the most prominent and relevant facts."[20] He refers to the "total background out of which judgments and choices are made."[21] Or again, there is reference to a Christian's "interpretative self-awareness."[22]

In summary, "reason informed by faith" is shorthand for saying that the reasoner (the human person) has been transformed and that this transformation will have a cognitive dimension through its invasion of consciousness. I think it true to say that the more profound the faith, the greater and more explicit will be the Christian consciousness—which is a way of saying that how faith (and theology) affects ethics can be seen best of all in the saints. But even we non-saints ought to be able to give an intelligible account of theology's influence. But that account is destined to be more or less incomplete because the transformation worked by faith is at a very profound level not totally recoverable in formulating consciousness.

With that in mind, I suggest that theology can relate to bioethics in three distinct but overlapping ways. I shall call these ways *protective, dispositive, directive.*

1. PROTECTIVE

Moral philosophers, following St. Thomas, have identified basic inclinations towards goods that define our well-being or flourishing. Even though these inclinations can be identified as prior to acculturation, still they exist as culturally conditioned. We tend toward values as perceived. And the culture in which we live shades our perceptions of values, a point made by Philip Rieff in *The Triumph of the Therapeutic* when he referred to "reasons that have sunk so deeply into the self that they are implicitly understood."[23] He argues that decisions are made, policies set not chiefly by articulated norms, codes, regulations and philosophies, but by these "reasons" that lie below the surface. Our way of perceiving the basic human values and relating to them is shaped by our whole way of looking at the world.

An example from bioethics will help here. In relating to the basic human values several images of human beings are possible, as Daniel Callahan has pointed out.[24] First, there is the power-plasticity model. In this model, nature is alien, independent of humans, possessing no inherent value. It is capable of being used, shaped and dominated by humans. We see ourselves as possessing an unrestricted right to manipulate in the service of our goals. Death is something to be overcome, outwitted. Second, there is the sacro-symbiotic model. In its religious forms, nature is seen as God's creation, to be respected and heeded. Nature is a trust; we are not masters, but stewards. In secular forms, humans are seen as a part of nature. Nature is a teacher and we must live in harmony and balance with it. Death is but a rhythm of nature, to be gracefully accepted.

The model which seems to have sunk deep and shaped our moral imaginations and feelings—and our perception of basic values—is the power-plasticity model. We are corporately *homo technologicus*. The best solution to the dilemmas created by technology is more technology. We tend to eliminate the maladapted condition (defectives, retarded, etc.) rather than adjust the environment to it: this is our cultural bias.

It can be persuasively argued that the peculiar temptation of a technologically advanced culture such as ours is to view and treat persons functionally. Our treatment—at least all too often—of the aged is a sorry symptom of this. The elderly are probably the most alienated members of our society. More and more of them spend their declining years in homes for senior citizens, in chronic hospitals, in nursing homes. We have shunted them aside. Their protest is eloquent because it is helplessly muted and silent. But it is a protest against a basically functional assessment of their persons. "Maladaptation" is the term used to describe *them* rather than the environment. This represents a terribly distorted judgment of the human person.

I want to argue that faith can be protective against such a collapse. It should and, I believe, does sensitize us to the meaning of persons, to their inherent dignity regardless of functionability. In this sense it aids us in staying human by underlining the truly human against cultural pressures to distort it. We might say that it is by steadying our gaze on the basic human values that are the parents of more concrete norms and rules that faith can exercise this protective function.

Let me put this another way. I have noted that the single, dominating, all-pervasive vitality in Jesus was the God-relationship. The human goods that define our flourishing (life and health, mating and raising children, knowledge, friendship, enjoyment of the arts) while desirable and attractive in themselves, are *subordinate* to this structural God-relationship.[25] Yet it is the characteristic of the redeemed but still messy human condition to make idols, to pursue these basic goods *as ends in themselves*. This is the radical theological meaning of secularization: the loss of the context which relativizes and subordinates these basic goods and prevents our divinizing them. The goods are so attractive that our constant temptation (our continuing enslavement, our bondage to the world, our constant need for liberation) is to center our being on them as ultimate ends, to cling to them with our whole being.

Jesus' love for us is, of course, primarily empowerment. But it is also, in its purity and righteousness, the standard against the type of collapse known as idolatry. Whatever he willed for us and did for us, he did within the primacy and ultimacy of the God-relationship. Since this relationship is our very being and destiny, his love took the form of a constant reminder of this momentous dignity to people hell-bent on their idolatries.

His love, as standard, suggests the shape of our Christian love for each other. It is conduct which reminds others of their true dignity, which reminds them of their being and destiny, and therefore which pursues, supports, protects the basic human goods *as subordinate*. Perhaps Barth had something like this in mind when he stated that the first service of others is witness—because the most urgent need of others is God himself.[26]

Vincent MacNamara has summarized as follows what I have called the "protective" function of faith:

> It seems to me that the fact that union with God is the most important component of welfare or happiness will affect choice both for oneself and for one's service of others. One's own flourishing will mean preserving that relationship above all: this will relativize some goods that a non-believer might regard as important and highlight some which he would regard as unimportant. It will mean that choices which will lead to a weakening of one's sense of the relationship or which will endanger it will be regarded as morally undesirable.[27]

2. DISPOSITIVE

The Christian of profound faith will reflect in his/her dispositions the very shape of that faith. That shape, as I have noted, is the
self-gift we call charity, love of God in others, charitable action. In an
illuminating study Edmund Pellegrino, M.D., shows how the central
dynamism of charity can shape moral choice within medicine. He argues that charity will influence: 1) the way the three dominant principles of medical ethics (beneficence, autonomy, justice) are interpreted;
2) the way the physician-patient relationship is construed; 3) the way
certain concrete choices are made. For instance, where beneficence is
concerned, Pellegrino argues that some form of benevolent self-efface-
ment (arguable on mere philosophical grounds) is a *minimum* obligation in an agapeistic ethic. The Christian physician sees him/herself
called to perfection, to imitate Jesus' healing. In this perspective appeals to exigency, fiscal survival, self-protection, the canons of a competitive environment are morally feeble, even totally unacceptable.

Similarly, where justice is concerned, faith-full Christians will
go beyond the strict calculus of duties and claims and exercise a
"preferential option" for the very ones whose moral claims on society
are difficult to establish: the poor, the outcasts, the sociopaths, the al-
coholic, the non-compliant in the care of their own health.

When he turns to the physician-patient relationship, Pellegrino
argues that a charity-based ethic would reject notions of health care as
a commodity transaction, of the physician as a businessperson. Like-
wise it would reject the relationship as one of contract for services, or
as one primarily for profit. The covenantal model is most consistent
with the perspectives and dispositions generated by charity. Pellegrino
does not argue for a fanatical devotion to medicine that would exclude
other obligations to family, self, society or country. Rather charity
disposes us to place these facets of medical practice in a morally defensible order.

Let me take another aspect of an ethic rooted in Christian faith,
an aspect that may also be considered dispositive. It is the paschal
mystery, the death-resurrection of Christ. Christians are accustomed
to viewing aging, suffering and dying within these perspectives.

Take aging as an example. Perhaps the most prominent quality
of the lives of the elderly is dependence. Yet, as Theodore Minnema
points out,[29] we are notoriously resistant to the idea of dependence.
Our national consciousness is shaped by the Declaration of Independence. And similar perspectives frame our individual attitudes.
Dependence is vulnerability. Independent autonomy is exalted as a

key marker of dignity. On this view there is a certain negativity that attaches to the passive virtues (meekness, humility, patience). Yet Christ's supreme dignity was manifest in dependence: "Not my will, but thine be done."

For this reason Drew Christiansen, S.J., developed what he calls a "theology of dependence." For most of our adult lives we ignore the dependence that ties us to other men and women. As Christiansen words it:

> We keep the realization of our need for others at arm's length by keeping busy. If we can produce enough, if we can win enough, if we can party enough, we don't have to think too long about the meaning of life. Moreover, by manipulating things and managing people, we convince ourselves of our freedom and mastery of the world, and so avoid admitting how much we owe to others and to God.[31]

Christiansen sees this avoidance of dependence as mistaken. Dependence is an opportunity, a call to let ourselves go, to open up to God, to cling in trust to a power beyond our control, to see more clearly than ever the source and end of life, much as Christ did in his dying dependence on the Father.

Dependence on others should be a sign of our more radical dependence on God. Since our freedom is intended to lead us to a deeper union with God, it is an interesting paradox that our deep dependence on God establishes our own radical independence: independence in dependence.

Thus from a theological perspective, dependent old age should represent a flowering, not a wilting. Or in Christiansen's words:

> Outside of faith, dependence threatens us with subjugation, and our self-assertion may lead to isolation and abandonment. But for those who believe in the Giver of life, the promise hidden in dependence is communion with the Source of life itself.[32]

Very similar things can be said about suffering and dying. From the perspective of faith, just as aging is not mere dependence and weakening, so suffering is not mere pain and confusion, dying is not merely an end. These must be viewed, even if mysteriously, in terms of a larger redemptive process: as occasions for a growing self-opening after Christ's example, as various participations in the paschal mystery. Such perspectival nuances may not solve clinical dilemmas nor are they in any way intended to glorify suffering and dying. But they powerfully suggest that in approaching such realities healing can never be seen as mere fixing; autonomy is not a mere "being left alone," but a condition for life-shaping; care is never merely material provision, but a "being with" that reinforces a sense of worth and dignity; dying can never be seen as "cosmetized passing" whose dignity is measured by the accumulation of minutes.

I have called such influences "dispositive" because they root in the primacy of charity in such a way that one is disposed to view all of life's moments as occasions for a more intense personal assimilation of the shape of the Christ-event.

3. DIRECTIVE

The biblical materials or stories that pass along the events that are the occasion of faith yield certain perspectives or themes that shape consciousness, and therefore constitute faith's informing of reason. I have attempted elsewhere to identify some of the themes that structure our ethical deliberation in biomedicine as the following: 1) Life as a basic, but not absolute value. 2) The extension of this evaluation to nascent life. 3) The potential for human relationships as that aspect of physical life to be valued. 4) The radical sociality of the human person. 5) The inseparability of the unitive and procreative goods in human sexuality. 6) Permanent heterosexual union as normative.[33]

Let me take just the first to illustrate the "directive" influence of theology on bioethics—life as a basic but not absolute good.

The fact that we are pilgrims, that Christ has overcome death and lives, that we will also live with Him, yields a general value judgment on the meaning and value of life as we now live it. It can be formulated as follows: life is a basic good but not an absolute one. It is *basic* because, as the Congregation for the Doctrine of the Faith worded it, it is the "necessary source and condition of every human activity and of all society."[34] It is not *absolute* because there are higher goods for which life can be sacrificed (glory of God, salvation of souls, service of others, etc.). Thus in John: "There is no greater love than this: to lay down one's life for one's friends."[35] Therefore laying down one's life for another cannot be contrary to the faith or story or meaning of humankind. It is, after Jesus' example, life's greatest fulfillment, even though it is the end of life as we now know it. Negatively, we could word this value judgment as follows: death is an evil but not an absolute or unconditioned one.

This value judgment has immediate relevance for care for the ill and dying. It issues in a basic attitude or policy: not all means must be used to preserve life. Why? Pius XII in a 1952 address to the International Congress of Anesthesiologists stated: "A more strict obligation would be too burdensome for most people and would render the attainment of the higher, more important good too difficult. Life, health, all temporal activities are in fact subordinated to spiritual ends."[36] In other words there are higher values than life in the living of it. There are also higher values in the dying of it.

What Pius XII was saying, then, is that forcing (morally) one to take *all* means is tantamount to forcing attention and energies on a subordinate good in a way that prejudices a higher good, even eventually making it unrecognizable as a good. Excessive concern for the temporal is at some point neglect of the eternal. An obligation to use all means to preserve life would be a devaluation of human life, since it would remove life from the context or story that is the source of its ultimate value.

Thus the Catholic tradition has moved between two extremes: medico-moral optimism or vitalism (which preserves life with all means, at any cost no matter what its condition) and medico-moral pessimism (which actively kills when life becomes onerous, dysfunctional, boring). Merely technological judgments could easily fall into either of these two traps. The medically effective could begin to define the humanly beneficial.

Thus far theology. It yields a value judgment and a general policy or attitude. It provides the framework for subsequent moral reasoning. It tells us that life is a gift with a purpose and destiny. Dying is the last or waning moments of this "new creature." At this point moral reasoning (reason informed by faith) must assume its proper responsibilities to answer questions like: 1) What means ought to be used, what need not be? 2) What shall we call such means? 3) Who enjoys the prerogative and/or duty of decision-making? 4) What is to be done with now incompetent, and always incompetent patients in critical illness? The sources of faith do not provide direct answers to these questions, in my judgment.

One way to indicate the directive importance of such general themes is by an example. Several years ago, in Louisville, I participated on a panel on the artificial heart. The panel included the mandatory Protestant (Robert Nelson), Catholic and Jew (the late Isaac Franck) along with Dr. William Lansing, President of Humana. The question arose as to whether the artificial heart works. Dr. Lansing stated: "When Bill DeVries and I decide that it doesn't work, the program will stop." I jumped on that and asked: "If the artificial heart gives you only an extra ten hours of life, or ten days, does it work?" Somewhat to my surprise—but not really as I look back on the incident—my colleague and friend, Dr. Franck, mumbled audibly "It works." Theology was only thinly disguised in such a reaction. I do not believe the Christian story would support such a response. It views life and death in light of the paschal mystery and this has a relativizing influence on both that I found lacking in Dr. Franck's judgment.

What I am proposing, therefore, is that theology—and I repeat that I understand that as reflection on Christian faith as explained—can influence bioethics in very important ways. Its function is not a *direct* originating influence on concrete moral judgments at the essential level—and in this I agree with autonomists like Fuchs, Schüller, Auer, Hughes, *et al.*—but on "morally relevant insights," in the words of Franz Böckle.[37] On this view faith and reason compenetrate to produce a distinct consciousness, a consciousness with identifiable cognitive dimensions or facets. I have tried to identify three such dimensions, overlapping as they are, as *protective* (or corrective), *dispositive* and *directive*.

Cumulatively, such influences attempt to show how faith informs reason. I believe the outcome of such "informing" is a distinct—though not utterly mysterious—way of viewing the world and ourselves and of hierarchizing values. To claim that such distinct outlooks and onlooks (theology) have nothing to do with bioethics is: 1) either to separate faith from one's view of the world (which is to trivialize faith by reducing it dualistically to an utterly other-worldly thing); or, 2) to separate one's view of the world from bioethics (which is to trivialize bioethics by isolating it from the very persons it purports to serve).

CHAPTER 12

The Malaise in Bioethics

It is admitted by a significant number of scholars that there is a pervasive dissatisfaction with the status quo of bioethical reflection in the United States. A sense of malaise is unmistakably present and hovers over the subject like a dark cloud. Most of the dissatisfaction points to the "principles approach as the regnant paradigm." It is said to be a dilemma-oriented, problem-solving, deductive, rationalistic, individualistic and rights-focused enterprise. By contrast there are repeated calls for less reliance on principlism, proximity to the lived-in existence, inclusion of the imagistic, symbolic, emotional dimensions; less absolutism, greater emphasis on the self as connected to others, modification of secularism in bioethical thought, etc. If these criticisms are accurate, bioethics of the past twenty years in the U.S. has powerfully reinforced the very problematic perspectives it should be challenging and correcting.

I agree that there is malaise. So much of what is written seems tired and predictable, only marginally relevant. But I am not sure that the diagnosis goes deep enough. If it does not, then we are involved with band-aids. What I mean is that these shifts in approach are not likely to occur in any lasting way through explicit effort on the part of ethicists alone. They will be a significant aspect of bioethics only if the practice of medicine itself is changed. For that is where the malaise originates. Medicine may have been content with the bioethical enterprise during twenty years because it was left comfortably unchallenged and free to go its businesslike way.

Some critics suggest that perspectival shifts in bioethics have to be made if bioethics is to be truly formative. The assumption is that if bioethics makes these shifts—"from above" so to speak—it will be much more relevant and formatively influential.

I have to wonder about that, even doubt it. The forces that are dissolving the culture of medicine as a profession have a certain independent and almost uncontrollable dynamic about them. Adjustments in bioethics will not change them. And unless they are changed, medicine will continue on its present course. Indeed, one could mount a fairly persuasive argument that bioethics in the United States in the past twenty years has developed peacefully and serenely because it has posed no threat to the major developments in medicine of the past twenty years. That means it has been irrelevant to the major transformation occurring, viz., the displacement of the culture of medicine as a profession.

I will use Catholic hospitals as a symptom for the substance of my concern. There are two facts that bring the issue into focus. First, Catholic hospitals have beautiful mission statements. We read references to continuing the healing mission of Jesus through comprehensive health care. There are statements about caring service for each individual, personalized patient care, the wholistic approach which weds competence and compassion. There are assertions about an option for the poor, about continuing Christ's redemptive presence.

Yet, secondly, everywhere I go I see Catholics involved in health care doubtful, perplexed, wondering whether they are viable, whether they ought to be in health care, asking about their identity, how they differ from non-Catholic institutions. There is a great deal of institutional navel-gazing. In sum, there is a gap between institutional purpose and aim, and personal conviction and involvement.

What is going on here? I believe that a strong argument can be made that the circumstances of late 20th century United States have weakened and sometimes dissolved the culture of the Catholic health care facility, the strength and transforming power of its vision. Could it be that dissatisfaction with principlism is but a superficial response and is transparent of much deeper longings and losses? I think so. And if this is true of Catholic hospitals, it is likely all the more true of other religiously-unaffiliated institutions and of the medical establishment in general.

Let me draw on Thomas Peters' and Robert Waterman's *In Search of Excellence* to make my point.[1] They note:

> As we worked on research of our excellent companies, we were struck by the dominant use of story, slogan, and legend as people tried to explain the characteristics of their own great institutions. All the companies we interviewed, from Boeing to McDonald's, were quite simply rich tapestries of anecdote, myth, and fairy

tale. The vast majority of people who tell stories today about T.J. Watson of I.B.M. have never met the man or had direct experience of the original, more mundane reality. Two Hewlett-Packard engineers in their mid-twenties recently regaled us with an hour's worth of "Bill and Dave" (Hewlett & Packard) stories. We were subsequently astonished to find that neither had seen, let alone talked to, the founders. These days, people like Watson and A.P. Geanini at Bank of America take on roles of mythic proportions that the real persons would have been hard pressed to fill. Nevertheless, in an organizational sense, these stories, myths and legends appear to be very important *because they convey the organization's shared values, or culture.*[2]

Peters and Waterman then continue to highlight the importance of culture.

Without exception, the dominance and coherence of culture proved to be an essential quality of the excellent companies. Moreover, the stronger the culture and the more it was directed toward the marketplace, the less need was there for policy manuals, organization charts, or detailed procedures and rules. In these companies people way down the line know what they are supposed to do in most situations because the handful of guiding values is crystal clear.[3]

If we ask why or how the guiding values are crystal clear, Peters and Waterman respond:

The shared values in the excellent companies are clear, in large measure, because the mythology is rich. Everyone at Hewlett-Packard knows that he or she is supposed to be innovative. Everyone at Procter & Gamble knows that product quality is the *sine qua non* . . . "Right from the start" said the late Richard R. Deupree when he was chief executive officer, "William Proctor and James Gamble realized that the interests of the organization and its employees were inseparable."

Poorer-performing companies often have strong cultures, too, *but dysfunctional ones.* They are usually focused on internal politics rather than on the product and the people who make and sell it. The top companies, on the other hand, always seem to recognize what the companies that set only financial targets don't know or don't deem important. The excellent companies seem to understand that *every* person seeks meaning (not just the top fifty who are "in the bonus pool").[4]

And so it goes with Johnson and Johnson, Maytag, Marriott, Bechtel, Boeing, Delta, Dana, Caterpillar, Wang, 3-M, Digital Equipment, etc.

Now what do we see here? The following: (1) Shared values or culture, and values shared throughout the company. (2) Values that are crystal clear. (3) Communicated by legends and stories. (4) Values that give meaning (motivation and inspiration) to the work of individuals.

I realize that it is somewhat anomalous to turn to business to clarify the importance of culture in Catholic health care when one of the vexing problems of such care is that it has been transformed into a business. The point of contact, however, remains the notion of culture. Culture is essential to the flourishing of institutions, whether they be Catholic hospitals or business corporations. When the culture is dysfunctional or absent, we usually see a company in disarray. We see a Catholic hospital questioning its identity. More to the point, we see a situation where "people's only security comes from where they live on the organization chart." We see people who have jobs, not great causes.

I think this may well have happened to many Catholic hospitals. They were organized around the "greatest story ever told" (of God's engendering deed in Jesus that transforms us and our world). Catholic hospitals exist to enact in the health care setting what God did in Jesus. Jesus is God's love for us in the flesh. The Catholic hospital exists, therefore, to be Jesus' love for the other in the health care setting. It has the daily vocation of telling every patient—especially the poor—and every employee how great they are, because Jesus told us how great we are and in the process empowered us. Yet I suspect this *raison d'être* has become practically dysfunctional. If that is the case, then the heart of the Catholic health care culture is gone. And if that is the case, then persons in this context will derive their meaning, significance and security from elsewhere, not from the great cause that defines their reason for being where they are. They will be performing a job only.

I have used the Catholic hospital as an example of the importance of culture. Something analogous can be said of the medical profession itself. There is a culture that distinguishes medicine from business. Physicians are rightly proud of it. Marvin R. Dunn, M.D., dean of the University of South Florida College of Medicine, noted that in the last ten years applications to medical school have fallen off. One of the reasons cited by Dunn "was that college students began to see medicine as more of a business than a profession."[6] For this reason Dunn concludes that "there is probably no more important area for us [physicians] all to work together than in the preservation of these values that continue to define medicine as a true profession."

What are those values, or what I have above called a culture? Dunn puts it as follows:

> Medicine is a unique profession. More than for any other, something seems to develop within the individual before formal medical education begins and to remain even after retirement from active practice. This is the human side. It is that something which separates the physician from the computer. It is the caring and compassion that makes medicine an art as well as science. It is the capacity for ethical concern for the total individual that invites patients to share in total confidence those intimate aspects of their lives that are shared with few or none other.

Better than anyone familiar to me Leon R. Kass has analyzed the meaning of "concern for the total individual." I will cite him at length because what he says lies close to the heart of the culture of medicine as a profession. The physician-patient *relationship* is too pale and unspecified a term to enlighten. Rather, drawing on Aristotle, Kass notes:

> The patient as beneficiary is, in a sense, the physician-at-work. The physician's being, manifested as physicianly activity, lives in the patient. Healing the patient manifests the physician's *own wholeness*, in its self-manifesting activity. As parents love their children, and teachers their students, so physicians their patients—for it is only in and through the patient that the doctor's being is actively realized, for the doctor himself.
>
> Medicine is thus not rightly described as a profession that requires self-sacrifice and self-denial. Anyone who enters it in this spirit is courting disappointment. Neither are the deepest rewards of medicine external to the activity. Anyone who thinks that money or prestige or honor alone will make the practice rewarding is courting discontent—for what will sustain him when the coffers are full and the tributes are paid? No, medicine calls you to intrinsically self-manifesting and self-fulfilling activity, in which your good and the patient's good coincide. In each daily encounter with your patients, you will serve yourself exactly in your efforts to help others, as you energetically respond to the call for help, exercising your art that makes help possible.
>
> But there is one more wrinkle to this self-sustaining activity of benefaction, which, as described so far, does not distinguish the

unique form of doing good that is physicianly. For it seems strange to say that the hip surgeon lives in the prosthesis he has implanted or that the internist is at work in the digitalis he has sent circulating in the cardiac patient's blood. To the extent that doctors are thought to act on the human being regarded scientifically as objectifiable body, to that extent the claim of living participation in the beneficiary rings somewhat hollow. The engineer is not the benefactor of the bridge; the plumber is not the benefactor of the pipes; the physician regarded as body engineer or plumber is not the benefactor of the body—silent, indifferent, private. If one regards the patient only as objectified body, then one may *take* care *of* the patient, but one does not yet *care for* the patient. Squaring the life and work of physician as benefactor with patient as beneficiary requires a *relationship* with the patient regarded not as body but *as embodied soul.* It requires converting the private and unsharable good of well-healed bodily parts into a common and consciously sought good, which in turn requires attentive, sympathetic, and concerned speech, as always, the bond of truly human associations.[7]

It is precisely certain shared values that make medicine a profession rather than a business. There may be other ways of stating those values, but many would think that Dr. Dunn is close to the mark and that Dr. Kass is right on it. When those values (that culture) are under threat, are weakened, or are more or less dysfunctional, the profession itself is threatened, weakened, or dysfunctional as a profession.

I see the dissatisfaction with principlism (deductive, rationalistic, individualistic, rights focused, etc.) as a symptom of a deeper malaise: the well-founded fear that the profession itself is profoundly threatened, perhaps even already severely undermined by the forces that make up the context of its practice in the United States. Put differently, an increasing number of people judge that Drs. Dunn and Kass have described a desirable but disappearing species.

If that is true, we all will be the poorer. For that reason it is essential to identify those characteristics or aspects that powerfully shape the context of the practice of medicine. Here I will list five, though there are probably many more, some perhaps even more formative than the ones I list.

1. DEPERSONALIZATION

There are three factors at work in the way we perceive and respond to health care problems. First, there is the growth of technology. Everything from diagnosis through acute care to billing is done by computer. Check the advertisements in any medical journal and it becomes clear that medicine and the machine are wed. This gives efficiency but inevitably some impersonality.[8] I mean in no way to bad-mouth technology in medicine. My own life owes its continuance on several occasions to "high-tech" medicine.

Second, there is cost and cost containment. Spiraling costs are due to many factors (e.g., sophistication of services, higher wages, more personnel, cost pass-along systems, paperwork, technology, inflation, fraud). In 1990 national health expenditures were projected to be 12% of the gross national product and they are well above that as I write. Per capita health care spending was $2566 compared to Canada's $1991. Seattle has more CT scanners than all of Canada.[9] A Gallup Poll done for the AMA revealed that 68% of patients disagreed with the statement "doctors' fees are usually reasonable."[10] Obviously the cost factor will force difficult decisions, sooner or later, soon at the latest.

Finally, we have *the multiplication of public entities.* By "public entities" I mean attorneys, courts, and legislatures. Thus we have the Patient Self-Determination Act of 1990 passed as part of the Omnibus Budget Reconciliation Act. We have had a series of trial cases: *Quinlan, Saikewicz, Fox, Spring, Perlmutter, Herbert, Conroy, Brophy, Cruzan.* We have *Roe v. Wade.* These are but the protruding tips of the icebergs.

Together these factors affect the very matrix of the healing profession. This matrix roots in the conviction that patient-management decisions must be tailor-made to the individual, to the individual's condition and values. They are *personal* decisions that must fit the individual like a glove to a hand. Yet the three factors mentioned above are rather *impersonal* factors. When they begin to preprogram treatment, they tend to depersonalize that treatment. A clear sign of this depersonalization is the constant physician complaint about loss of autonomy. John Lee Clowe, M.D., president of the AMA, stated that "based on the letters I receive from around the country, there is no question in my mind that the loss of autonomy is the most troubling trend physicians in this country face."[11] Complaints about loss of autonomy escalated after 1983 with the introduction of Medicare's 467 Diagnostic Related Groups.

2. SECULARIZATION

The very forces that lead to depersonalization of health care can robustly support the secularization of the medical profession. By "secularization" I refer to the divorce of the profession from those values (that culture) that make health care a *human service*. Or stated somewhat more aggressively, it is an increasing preoccupation with factors that are peripheral to and distractive from holistic human care (competition, liability, government controls, finances).

There are any number of symptoms of this drift toward secularization. One is the fact that physicians are leaving the profession. A survey of physicians done in 1989 by the Gallup Organization revealed that a considerable number of physicians definitely would not (14%) or probably would not (25%) go to medical school if they were in college now, knowing what they know about medicine.[12]

Another symptom is the reason given by physicians for their discontent. Basically it is a souring of the physician-patient relationship. Dr. Paul Bearman, director of urgent care at Park Nicollett Medical Center in Minneapolis put it this way: "The ability to have the same kind of relationship. I think that's gone. There is the feeling that you could just replace one physician with another and that's unfortunate. A lot of the really good doctors feel bad."[13] Dr. William Roper, deputy director of domestic policy in the White House, stated: "I am worried about the growing disenchantment of the average doctor . . . I fear that the loss of faith by doctors will make them less caring and compassionate."[14] Perhaps it already has. Of 1500 people polled by Gallup in 1989, 67 percent said that doctors are too interested in making money and 57 percent agreed that "doctors don't care about people as much as they used to."[15]

Behind such an erosion of the physician-patient relationship is the loss of a culture of compassion and care. It is being replaced by a business ethos. As Lawrence Altman and Elizabeth Rosenthal summed it up: "The image of the dedicated physician toiling long hours for the good of his patients is fading fast, replaced by salaried doctors who work 9 to 5."[16] Many physicians feel that what they do is "a job."

When medicine is reduced to a business, physicians begin acting like businesspeople. As Dr. Edmund Pellegrino has observed, they claim the same rights as the businessperson—that is, to do business with whom they choose. Medical knowledge is viewed as something that belongs to the physician and that can be dispensed on her own terms in the marketplace, and illness is seen as no different from any other need that requires a service.[17] It is this ethos that James Gorman bashes in his wonderful tongue-in-cheek piece "The Doctor Won't See You Now."[18]

I am not interested in assigning blame for this secularization of medicine. Physicians would doubtless point to their eroded autonomy (controls), diminished prestige, increased liability exposure, reduced compensation, etc. Others would lay the blame squarely on the profession. I shall not referee this dispute here. I simply want to note the fact of secularization and the replacement of the professional culture by the business ethos.

Once the profession is secularized, physicians will begin to make secularized judgments. One such is that the physician is free to treat or not treat AIDS patients. Thirty percent of the physicians polled by the AMA made such a judgment. I can only view this as extremely ominous. Another, in my opinion, is the refusal to treat Medicaid patients.

Another judgment that could easily convey a full-blown secularization is the following: "I will not impose my values on my patient." Of course, there is a perfectly healthy and orthodox understanding of this statement. It is: In designing patient management regimes, I will take appropriate account of the patient's background, education, age, values, preferences, etc. The noxious and secularized reading is this: I will do anything the patient prefers and requests. Here the physician is reduced to a technological tool of the patient, conscripted to do the patient's bidding for a price.

It is easy to see why the secularization of medicine feeds off of (I do not say "caused" because it is unclear which caused which) an absolutized notion of patient autonomy. When autonomy is absolutized, very little thought is then given to the values that ought to inform and guide the use of autonomy. Given such a vacuum, the sheer fact that the choice is the patient's tends to be viewed as the sole right-making characteristic of the choice. That trivializes human choice. It is no coincidence that the notorious Jack Kevorkian is drum major for an absolutized autonomy. "In my view the highest principle in medical ethics—in any kind of ethics—is personal autonomy, self-determination. What counts is what the patient wants and judges to be a benefit or a value in his or her own life. That's primary."[19] Stop. Period. No qualifications. As Leon Kass notes: "The autonomy argument kicks out all criteria for evaluating the choice, save that it be uncoerced."[20] And it is no coincidence that Kevorkian regards medicine as a "strictly secular endeavor." It should be entirely separate from religious ethics. His example: a Catholic doctor should be prepared to provide an atheistic woman with an abortion.[21] Behold the indissoluble union of a secularized medicine with absolutized autonomy that trumps every other consideration. In this system Kevorkian has become what he provides: a machine.

3. THE EMERGENCE OF PUBLIC MORALITY

Nearly everyone has heard the term "public morality" and is vaguely conscious of the need of public morality. But what does the term mean? It suggests that the pursuit of the basic goods that define our well-being has increasingly been shifted from private one-on-one acts and has been put into the public sphere. That means that bioethics will have to have much more to say at the level of policy-making than it has. Until quite recently it has been much more concerned with the level of individual decision. "But," as Daniel Callahan correctly notes, "on a national scale those decisions are going to be over-shadowed by large structural, moral and political decisions. It is these decisions that will eventually shape the individual decisions."[22]

I will begin by stating what public morality is not. First, it is not simply public participation in the directions and priorities of medical practice, research, and health care. If public morality is understood in this way, it easily becomes a merely formal affair, a matter of structuring dialogue to include representative participants.

Second, it is not merely law or public policy. One of the prime tests of law is its own "possibility," as John Courtney Murray words it,[23] or its feasibility, ". . . that quality whereby a proposed course of action is not merely possible but practicable, adaptable, depending on the circumstances, cultural ways, attitudes, traditions of a people, etc." Public policy must, therefore, take account of some very pragmatic considerations in a rather utilitarian way. Reducing public morality to public policy would be to undermine public morality.

A clearer grasp of the meaning of public morality becomes possible when we consider the contemporary context of health care delivery. Individual decisions will, of course, remain and will remain important. But increasingly, the services of physician to patient are mediated by institutions. Such institutions have become partners in health care delivery. Thus we have group practice, third party carriers, legislative and administrative controls (e.g., Food and Drug Administration), etc.

Groups (whether universities, insurance companies, or the government) have interests and concerns other than the immediate good of the patient. Thus the government has a legitimate interest in population control, in reducing welfare rolls, in control of illegitimacy, in the advancement of diagnostic, therapeutic, preventive medicine, in balancing the budget, in protecting life. Teaching and research hospitals have a concern for the health of future generations.

This suggests that whenever other values (than the patient's) are the legitimate concern of the mediator of health care, the good of the individual patient becomes one of several values in competition for priority. It further suggests that the individual is in danger of being subordinated to these values.

As I understand the term, "public morality" is the pursuit of these other values without violating the needs and integrity of the individual. It is a harmonizing of public concerns with individual needs. These "other values and concerns" constitute the public dimension of biomedicine because they represent concerns other than and beyond the individual. In Callahan's words: "Ways will have to be found to balance that ethic [patient-centered] off against the legitimate interests of the public . . ."[24]

Callahan has summarized this matter splendidly. He argues that the allocation of resources, the development of a just health-care delivery system, the adjudication of the rights and claims of different competing groups "are and will be the important moral problems of the future." These problems will "force biomedical ethics to move into the mainstream of political and social theory, beyond the model of the individual decision-maker, and into the thicket of important vested and legitimate private and group interests." Establishing the proper balance between individual patient-centered concerns and other legitimate interest is what I mean by the term "public morality."

When biomedicine is mediated by groups with other (than the individual's) concerns, the medical-research establishment is thereby deeply inserted into the value perspectives of society at large, and begins to be shaped by these perspectives and priorities. One need not be a Cassandra to note that in the United States top cultural priorities are technology, efficiency, comfort. This means that these priorities will unavoidably penetrate the "medical-research complex" and shape its directions. It requires no stretch of the imagination to see how deleteriously such values can impact the professional culture of medicine.

4. THE MARKET-DRIVEN HEALTH CARE SYSTEM

By market-driven I mean institutions whose existence and policies are heavily dictated by the economic factor. In such an atmosphere, one thing is clear: the institution is financially viable or it does not survive ("No margin, no mission").

There are telltale indicia all around us that point to the ascendancy, even primacy of the economic factor, and perhaps especially the competitive environment. Hospitals have marketing directors. They experience pressures from HMOs, which will increasingly feel pressure from PPOs. Health care institutions must train a keen institutional eye on Diagnostic Related Groups. Between 1980 and 1986, 414 hospitals closed. Predictions vary but some estimates foresee the closure of 700 more by 1995. Increasingly hospitals are forced into joint ventures and mergers. Essential services (e.g., trauma centers) do not support themselves. The dumping syndrome is alive and well, even if in subtle and changing ways. Acquisition decisions, hiring practices, incentive proposals are often closely market-related.

This litany could be continued almost indefinitely; but that is unnecessary. Above I pointed to cost-containment concerns and related them to depersonalization. My focus is somewhat different here. When institutions are swept into preoccupation with their financial status, their sense of mission can be swallowed up in the process. And when that happens, the culture of the profession can be severely tested. The professional culture of medicine should find reinforcement in institutions, not threats. A symptom of my concern here is the growing literature on the fiscal responsibilities of physicians, and on physician's as fiscal gate-keepers. This issue is much more intense now than it ever was in the past.

5. THE CRISIS OF NURSING

It is obvious that nurses are an essential aspect, probably the most important aspect, of hospital care, and health care more generally. What is not so obvious is that if there is a nursing crisis, that has the potential of affecting negatively the culture of medicine.

Why so? Physicianly care is care of the *person,* as Kass pointed out. Therefore, it combines the collaborative contributions of many people: physicians, nurses, pastoral care people, para-medical personnel. If one element is in crisis, the whole collaborative team will be affected. Nurses are an especially valuable adjunct in this collaboration. So often they bring, besides their technical competence, a special presence, communication, support, shared faith, empathy. Quite simply they often make the difference between healing and mere fixing.

The crisis is a shortage of nurses. There are many reasons for this. One of the key dissatisfactions of nurses is the absence of satisfying professional relationships with physicians.[25] Some others are: small financial rewards compared to responsibilities; limited autonomy in clinical situations; little involvement in hospital management decisions regarding standards of practice and support services; disarray in titling and educational preparation of nurses (the American Nursing Association wants all nurses to have the four-year baccalaureate degree, but two-thirds enter practice with an associate degree or a diploma); Medicare's Prospective Payment System wherein economic incentives to reduce the length of hospital stays mean the same care must be given in less time; unpopular working hours and shift rotations and absence of adequate support personnel—and all of this at the very time of the proliferation of alternative health delivery plans that provide nurses with new career opportunities.[26]

I have mentioned five different aspects or characteristics that make up the context of the practice of medicine in the United States today: depersonalization, secularization, the emergence of public morality, the market-driven system, and the crisis of nursing. These are obviously interrelated and overlapping. Thus the crisis of nursing is clearly related to the secularization of medicine. Depersonalization and secularization are related, as are the emergence of public morality and market-driven health care.

My interest, however, is that cumulatively these forces are capable of, indeed are, undermining the culture that makes medicine a profession. Contemporary medicine has gone a long way toward becoming a business and a business that is heavily self-interested. Everybody from physicians, nurses, administrators, politicians, bioethicists to patients (now called "consumers") is screaming bloody murder about this. But on it goes. As I noted at the outset, the problem is the displacement of the culture of medicine as a profession.

Let me appeal to a symbol to illustrate my point. As I write, the National Conference of Catholic Bishops is in the process of updating the *Ethical and Religious Directives for Catholic Health Care Facilities*. One can predict what the ultimate product will look like. There will be basic values stated to which we are committed (e.g., sanctity of life) and these will be hammered out in more concrete directives about abortion, experimentation, care of the dying, transplantation, etc. They will be voted on by the bishops and become official policy—as if such guidance and directives were responding to the real problems of Catholic health care institutions. They are not. These institutions exist in a climate that dispossesses them of their culture. They are losing their souls, so to speak. *That* is the problem that should rivet our attention.

Something similar can be said of the field of bioethics. If it simply makes strategic adjustments, it will continue to march, in a disciplined and orderly way to be sure, parallel to the truly formative developments in the field. If, on the other hand, those forces that have been dissolving the culture of the medical profession can be honestly faced and effectively dealt with, then we might be pleasantly surprised to see needed adjustments occur almost spontaneously, "from below" so to speak. For a genuine professional culture would be in place to suggest, nourish, support, even demand such adjustments.

Can these forces be faced and dealt with effectively? I honestly do not know. It may be unduly pessimistic to put it this way, but major cultural shifts or conversions (and that is what is called for here) so often occur only via catastrophe and suffering. Is it excessive to believe that until we feel *painfully, corporately,* and *personally* the results of the dissolution of the professional culture in medicine nothing will change? In this sense truly helpful revisions in bioethics may be painful, because they will be conditioned by changes in the forces that shape medicine.

One may legitimately wonder what the reflections presented above have to do with theology. In my view, a great deal. Medicine has what some have called its own "internal" morality. Philosopher Robert Sokolowski notes that the good of the medical art is the health of the individual or community. He continues:

> In acting according to his art the physician also seeks the good of the patient. Because the art of medicine aims at something that is a good for the patient, the doctor, in the exercise of his art, seeks the medical good of the patient as his own good. He pursues professionally what is good for another . . . The nature of his art . . . makes him, in the good exercise of his art, not only a good doctor but also essentially a good moral agent, one who seeks the good of another formally as his own. The doctor's profession essentially makes him a good man, provided he is true to his art and follows its insistence.[27]

This morality internal to the medical profession is even more resplendent when viewed through the eyes of Christian theology. In the Christian understanding, the encounter of persons has a certain structure.

It is the categorical moment for the faithful activity in love that describes the very being of the "new creature." It is literally our way of loving God in this context. It is the vertical in the horizontal, or, as Joseph Sittler puts it, "Love is the function of faith horizontally just as prayer is the function of faith vertically."[28] This is true of both the curing and the caring dimensions of health care. If we do not view health care in this way, we interpret and restrict its reality short of the depths of faith. The Decree on the Apostolate of the Laity of Vatican II, after noting that Christ made the commandment of love his own and endowed it with new meaning, states: "For he wanted to identify himself with his brethren as the object of this love when he said, 'As long as you did it for one of these, the least of my brethren, you did it for me.'"[29] But if this profound structure of the health care encounter is to be lived, "certain fundamentals must be observed. Thus attention is to be paid to the image of God in which our neighbor has been created, and also to Christ the Lord to whom is really offered whatever is given to a needy person."[30]

If the medical encounter is viewed and lived in this way, it would be both guided by and generative of the moral dispositions and perspectives implied in Christ's phrase "as I have loved you." One need not understand this as a psychological "immediacy." I am speaking rather of the profoundest ontological structure of the encounter, fully disclosed in and by Christ, a structure we perceive only dimly (in faith), but one that ought to be the organizing shape and power of our responses. This is nothing more nor less than the encounter to which Christ enjoined his followers. This is exactly what the "Decree on the Apostolate of the Laity" meant when it urged professional people to remember that in fulfilling their secular duties of daily life, "they do not disassociate union with Christ from that life."[31] It further urged professionals to "see Christ in all men whether they be close to us or strangers."[32]

If health care personnel view their profession in this way, I believe we can reasonably predict three important results. First, there will be the growth of those dispositions that nourish, protect, and support the medical encounter as a truly human (not merely technological) one: compassion, honesty, self-denial, and generosity.

Second, we may reasonably expect that a profession deeply penetrated with persons of such faith and such dispositions will be transformed. The "Decree on the Apostolate of the Laity" states of persons of faith that "their behavior will have a penetrating impact, little by little, on the whole circle of their life and labors."[33] It regards this as the "penetrating and perfecting of the temporal sphere." I take it as indisputable that, in a time of high technology and growing impersonality in health care, this would be a truly desirable leavening influence. Faith creates sensitivities in the believer beyond natural capacities. It bestows sensitivity to "dimensions of possibility" not otherwise suspected.

Third, this "penetrating and perfecting of the temporal sphere" will be guided by the phrase "as I have loved you." Therefore it will be permeated with the ultimacy and absoluteness of the God-Relationship, and the corresponding relativizing of other human goods. In health care delivery this can be very important.

The characteristic temptation of the ethos of the medical profession is to idolize life and the profession's ability to preserve it. The manifestation of this is the abandonment of patients when cure is no longer possible and death is imminent. For many physicians death is defeat. ("No one dies on my shift.") This can skewer and distort the ministry of health care, decontextualize its instrumentalities, technologize its value judgments, and bloat its practitioners—to say nothing of limitlessly expanding its cost.

If medicine is indeed being transformed into a business, then the theologian must view this as a disaster. It involves a crucial displacement and disharmony at the heart of the medical art. What is supposed to be a privileged encounter, indeed a graced one (a source of healing and growth for both physician and patient) has become a means. The theologian views the physician encounter with the patient as the physician encounter with Christ. It is precisely for that reason that the theologian legitimately expects the three results mentioned above.

When, however, the crucial encounter of physician with patient is displaced into a business context, not only is the professional ethos (compassion, honesty, self-denial, generosity) exposed to erosion, but we all will be deprived of the transforming effect of faith alive in a physician.

To the theologian that is unacceptable.

CHAPTER 13

Hidden Persuaders:
Value Variables in Bioethics

The late, great theologian Karl Rahner once noted that moral analyses frequently reflect basic assumptions and cultural variables that operate behind them. He referred to such assumptions as "global prescientific convictions." We might translate that as massive cultural biases. At any rate, Rahner stated that such convictions are responsible for the impression that certain "proofs" in moral theology assume from the outset the conclusion they purport to establish. In this fashion the conclusions are "smuggled into the premises of the argument."[1] *Hineingesmuggelt* is Rahner's sonorous word. He urged that one of moral theology's important tasks is the exposure and demolition of such prescientific convictions.

What Rahner calls "global prescientific convictions" Harry Stack Sullivan once described as "reasons" that have sunk so deeply into the self that they are implicitly understood. Such reasons constitute the unwitting aspect of a culture and are much more responsible for its tone and direction than explicit laws and policies.

I believe we could find several "global prescientific convictions" in the Church's nineteenth-century analysis of religious freedom (e.g., certain convictions about the state as ideally Christian). The same could be said of the notions of "natural" and "unnatural" as they weave themselves in and out of discussions of reproductive technology and genetic engineering. The subordinate status of women in society and the Church is another such conviction.

My contention here is that bioethical thought—and indeed health care planning in general—can be profoundly influenced by certain cultural assumptions, trends, unexamined attitudes, biases—what I shall call "value variables." I will list ten candidates here with the happy admission that more and others might qualify. Two things should be noted about these value variables: they are more or less implicit, and they are intertwined in such a way that they often feed off each other.

1. THE DENIAL OF MORTALITY

Of course, it is impossible to deny mortality. What is possible, however, is to organize health care in such a way that it seems to imply rejection of the fact. Daniel Callahan puts it as follows:

> Our toughest problem is not that of a need to ration health care, though that will be necessary. It is that we have failed, in our understandable eagerness to vanquish illness and disability, to accept the implications of an insight available to all: We are bounded and finite beings, ineluctably subject to aging, decline and death. We have tried to put that truth out of mind in designing a modern healthcare system, one that wants to conquer all diseases and stay the hand of death.[2]

Thus, Callahan continues, "We have defined our unlimited hopes to transcend our mortality as our needs, and we have created a medical enterprise that engineers the transformation."

The symptoms of this rejection of the fact of mortality abound.

Item: a wealthy society like ours must not allow anyone to die who can be saved. Witness the end-stage renal disease program of 1972 providing government-paid dialysis for all who need it. Indeed a 1987 Harris poll revealed that most people (71% to 26%) believe that "health insurance should pay for any treatments that will save lives, even if it costs one million dollars to save a life."

Item: Intensive care units are overused; too frequently they resemble high-tech hospices. As Joseph A. Califano, Jr., puts it: "A substantial number of patients admitted are elderly, in chronically poor health, with little chance for short-term survival."[3] Many patients are either too sick or not sick enough.

Item: Nearly 30 percent of Medicare's money goes to patients with less than a year to live. This figure has not varied appreciably in the last fifteen years.[4]

Item: Patients in a persistent vegetative state are maintained for prolonged periods by artificial nutrition and hydration (e.g., Nancy Cruzan). Most people judge this prolongation to be needless, heedless and aimless—indeed a pursuit of the temporal that potentially blurs the eternal.

Christopher F. Koller summarizes as follows: "Health care has much more important things to offer than the false hope of immortality."[5]

2. THE EUGENIC MENTALITY

By this phrase I refer to positive eugenics, the preferential breeding of superior individuals or genotypes. At the heart of such an attitude is an intolerance of imperfection. I will use two happenings to make my point. The first was the *in vitro* fertilization debate in this country. I was privileged to be on the 13-member Ethics Advisory Board of the Department of Health, Education and Welfare (HEW), which deliberated on this matter for the federal government. While taking testimony throughout the country, I became aware of an interesting attitude on the part of a considerable number of people. It was the "consumer-item mentality" toward the child—"Give me blue eyes this time." The second incident was Robert K. Graham's announcement on May 25, 1982, of the establishment of the Repository for Germinal Choice. Graham was seeking out the sperm of superior individuals (e.g., Nobel Prize winners like Dr. William S. Shockely) to produce—I use the word deliberately—genetically superior persons. "We only go with the most superlative males," boasted Graham. Since that time, similar repositories (sperm banks) have become quite common, offering brochures that state the donor's race, education, hobbies, weight—and yes, eye color.

These two events occurred in a twofold cultural context. First, prenatal diagnosis is increasingly sophisticated. We have amniocentesis, chorionic villus biopsy, ultrasonography and maternal serum alpha feto-protein testing for neural tube defects. Second, abortion is a culturally accepted form of health care.

The consumer-item mentality toward children, combined with sophisticated prenatal diagnosis, will lead to an increasing emphasis on eugenics. Telling symptoms of this mentality are already apparent. We hear people refer to "the right to a healthy child." Implied in such loose talk is the right to discard the imperfect. What is meant, of course, is that couples have a claim to those reasonably available means to see that their children are as healthy as possible.

Barbara Katz Rothman has noted the erosion of the unconditional acceptance of the child implicit in "quality" thinking. She asks,

> What does it do to motherhood, to women, and to men as fathers too, when we make parental acceptance conditional, pending further testing? We ask the mother and her family to say in essence,

"These are my standards. If you meet these standards of accept-
ability, then you are mine and I will love and accept you totally.
After you pass this test."[6]

Furthermore, recently we have seen several cases of "wrongful
life" where the child himself or herself is the plaintiff.[7] Recent neona-
tal intensive care cases have revealed an alarming attitude on the part
of some people, including physicians. The options narrow to a healthy
child or a dead child. We have donor insemination. We have pre-implantation diagnosis for some genetic defects. The National Institutes
of Health are already involved in genetic correction of some diseases.
Someday soon, researchers will contemplate a more thorough cure,
that of correcting the defective gene in the germ line cells (ova or
sperm). As an editorial in *The New York Times* noted:

> Repairing a defect is one thing, but once that is routine, it will
> become much harder to argue against adding genes that confer
> desired qualities, like better health, looks or brains. There is no
> discernible line to be drawn between making inheritable repairs
> of genetic defects, and improving the species.[8]

"Improving the species" belongs to what we call "positive eugenics." It raises a host of unanswerable questions: what qualities are to
be maximized? Who decides? Which defects are too burdensome?
Who decides? Every thoughtful commentator runs from questions like
these as if they were the plague. These are just some of the dilemmas
of positive eugenics. Far too few people advert to the fact that when
we program for high IQ, we can begin to value the person in terms of
the quality. In other words, we reduce the whole to a part. People
who do that are on their way to doing other things civilized societies
should abhor.

This eugenic mentality is powerfully supported by the developing notions of disease and health. The term "disease" has had an interesting evolutionary history, and, therefore, so has the term "health."

The word "disease" first meant an identifiable degenerative or
inflammatory process, which, if unchecked, would lead to serious organic illness and sometimes eventually to death. The next stage of
development was statistical: At least some diseases were identified by
deviation from a supposed statistical norm. Thus we referred to *hyper*-
thyroidism or *hypo*cholesterolemia, *hypo*glycemia, etc. One was said
to be unhealthy, to have a disease, if he or she were *hypo* or *hyper*
anything. The person was unhealthy not in the sense of an existing,
tangible degenerative process, but in the sense that the individual was

more likely than others to suffer some untoward event, what my late colleague Dr. André Hellegers impishly called "hyperuntowardeventitis."

The third notion defines disease as inability to function in society. For instance, a good deal of surgery being performed to enlarge breasts, to shrink buttocks, to tuck tummies, to remove wrinkles—in brief, to conform to someone's notion of the attractive and eventually of the tolerable. We live in a society that cannot tolerate aging. At some point, then, this question arises: Who is the patient here? Who is sick—the individual, or society? I mean, of course, that this broad understanding of "health" can too easily reflect the sickness in society's judgments about the meaning of the person. In our time and in some societies, people are hospitalized because of nonconformity. That suggests that the notion of "health" is becoming increasingly nonsomatized and getting out of control.

The final stage of development is the definition of health popularized by the World Health Organization. According to WHO, health is a "state of complete physical, mental, and social well-being, not simply the absence of illness and disease." This description of health was adopted in the 1973 abortion decisions of the U.S. Supreme Court. The Court stated that the "medical judgment may be exercised in the light of all factors—physical, emotional, psychological, familial, and the woman's age—relevant to the well-being of the patient."[9]

Through the expansion of the notions of health and disease, contemporary medicine is increasingly treating people's desires in a move toward a society without discomfort. In the process some basic human problems are being medicalized.

3. GOOD HEALTH CARE = EFFICIENT RESCUE MEDICINE

When people think of health care they usually think of sick care. Joseph Califano puts it this way:

> Heart disease is America's number-one killer. Daily newspapers and television dramas give the impression that coronary bypass surgery, modern cardiopulmonary techniques, miracle hypertension pills, human heart transplants, and in the future, animal and artificial heart transplants are the way to battle heart disease.
>
> Right?
>
> Couldn't be more wrong.
>
> Since 1970 our nation has experienced a dramatic 25 percent decline in deaths from coronary heart disease. The major reasons? Improved eating habits—the reduction in cholesterol—accounted

for almost one-third of the drop. The decline in cigarette smoking was responsible for another quarter. So individuals, by changing personal habits, were responsible for more than half the decline in deaths from heart disease. In contrast, coronary care units accounted for only 13.5 percent; cardiopulmonary resuscitation, 4 percent; bypass surgery 3.5 percent; and the widely used hypertension pills only 9 percent. Deaths from stroke are also sharply down for much the same reasons.[10]

Califano goes on to point out that virtually all the factors that substantially increase the likelihood of heart disease are in the patient's control, not the physician's.

But on we go, and our bias toward acute care means not only neglect of health care, but a one-sided emphasis on cure to the neglect of care, and that in an aging society at the very time when what is needed is *more* caring. Christopher Koller states: "Clinically, patients and providers alike often forsake the collective art of caring for the individualized science of curing."[11] And why not? After all, as Dr. Timothy Quill notes, "We overtrain doctors to extend life. We undertrain them to address human suffering."[12] His example: the attempt to resuscitate an 80-pound, 80-year-old man ravaged by lung cancer whose bones fracture under the pressure of CPR.

Daniel Callahan points out that caring is not emphasized for physicians in the way that medical knowledge and technical skills are stressed. "The ability to care requires a capacity to acknowledge our own mortality and our common vulnerability as well as to understand the privacy and hiddenness of much pain and suffering in others, an understanding that requires imagination."[13]

4. ABSOLUTIZATION OF AUTONOMY

I adverted to this in the previous chapter. But it bears repeating. Until the last few decades, medicine was practiced in a highly paternalistic way. Paternalism refers to a system in which treatment decisions are made against the patient's preferences or without the patient's knowledge and consent. The past twenty years have seen a reaction against such paternalism and the flowering of patient autonomy.

What can easily be missed is that reactions have a way of becoming overreactions. In the religious sphere, a reaction against authoritarianism can usher in anarchy. In an overreaction against paternalism, autonomy has been absolutized. As I noted above, the symbolic cheerleader for this absolutization is Dr. Jack Kevorkian, who states:

> In my view the highest principle in medical ethics—in any kind of ethics—is personal autonomy, self-determination. What counts is what the patient wants and judges to be a benefit or a value in his or her own life. That's primary.[14]

Period.

The offshoot of this absolutization is that very little attention is given to the values that ought to guide the use of autonomy. The sheer fact that the choice is the patient's is viewed as the sole right-making characteristic of the choice. This attitude has impoverished the presentation of the pro-choice position on abortion. Choices, however, may be good or bad, and unless we confront the features that make choices good or bad, autonomy usurps the evaluation. When it trumps every other consideration, autonomy has been overstated and distorted and leads to what Bruce Jennings calls "the terrible singularity, the chilling aloofness of the sovereign moral will."[15]

5. DIGNITY AS INDEPENDENCE

We often hear people, especially the elderly, declaring, "I don't want to be a burden." The idea of depending on others seems almost un-American. Depending on others is foreign to our notion of human dignity. Human dignity means independence, much as national dignity is anchored in the Declaration of Independence.

Witness this clip from *USA Today*:

> Cynthia Powelson knew it was time to die. She'd tried surgery, chemotherapy, acupuncture and meditation. She couldn't eat or drink. And her gastric tumor had grown so large she appeared six months pregnant. Doctors said she wouldn't live a year. The graduate student, 37, gathered family at her suburban Rochester, New York, home, married her longtime love, then had her feeding tube removed. She died 12 days later. Life was out of control. Death was on her terms. Having some say in death, as Powelson did, has become a national obsession.[16]

I am not criticizing Cynthia Powelson's decision, not at all. Nor is it appropriate to glamorize dependence. Our discomfort with dependence is quite understandable. But for too many people dignity is *totally* incompatible with dependence. Thus dignity—as in death with dignity—means death in my way, at my time, by my hand.

All I would argue here is that our notion of dignity must incorporate the reality of dependence. Christians realize that Christ displayed great dignity in dependence: "Not my will but thine be done." Christians do not view dependence as depriving us of our dignity, but as a sacrament of our openness to and dependence on God. In the fragility of dependence, we are invited to cling to and trust in a power beyond our control. In this sense, a rejection of interdependence is closely tied to rejection of creaturehood and mortality. An Anglican study group put it this way:

> There is a movement of giving and receiving. At the beginning and at the end of life receiving predominates over and even excludes giving. But the value of human life does not depend only on its capacity to give. Love, *agape,* is the equal and unalterable regard for the value of other human beings independent of their particular characteristics. It extends especially to the helpless and hopeless, to those who have no value in their own eyes and seemingly none for society. Such neighbor-love is costly and sacrificial. It is easily destroyed. In the giver it demands unlimited caring, in the recipient absolute trust. The question must be asked whether the practice of voluntary euthanasia is consistent with the fostering of such care and trust.[17]

6. THE SECULARIZATION OF MEDICINE

I adverted to this in the previous chapter but let me add a few details here. The average physician spends 7.5 hours a week on utilization review problems, nearly nine full work weeks a year. Physicians increasingly regard their expertise as their own possession to be dispensed in the marketplace on their terms. Thus, as I noted above, 30 percent have said that, were they free to choose, they would not treat AIDS patients. Sixteen percent of physicians now advertise, thus reinforcing the impression of medicine-as-business.

One result of this transformation is that physicians are leaving the profession. As Dr. Raymond Scalettar, chairman of the AMA Board of Trustees, put it: "You never used to hear of a physician retiring unless he was ill or disabled. This wasn't work. This was a calling. Now it has changed."[18] The nature of that change is captured by Seattle physician Michael McCarthy: "I like the emotional side of medicine. But this isn't about emotion anymore, it's a business."[19]

When medicine becomes a business, the physician-patient relationship is eroded by being made a means to a further end.

7. THE INTERVENTIONIST MENTALITY

This value variable is very close to the emphasis on "rescue medicine" discussed under Number 3 above, but it is somewhat broader. Corporately, we Americans are *Homo technologicus*. We believe that the best solution to the dilemmas created by technology is more technology. Thus, Glennon Hospital in St. Louis spends $400,000 to treat lead poisoning rather than attempting to correct the problems in the homes where lead poisoning originates. We use pesticides and discover only later that they are carcinogens. We tend to eliminate the maladapted condition (disabled, retarded, etc.) rather than adjust the environment to it.

The high-water mark of this interventionist mentality was the declaration of the late Joseph Fletcher that "laboratory reproduction is radically human compared to conception by ordinary heterosexual intercourse." The surest symptom that something is awry here is that the fun has gone out of things.

8. CONFUSION OF THE LEGAL AND MORAL

It is the temptation of the Anglo-American tradition to identify legal and moral issues. We are a pragmatic and litigious people for whom law is the answer to all problems, the only answer and a fully adequate answer. Thus, many people confuse morality and public policy. If something is removed from the penal code, it is viewed as morally right and permissible. And if an act is seen as morally wrong, many want it made illegal. Behold the "there ought to be a law" syndrome.

When these two spheres, interrelated as they are, get confusedly identified, then the moral arguments establishing the one or the other also are confusedly identified. Since public policy must be sensitive to a whole host of pragmatic considerations (e.g., enforceability, pluralism of conviction, social costs, social priorities) collectible under the term "feasibility," it is possible for moral argument to be affected—indeed, corrupted—by such considerations. Furthermore, it is possible that the tactics used so often to move public policy can come to be regarded as "moral arguments." An example can be drawn from the late 1960s and early '70s when "gut feelings," confrontation, symbolic acts of protest, and other forms of nondiscursive exchange prevailed over analytic discourse and were frequently regarded as adequate warrants for *moral* stances. The prophet was confused with the philosopher. As a result we experienced a loss of accountability to reason.

9. MORALITY AS PURELY PERSONAL

We often hear such declarations as: "It is not my concern what another does." "Each person must decide for him or herself." "Who am I to determine another's morals?" Or again, "I do not myself accept abortion, but I do not want to impose my morality on others." Such statements spring from a lonely individualism that supposes that you and I are islands, individual and isolated from the society and atomized within it.

One of the major mischiefs of this individualism is our failure to see the social dimension of many problems (physician-assisted suicide, abortion, reproductive technologies, human sexuality). A view of abortion as a matter of individual choice, for example, divides people, while abortion seen as a social problem could bring people together. Nearly everyone would agree that the conditions that lead to abortion (poverty, lack of education, broken families, lack of recreational alternatives, etc.) should be corrected.

Or again, sexual activity is often viewed as a purely private matter. Robert McAfee Brown recently underlined how false that view is.[21] Sexual relationships are microcosms of society. A loving atmosphere in the home can flow out into society. An inhumane and violent social atmosphere can turn on the family and shatter it. Sexual and social issues are inseparable. Or better, sexual issues are social issues.

10. FUNCTIONAL ASSESSMENT OF THE PERSON

I believe it safe to say that many Americans unwittingly operate from a rather crude utilitarianism in many of their moral judgments. "If it produces good results, what can be wrong with it?" This bias toward producing results will naturally lead to an evaluation of people as producers. They will be regarded, supported, protected in terms of their functionability or value to society. If this is the silently operating criterion, it is clear who will suffer.

The Implications of Value Variables. If I am correct in identifying these value variables, then it is clear that they will profoundly affect how we think about bioethical problems, and especially health care reform. When these variables are shaken and mixed, I strongly suspect that they will yield thought patterns that will overvalue and overstate longevity, independence, autonomy (of both patient and physician), technology, curing (to the neglect of caring), youth, individualism, doing (vs. being), and competition. Correspondingly, they will yield thought patterns that undervalue and understate mortality, dependence, caring, the social dimension of choices, limits of technology, aging, being (vs. doing and producing), and cooperation (vs. competition).

I expect such hidden persuaders to generate stiff resistance on the part of patients, physicians, and hospitals to the type of sacrifice that will be required by true healthcare reform. The wagons are already circling. Indeed if such reform is to occur, it will require something akin to a cultural conversion. If you are optimistic, you will believe that such conversion is possible without the turbulence of catastrophe. But if you are pessimistic . . .

CHAPTER 14

Who or What Is the Preembryo?

First, a word about my title. It reads "Who or What is the Preembryo?" Indeed for the rest of this chapter I shall refer to the preembryo. The word is about that such a usage has sinister motivations. I have heard it often. For instance, Dr. Michael Jarmulowicz asserts that this term was adopted by the American Fertility Society and the Voluntary Licensing Authority in Britain "as an exercise of linguistic engineering to make human embryo research more palatable to the general public."[1] I am afraid Jarmulowicz has a firm grasp on a preconceived idea that has led to a premature conclusion. I trust it was not premeditated.

I cannot speak for the VLA; but I can for the AFS. I was a member of its ethics committee that discussed and adopted this terminology. Our discussion had nothing to do with embryo research or even more generally with moral status. "Preembryo" was used because the earliest stages of mammalian development do not primarily involve formation of the embryo and its parts but the establishment of the nonembryonic trophoblast. As Clifford Grobstein, a distinguished basic scientist and a member of the AFS ethics committee, concludes: "The scientific rationale for the term preembryo, accordingly, is its greater accuracy in characterizing the initial phase of mammalian and human development . . . The status implications of such a change in terminology were not at issue in the discussion."[2]

The status of the preembryo is a question with very practical implications. Some of these are the following: 1) what may be done to preembryos before transfer; 2) whether all preembryos must be transferred; 3) what may be done to preembryos that are not transferred.[3] Furthermore, emergency treatment of rape cases may be affected by the status of the preembryo.

Not all proposed clinical experiments directly affect the preembryo. This would be true of cytoplasmic transfusion. If eggs are harvested prior to peak maturity, they often fail to yield a pregnancy when transferred. Assuming that this is due to the immaturity of ovum cytoplasm, researchers contemplate transfusing ova with the cytoplasm of mature ova. Other procedures are basically therapeutic. This is the case with removal of excess pronuclei. It can happen that more than one sperm enters an ovum. This results in the formation of three pronuclei. Such ova develop either not at all or abnormally (a molar pregnancy).

Some actual or projected protocols directly affect the preembryo. This is true of cryopreservation. Cryopreservation of extra preembryos decreases the number of stimulated egg recovery cycles for individual women and provides added flexibility in transfer protocols. Yet thawing is not a completely benign process. Significant numbers of preembryos die in the process. Moreover, cryo-injury cannot be altogether excluded. Down the road a year or ten lies pre-implantation genetic diagnosis. This would involve the removal of several cells from a preembryo developing *in vitro*. The DNA of these cells would be diagnosed and then only genetically normal preembryos would be transferred. With our growing knowledge of single gene defects and the rapid advance of amplification technology, it is not difficult to imagine scientists embarking on a variety of micromanipulations of the preembryo "in order to learn something."

The status of the preembryo is, of course, not a new problem. Any number of advisory committees have addressed it. For instance, the Ethics Advisory Board agreed in 1979 that "the human embryo [meaning what here is called the preembryo] is entitled to profound respect, but this respect does not necessarily encompass the full legal and moral rights attributed to persons."[4] The Warnock Committee in 1984 stated a similar position when it asserted that "the human embryo . . . is not under the present law of the United Kingdom accorded the same status as a living child or an adult, nor do we necessarily wish it to be accorded the same status. Nevertheless, we were agreed that the embryo of the human species ought to have a special status."[5] The Ontario Law Reform Commission (Canada) took this same view in 1985.[6] I think it fair to say that most groups that have addressed this question have arrived at a similar judgment. The most prominent exceptions are to be found in official Catholic statements to which I now turn.

Prior to 1869 there was for centuries vigorous debate about when the fetus was ensouled (or animated). Most held for delayed animation, a position still defended by some contemporary authors (e.g., Joseph Donceel, S.J.). The distinction between the ensouled-noninsouled fetus was largely concerned with canonical penalties since all interruptions into the reproductive process were condemned as immoral. In 1869 Pius IX dropped reference to the "ensouled fetus" in the excommunication for abortion. Thus excommunication was incurred for any abortion, even the earliest. It is understandable, then, why recent Catholic literature would use the phrase "from the moment of conception" in its formulations of the abortion prohibition. Let a few examples suffice. Thus Vatican II stated: "From the moment of conception life must be guarded with the greatest care."[7] This phrase can be found over and over again in episcopal pastoral letters and papal addresses. An example is the *Charter of the Rights of the Family* published by the Holy See. It states: "Human life must be absolutely respected and protected from the moment of conception."[8] A very recent and pertinent statement is that of John Paul II. Speaking to a group of scientists in 1982 he declared: "I condemn, in the most explicit and formal way, experimental manipulations of the human embryo, since the human being, from conception to death, cannot be exploited for any purpose whatsoever."[9] Conception is understood as fertilization in these documents, though the two concepts are not necessarily identical. By that I mean that fertilization is a biological term; conception need not be. It is still not absurd to ask: when should a woman be said to conceive? In a letter to the Duke of Norfolk on the Human Fertilisation and Embryology Bill, Cardinal Basil Hume seems implicitly to acknowledge this distinction. He writes: "I would assure you that there is no doubt that the Church's official teaching is that human life is to be protected from the first moments of fertilization."[10]

The two most recent documents dealing with the status of the preembryo are the *Declaration on Procured Abortion* (1974)[11] and *Donum vitae* (1987).[12] For the present I want only to state their conclusions rather than thoroughly analyze their arguments.

The *Declaration on Procured Abortion* is explicitly concerned with abortion and its legal regulation, and therefore, its chief concern is established pregnancy. But it does make all-encompassing remarks about the protection of human life. Thus:

In reality, respect for human life is called for from the time that the process of generation begins. From the time that the ovum is fertilized, a life is begun which is neither that of the father nor of the mother; it is rather the life of a new human being with his own growth. He will never become human if he were not human already.[13]

Then the Declaration makes two points. First it states that modern genetic science brings "valuable confirmation" to this perspective since it shows that from the very beginning the genetic package is in place. "Right from fertilization is begun the adventure of a human life."[14]

Second, the Declaration states that its conclusion stands independently of "the discussions on the moment of animation." Such discussions the Declaration "expressly leaves aside." We shall see its argumentation for its conclusion below.

What is clear, then, from the Declaration is that human life must be protected from fertilization, even though the Declaration explicitly refrains from asserting that the person is present *ab initio* (for if the soul is not present, the person is not).

Donum vitae is even more interesting. The Congregation for the Doctrine of the Faith asserts that it "is aware of the current debates concerning the beginning of human life, concerning the individuality of the human being and concerning the identity of the human person."[15] It immediately cites the *Declaration on Procured Abortion* about the presence of genetic programming from the beginning. Then it states most interestingly:

The conclusions of science regarding the human embryo provide a valuable indication for discerning by the use of reason a personal presence at the moment of this first appearance of a human life: how could a human individual not be a human person?[16]

It then notes that the magisterium has "not expressly committed itself to an affirmation of a philosophical nature" as to whether personhood coincides with fertilization.

In summary, then, the CDF looks at genetic uniqueness and on this basis is strongly inclined to see a personal presence from fertilization. On this basis it makes two remarkably different statements. 1) It *is* a person ("How could a human individual not be a human person?"). 2) It *must be treated as* a person ("The human being is to be respected and treated as a person from the moment of conception.") What is called a preembryo here has rights and indeed "a right to the same respect that is due to the child already born and to every human person." Harmful nontherapeutic experimentation is a "crime against their dignity as human beings" and destruction of preembryos is abortion.

I want now to turn to embryological science to see what help it can offer. Two things must be kept in mind, and in a sense in tension. First of all, as the *Declaration on Procured Abortion* notes, it is not the competence of science to decide the question of ensoulment (or personhood). "It is a philosophical problem."[17] On the other hand, as *Donum vitae* notes, the conclusions of science provide a "valuable indication" for reason's deliberations about personhood. We might say that if science cannot decide the question of personhood, neither can it be decided without science.

What then does science tell us? I will rely unblushingly on several sources.[18]

The union of sperm and ovum at fertilization yields a new hereditary constitution (genome), a unique genetic individual. This single fusion cell (zygote) has the theoretic potential to become an adult—a potential that is theoretic and statistical because relatively few actually achieve this in the natural process. It is to be noted that the genetic individual is not as yet developmentally single (a source of only one individual) until a single body axis has begun to form, near the end of the second post-fertilizational week when implantation is underway.

After fusion of egg and sperm the zygote (the single initial cell) undergoes successive equal divisions (cleavage) with little intervening growth. The product cells (or blastomeres) become successively smaller but the size of the aggregate is about the same. After three divisions the aggregate contains eight loosely associated cells.

Several things should be noted here. At this stage we know from other mammals that each cell (blastomere) has the same potential as the zygote. If separated from the others it can produce a complete adult. Furthermore, if two 8-cell stages of different parentage are fused, a single adult is still produced. As the AFS committee put it:

> Current scientific interpretation of these and other results from animal experiments is that first cleavage divisions in mammals produce a packet of cells, each of which still has the full developmental potential of the zygote, i.e., to produce a complete adult . . . Stated another way, at the 8-cell stage the developmental singleness of one person has not yet been established.[19]

The second thing to be noticed is that beyond the 8-cell stage the individual blastomeres begin to lose their zygote-like properties. The individual blastomeres are increasingly adherent. As the AFS report notes: "The impression now conveyed is of a multicellular entity, rather than a loose packet of identical cells."[20] This multicellular entity (blastocyst) has an outer cellular wall, a central fluid-filled cavity and a small gathering of cells at one end known as the inner cell mass. Developmental studies show that the cells of the outer wall become the trophoblast (feeding layer) and are precursors to the later placenta. All of these cells are discarded at birth.

As the blastocyst is attaching to the uterine wall the inner cell mass becomes more adherent and organizes into two layers that make up the embryonic disc (primitive body axis). The indication that this is happening is the appearance of the primitive streak. It is at this point that developmental individuality or singleness is established.

Two conclusions should be underlined here. First, these facts indicate that early events in mammalian development concern above all the formation of extraembryonic rather than embryonic structures. "This means that the zygote, cleavage and early blastocyst stages should be regarded as preembryonic rather than embryonic."[21] As Howard Jones words it: "While the embryoblast segregates and is recognizable toward the end of this stage [preimplantation], it consists of only a few cells, which are the rudiment of the subsequent embryo."[22]

Second, as the scientist Clifford Grobstein has noted, genetic individuality and developmental individuality do not coincide. At fertilization, he notes, "uniqueness in the genetic sense has been realized, but, for example, unity or singleness has not. The zygote, with its unique genome, may give rise in either natural or induced twinning to two or more individuals with identical heredity. In some species this occurs naturally and regularly. Moreover, in mice (and probably in most if not all mammals including humans) cells of two or more different genotypes can be combined to form one embryo which develops into an adult that is a mosaic of more than one genotype."[23]

Before leaving this scientific overview, several other points should be mentioned. First the product of fertilization may end up as a tumor, a hydatidiform mole, or worse, a chorioepithelioma. Quite aside from such anomalies, there is enormous loss of fertilized ova prior to implantation, conservative estimates hovering around the two-thirds figure.

What is to be made of these facts? Here I will proceed in three steps, corresponding to three sources of moral reflection: 1) The *Declaration on Procured Abortion*; 2) *Donum vitae*; 3) theological reflection.

1. THE *DECLARATION ON PROCURED ABORTION*

As noted, the Declaration sees in science "valuable confirmation" for protection of germinating life from fertilization. By "valuable confirmation" it refers to genetic individuality. It has nothing to say about developmental individuality. But since the crunch issue is not ultimately scientific, but moral-philosophical, the CDF states its principle: "From a moral point of view this is certain: even if a doubt existed concerning whether the fruit of conception is already a human person, it is objectively a grave sin to dare to risk murder."[25] In brief, then, the CDF is admitting the presence of doubt about personhood but asserting the immorality of acting in the face of such doubt. The age-old chestnut: when the hunter doubts about what moves in the underbrush, whether animal or human person, there is a *certain* obligation not to shoot. I shall return to this below.

2. *Donum vitae.* As I noted above, *Donum vitae* makes two different statements: the preembryo *is* a person; it *must be treated as* a person. These are different statements because even if one conceded that the preembryo is not yet a person, there might be powerful and persuasive reasons for holding that it ought to be treated as a person, *at least most of the time.* I shall return to this below, especially the italicized qualifier; for it represents the heart of the position I want to propose.

Let me say first off that *Donum vitae* makes absolutely no use whatsoever of the distinction between genetic individualization and developmental individualization. For the CDF, if the preembryo is genetically individualized, it is individualized in the most radical sense. For it asks: "How could a human individual not be a human person?" A possible, and in my judgment, sufficient response to this question is: "by not yet being a human individual (developmentally single)." Yet *Donum vitae* shows no awareness that in its early stages neighboring cells are loosely associated, that the cells of the inner cell mass of the early blastocyst are "little different in developmental capability from the zygote. Each can contribute to any part of the embryo, and separation of the mass into two parts can still yield two or more embryos."[26] It shows no awareness that only with implantation do we have primary embryonic organization.

That a biologically stable subject is not present *ab initio* seems factually established as long as twinning and recombination are possible. That it should be present as a minimal (necessary but not necessarily sufficient) biological substrate for personhood should appeal strongly to those in a tradition that originally defined person as "*naturae rationalis individua substantia*."[27] Thomas refers to "*incommunicabilis*" and "*subsistentia*."[28] The heart of these definitions, originally concerned with the Trinity and Incarnation, has come down to modern times so that person still refers to "the actual unique reality of a spiritual being, an undivided whole existing independently and not interchangeable with any other."[29]

The second assertion of *Donum vitae* is that the preembryo must be treated as a person. It does not develop this extensively, except to say that it must be treated as a person because it *is* a person ("How could a human individual not be a human person?"). It is a person because it is genetically unique. Yet it explicitly acknowledges that "the Magisterium has not expressly committed itself to an affirmation of a philosophical nature"—which, of course, is precisely what the assertion of personhood is.

3. THEOLOGICAL REFLECTION

Obviously, the question of personhood and its constitution is both critical and controversial. It is critical because it may determine what we conclude it is morally appropriate or inappropriate to do with preembryos. Specifically, if they are persons then they have rights, and presumably that most fundamental right to life. If they are not persons, then we must investigate the claims they make on us as those en route to personhood.

That the matter is controversial is obvious. The strongest case for personhood *ab initio* I have heard argues from the fact that there is no stage of nascent development that is so significant that it points to a major qualitative change: not implantation, not quickening, not viability, not birth. As John Mahoney, S.J., summarizes: "Failing all these alternatives, then, the conclusion necessarily pointed to is that no intervening qualitative change has taken place, but only continuous development of the potentialities which the ensouled human person has possessed from the time it was conceived."[30]

Some years ago the Belgian bishops cited *Abortus Provocatus*, a study issued by the Center of Demographic and Family Studies of the Belgian Ministry of Health:

There is no objective criterion for establishing, in the gradual process of development, a limit between "nonhuman" life and "human" life. In this process each stage is the necessary condition for the following and no moment is "more important," "more decisive" or "more essential" than another.[31]

More recently T.F. Torrance has put it this way:

If . . . we want to think of the human embryo as "potentially person," that must be taken to mean, not that the embryo is in the process of becoming something else, but rather that the embryo continues to become what he or she already is.[32]

In the simplest terms, no one in this world exists who did not exist as a preembryo. As Bishop Mario Conti, bishop of Aberdeen (England) writes: "Human beings commence their lives at fertilization." This he sees as the "common sense view."[33]

In contrast to this is the view that demands a certain biological stability in the organism before personhood is possible. This stability is not present prior to the stage of primary embryonic organization. "The first sign that primary organization is underway is the appearance of what is called the primitive streak."[34] Prior to this time twinning and recombination can occur. In other words, primary embryonic organization is the time when singleness is being established.

Donum vitae demurs. It states: "The conclusions of science regarding the human embryo provide a valuable indication for discerning by the use of reason a personal presence at the moment of this first appearance of human life." This is *not* what the conclusions of science provide if beyond genetic uniqueness there is also required developmental uniqueness.

Bishop Mario Conti has attempted to undermine this conclusion by locating developmental individuality earlier. He writes:

However, long before the formation of the primitive streak there is already differentiation of cell function so that the inner cell mass present at the fifth day represents a distinct center of organization within the embryo playing a role analogous to that associated with the later primitive streak. (In the case of identical twins there are two distinct inner cell masses at this stage.) If the individual is already established at the fourteenth day with the primitive streak, the same individual is already established at the fifth.[35]

It would be immodest of me to try to referee this basically scientific point. Let me rather cite Professor R.V. Short of the Department of Anatomy and Physiology (Monash University, Melbourne). To Conti's statement he says:

> It is also untrue to state that in the case of identical twins there are two distinct inner cell masses at the fifth day. When spontaneous cleavage of the embryo is delayed until eight or more days after fertilization, the two resulting embryos have come from a single inner cell mass, and share one common set of all placental membranes.[36]

Where does this leave us? Norman Ford's book *When Did I Begin?* lays out the facts of embryological development with admirable precision and objectivity. He knows the difference between genetic uniqueness and developmental individuality. Yet, interestingly and strangely, he agrees with the conclusions of *Donum vitae* (presumably that the preembryo must be treated as a person). He puts it as follows:

> Wherever there are reasonable doubts about the personal status of the early embryo, moral principles, without prejudice for the search for truth, require that the human embryo from conception be treated as a person.[37]

There are two key elements in Ford's statement: moral principles and reasonable doubts.

First, the moral principles. It has been accepted teaching in Catholic theology for many decades that one is free to act on the basis of a doubtful obligation based on a doubt of fact provided that one does not thereby risk harm to a third party. The doubt of fact, in this case concerns the personhood of the preembryo, the presence of a person. Because the doubt cannot be resolved, the risk to a third party remains and a doubtful fact does not convert to a doubtful obligation.[38]

The traditional illustration: the hunter who doubts about the object moving in the underbrush, whether it is an animal or a person. It was said that he had a *certain* obligation not to shoot. As the axiom went: *Idem est in moralibus facere et exponere se periculo faciendi.*[39] Thus the preembryo must be treated as a person.

The principle (of tutiorism) appealed to by Ford fails to mention several things. First it does not mention the circumstances of the hunter.[40] Is the hunter perhaps a starving hunter, or one on whom others depend for their lives? Would such circumstances not purge the risk of imprudent recklessness? It is precisely the freedom not to shoot that renders shooting a morally imprudent risk and brings into play the axiom *Idem est in Moralibus*. . . .

Second, Ford does not enter into a discussion of the degree of doubt when he refers to "reasonable doubts" about the personhood of the fetus. "Unless," he says, "my thesis is shown to be certainly true, I hold, in accord with *Donum vitae,* that morality requires that the human embryo be treated as a person from conception."[41] That is, I think, too sweeping. "Certainly true" is the type of certainty we rarely have and, more importantly, rarely require for human action. I agree with John Mahoney, S.J., when he states that "the most one can regularly hope for, as Aristotle and Aquinas realized, is certainty sufficient to justify a choice of action."[42] Such certainty is constituted by the presence of very strong reasons for maintaining a particular view.

Are there very strong reasons for maintaining that the preembryo is not yet a person? I believe so. In this I agree entirely with Mahoney. He sees the "probability" that the preembryo is a person as "a possibility at most."[43] There are two arguments officially adduced to defend personhood *ab initio.* The negative (absence of any subsequent development so significant as to indicate a qualitative change) he regards as "upon further examination to carry little, if any, force." The possibility of twinning and recombination are key here. The positive argument (from genetic uniqueness), an argument used by the *Declaration on Procured Abortion* and *Donum vitae,* shows only genetic, not developmental uniqueness. Mahoney concludes that the opinion holding the move toward personhood to be a process is "a quite impressively strong one."[44] Similarly he argues that the risk of destroying a person at this stage is "correspondingly slight." I would conclude that Ford's moral assertion (the preembryo *must be treated* as a person because there are reasonable doubts about whether it is a person) is not a defensible conclusion in the light of most recent scientific data. And if the preembryo is not yet a person, it cannot be the subject of human rights.

This does not mean, however, that preembryonic human life is simply disposable tissue. Not at all. I want to raise two considerations here that must be carefully weighed as we try to discern our obligations toward preembryonic life. The first is potential. Under favorable circumstances the fertilized ovum will move through developmental individuality, then processively through functional, behavioral, psychic and social individuality. In viewing the first stage one cannot afford to blot out subsequent stages. Granted, the statistical potential of any given preembryo is significantly reduced. Yet it remains potential for personhood and as such deserves profound respect. This is *a fortiori* weighty for the believer who sees the human person as a member of God's family and the temple of the Spirit. Interference with such a potential future cannot be a light undertaking.

The second consideration concerns our own human condition. I want to gather these reflections under the notion of uncertainty. There is uncertainty about the controllability of human research enthusiasms. That is, if we concluded that preembryos need not be treated in all circumstances as persons, would we little by little extend this to embryos (established pregnancies)? Would we gradually trivialize the reasons justifying preembryo manipulation? These are not abstract worries, I assure you. I have experienced their realization. Furthermore, there is uncertainty about the effect of preembryo manipulation on personal and societal attitudes toward nascent human life in general. Will there be further erosion of our respect? I say "further" because of the widespread acceptance and practice of abortion. There is grave uncertainty about our ability to say no and backtrack when we detect abuses, especially if they have produced valuable scientific and therapeutic data. Medical technology has a way of establishing irreversible dynamics.

Let me conclude with two proposals, one a moral statement, the other a practical policy.

The moral statement. In view of the fact that the preembryo is not yet a person and that its statistical potential for becoming such is greatly reduced, it is not clear that nontherapeutic experiments can be excluded in principle. However, because the preembryo does have intrinsic potential—and is in a sense *personne en devenir*—and because of the many uncertainties mentioned above, I would conclude that there are good grounds for concluding that the preembryo should be treated as a person—that this "should" is a *prima facie* obligation only, albeit a strong one.

This is virtually identical in substance with the conclusion reached by John Mahoney, S.J. After noting that depriving a preembryo of its future cannot strictly be called homicide, Mahoney says of actions that terminate its existence:

> Even in the very earliest days, moreover, such an action could not responsibly be undertaken for any but most serious reasons, going far beyond considerations of convenience or scientific curiosity, and affecting either that being's own prospects for the future, as in cases of genetic abnormality, or the life and welfare of others, as in cases of rape and incapacity in a woman to carry a child to term without risk to herself.[45]

My second proposal is procedural. Because this matter is so important and yet so controversial, any exceptions from the *prima facie* duty to treat the preembryo as a person should be based on criteria established at the national level. For this reason I dissented from the report of the ethics committee of the American Fertility Society. That committee had demanded approval of an Institutional Review Board for experimentation on preembryos. My dissent read: "The matter is of such grave public importance that approval of preembryo research should depend on conformity with guidelines established at the national level."[46]

One final note by way of conclusion. Does the analysis in this paper correspond with current official Catholic formulations? No, not in every respect. I have indicated that the two key Catholic documents (*Declaration on Procured Abortion, Donum vitae*) do not consider developmental individuation, a point central to my paper.

I must point out, however, that John Mahoney's analysis is practically identical with mine in his *Bioethics and Belief*. Mahoney's book, containing an *imprimatur*, was published in 1984. In 1986 the *imprimatur* was removed. In a joint statement, Mahoney and Rt. Rev. Ralph Brown, vicar general of the Archdiocese of Westminster, explained why the imprimatur was withdrawn. At one point they state that the imprimatur is no more than a "declaration that a book or a pamphlet is considered to be free from doctrinal or moral error."[47] This does not totally disperse one's anxiety. But then they state very interestingly: "However, the question can arise, particularly in light of the passages of the Second Vatican Council quoted above, as to whether a work which contains passages which are at variance with the Church's current official teaching on a particular moral matter is to be considered by that fact as containing moral error." If history is our guide, the answer to that question is a clear "no." Being "at variance with the Church's current official teaching" is not tantamount to being wrong. If it were, the above reflections would be an exercise in intellectual folly and unquiet conscience.

CHAPTER 15

Abortion: The Unexplored
Middle Ground

During the Republican National Convention (August, 1988) I listened to an interview on abortion involving Jerry Falwell and Faye Wattleton (president of Planned Parenthood). Falwell kept insisting on the fact that unborn babies were the last disenfranchised minority, voiceless, voteless and unprotected in the most basic of civil liberties. Wattleton's statements all returned to the concept of privacy and the woman's right to decide whether she would or would not bear a child. It was a tired old stalemate. Neither party budged an inch. The moderator concluded that their only common ground was that this is a great country in which people are free to disagree.

Unfortunately, the Falwell-Wattleton exchange is a symbol of the way discussions on abortion are often conducted. One point is picked as central and then is all but absolutized. The discussion goes nowhere, except perhaps up on the mercury scale. Everything returns to the single absolutized dimension and is interpreted in light of it. Thus, where nonviolent demonstrations at abortion clinics are concerned, Falwell sees them as catalytic signs of hope for a transformation of consciousness and a growing rejection of abortion. Wattleton sees them as unconstitutional and violent disturbances of a woman's prerogative to make her own choice.

Are we doomed forever to this kind of dialogue of the deaf? Perhaps so. This is especially the case if the single issue identified as central by either party is indeed plausibly just that. An important difference in these "central issues" should be noted here. Falwell—and those who share his view—are speaking primarily of the *morality* of abortion and only secondarily (but a close second) about public policy or the civil rights of the unborn. Wattleton says little about morality (though she implies much) but puts all her emphasis on what is now constitutional *public policy.* On his level, I believe Falwell is right. On her level, Wattleton is right (in the sense that *Roe v. Wade* does give the woman a constitutional right). Two planes passing in the night at different altitudes.

What rarely gets discussed in such heated standoffs is what public policy *ought to be,* especially in light of *what morality.* The linkage of these two in a consistent, rationally defensible and humanly sensitive way almost always falls victim to one-dimensional gavel-pounding. It never gets discussed. Unless this linkage is made more satisfactorily in the public consciousness than it has been, any public policy on abortion is going to lack supportive consensus and continue to be seriously disruptive of social life. The terms "pro-choice" and "pro-life" will—misleadingly—continue to define and divide our citizenry.

Is there a way of enlarging the public conversation so that a minimally acceptable consensus might have the chance to develop? I am probably naive to think so. But I have seen more unexpected and startling things happen (e.g., Vatican II). In this spirit I want to suggest that there are quite a few things that Falwell and Wattleton could agree on beyond the edifying puff that this is a great country because people are free to disagree. I will call these things "the unexplored middle ground." It is my suggestion that if we talked more about this middle ground, maybe, just maybe we would establish a public conversational atmosphere with a better chance at a peaceable public policy. I say "maybe, just maybe" because I am not at all optimistic. Still it is worth a shot.

Before listing possible elements of this "unexplored middle ground," I want to make three introductory points. First, diverting attention to the middle ground is not an invitation to compromise. To attempt to discover what we might agree on is not to forfeit our disagreements. It is only to shift the conversational focus. It is to discuss one's convictions with a different purpose, with different people, in a different way.

Second, my own *moral* position on abortion is abundantly clear from previous writings.[1] So is my conviction that *Roe v. Wade* is not an adequate policy reflection of the convictions of a majority of Americans. But that should in no way hinder the search for a middle ground. It should, however, warn the reader that what I propose as "middle ground" could very possibly be influenced by these postures.

Specifically, what kind of consensus I would like to see develop and be reflected in policy is not unrelated to my own convictions. This prospective consensus will undoubtedly shape my identification and wording of the "unexplored middle ground." Indeed, some—from both sides—will undoubtedly see my middle ground as a poorly disguised presentation of only one point of view, hardly in the middle. I acknowledge the possibility in advance, but forge ahead nonetheless.

Third, when I speak of a common ground I do not mean that all or many now factually agree on these points. I mean that there is solid hope that they can be brought to agreement.

ELEMENTS OF A MIDDLE GROUND

1. THERE IS A PRESUMPTION AGAINST THE MORAL PERMISSIBILITY OF TAKING HUMAN LIFE

This means that any individual or society that would sanction this or that act of intentional killing bears the burden of proof. Life, as the condition of all other experiences and achievements, is a basic good, indeed the most basic of all goods. To think that it may be taken without publicly accountable reason is a return to moral savagery. For this reason all civilized societies have rules about homicide, much as we might disagree with their particulars.

I take the presumption stated above to be the substance of the Christian tradition. The strength of this presumption varies with times and cultures. Cardinal Joseph Bernardin has noted that the presumption has been strengthened in our time.[2] By that he means that in the past capital punishment was viewed as a legitimate act of public protection. Furthermore, war (in which killing was foreseen) was justified on three grounds: national self-defense, the recovery of property, the redressing of injury. Now, however, many (including several recent popes) reject capital punishment and view only national self-defense as justifying violent resistance. While such applications remain controversial, they are not the point here. The key point (or principle) is the presumption against taking human life.

2. ABORTION IS A KILLING ACT

So many discussions of abortion cosmetize the intervention as "the procedure" or "emptying the uterus" or "terminating the pregnancy." By saying that abortion is a "killing act" I do not mean to imply that it cannot be justified at times. That issue is not raised in the statement. I mean only that the one certain and unavoidable outcome of the intervention is the death of the fetus. That is true of any abortion, whether it be descriptively and intentionally direct or indirect. If the death of the fetus is not the ineluctable result, we should speak of premature delivery. To fudge on this issue is to shade our imagination from the shape of our conduct and amounts to anesthetizing self-deception. All of us should be able to agree on this, whether we consider this or that abortion justified or not.

A final gloss, I pass over here (with no intention of ignoring it) *a key issue*. It is this: at what point does interruption of the reproductive process merit the name "abortion"? That is a very legitimate question. I mean that there are plausible reasons for saying that only interruption of an *implanted* fertilized ovum deserves this name. I do not enter the discussion here because I do not want to distract from the main assertion—one that applies to the 1.3-1.5 million abortions done per annum in this country.

3. ABORTION TO SAVE THE LIFE OF THE MOTHER IS MORALLY ACCEPTABLE

This may strike many as irrelevant. Why even bother to mention it? For one reason: those who are morally opposed to abortion frequently see their position caricatured into unrecognizability. That only intensifies opposition and polarization.

Let me cite a recent instance. The *New York Times*, hardly celebrated for its serene objectivity in this realm, in an editorial on George Bush's supposed gender gap, reported the Republican platform as follows: "'That the unborn child has a fundamental individual right to life which cannot be infringed.' In other words, given a choice between saving the fetus or the mother, the mother must die."[3]

That interpretation of a "fundamental individual right to life" is so distorted that it comes as close as imaginable to editorial hucksterism. Those who formulate their convictions in terms of a "fundamental right to life" by no stretch of the imagination deny a similar right to the mother. Nor does such a general statement even address situations of conflict. It is language that is meant to restate the presumption mentioned in my first point, but carried into the abortion context.

Presumptions can at times be overcome. Here it would be useful to recall the statement of J. Stimpfle, bishop of Augsburg: "He who performs an abortion, *except to save the life of the mother*, sins gravely and burdens his conscience with the killing of human life."[4] The Belgian bishops made a similar statement.[5]

Agreement on this point may seem a marginal gain at best. But in the abortion discussion, *any* agreement can be regarded as a gain, especially when it puts caricatures to rest.

4. JUDGMENT ABOUT THE MORALITY OF ABORTION IS NOT SIMPLY A MATTER OF A WOMAN'S DETERMINATION AND CHOICE

Pro-choice advocates often present their position as if the woman's choice were the one and only right-making feature in the judgment of abortion. But I believe that very few if any *really* mean this, at least in its full implications. It is simplistic and unsustainable. Taken literally, it means that *any* abortion, at *any* time, for *any* reason, even the most frivolous, is morally justified if only the woman freely chooses it. That is even incompatible with the admittedly minimal restrictions of *Roe v. Wade*. I know of no official church body and no reputable philosopher or theologian who would endorse the sprawling and totally unlimited acceptance of abortion implied in that criterion. It straightforwardly forfeits *any and all* moral presumptions protective of the unborn. In this formulation, fetus becomes blob—stop.

Conversation about the italicized statement above will not, I am sure, bring overall agreement on the abortion issue. But it might lead to a more nuanced formulation on the part of those identified with the pro-choice position. It might also lead to a greater sensitivity on the part of some pro-lifers to the substantial feminist concerns struggling for attention and expression in the pro-choice perspective.

5. ABORTION FOR MERE CONVENIENCE IS MORALLY WRONG

This is but an explicitation of the above point. Once again, agreement on this point may seem to represent precious little gain. And even agreement might be quite difficult and fugitive because of the definitional problem in the phrase "mere convenience." One person's inconvenience is another's tragedy, etc. Yet for those not hopelessly imprisoned in their absolutisms, I think agreement is possible if discussion is restrained.

Furthermore, such discussion could be remarkably fruitful. How so? Those who agree with the statement—and that would include some, perhaps many "pro-choicers"—will have to say eventually *why* such abortion is morally wrong. There is only one direction in which such a discussion can go: straight to the whys and wherefores of the claims of nascent life upon us.

6. THE CAUSES THAT LEAD TO ABORTION SHOULD BE ABOLISHED INSOFAR
AS POSSIBLE

I refer to poverty, lack of education, lack of healthy recreational
alternatives to sexual promiscuity among teenagers and so on. Nearly
everyone agrees with these prescriptions. They should be emphasized
much more than they are. In other words we have tended to approach
abortion too exclusively as a problem of *individual choice*. Left there
it tends to divide people. Were it also approached as a *social problem*,
it could easily bring together those with opposed positions at the level
of individual choice.

7. ABORTION IS A TRAGIC EXPERIENCE TO BE AVOIDED AS FAR AS
POSSIBLE

Regardless of one's moral assessment of abortion, I believe most
people could agree that it is not a desirable experience in any way. It
can be dangerous, psychologically traumatic, generative of guilt feelings, divisive of families. And, of course, it is invariably lethal to
babies. No amount of verbal redescription, soothing and consoling
counselling or musical accompaniments can disguise the fact that people would prefer to achieve their purposes without going through the
abortional procedure. It is and always will be tragic.

8. THERE SHOULD BE ALTERNATIVES TO ABORTION

This is a kind of corollary to the preceding point. *Its urgency* is
in direct proportion to the depth of our perception of abortion as a
tragic experience. It seems to me that the need for alternatives should
appeal above all to those who base their approach on a woman's freedom of choice. If reproductive choice is to be truly free, then alternatives to abortion ought to be available. By "alternatives" I refer to all
the supports—social, psychological, medical, financial, religious—that
would allow a woman to carry her pregnancy should she choose to do
so. Expanding the options is expanding freedom. I shall return to this
below.

9. ABORTION IS NOT A PURELY PRIVATE AFFAIR

Roe v. Wade appealed to the so-called "right of privacy" to justify its invalidation of restrictive state abortion laws. Furthermore, the
public debate often surfaces assertions about a woman's "control over
her own body." Such appeals either create or reinforce the idea that
abortion is a purely private affair. It is not—at least not in the sense
that it has no impacts on others than the woman involved. It affects

husbands, families, nurses, physicians, politicians and society in general. We ought to be able to agree on these things because they are documentable facts.

What I am proposing here as an element of the "unexplored middle ground" is that the term "privacy" is a monstrously misleading term to underline the primacy of the woman's interest in abortion decisions. Communal admission of this point—hardly controversial—would clear the air a bit and represent a purification of the public conversation.

10. ROE V. WADE OFFENDS VERY MANY PEOPLE. SO DID PREVIOUS PROHIBITIVE LAWS

These are simple factual matters where agreement—at least for those who acknowledge facts—is not optional. But to place them together invites people out of their defensive trenches. In other words, it compels them to examine perspectives foreign to their own as they explore why this could possibly be the case. Such a possibility represents a patency that is presently not in evidence in the public conversation.

11. UNENFORCEABLE LAWS ARE BAD LAWS

Unenforceability may stem from any number of factors. For instance, a public willingness to enforce the law may be lacking. Or the prohibited activity may be such that proof of violation will always be insufficient. Or again, attempts to enforce might infringe other dearly treasured values. Whatever the source of the unenforceability, most people agree that unenforceable laws undermine the integrity of the legal system, and the fabric of social life.

Our own American experience with prohibition should provide sufficient historical education here. Its unenforceability stemmed from all the factors mentioned above and more. It spawned social evils of all kinds. In this respect Senator Patrick J. Leahy (D.-Vermont) once remarked that amendments should not be used to create a consensus but to enshrine one that exists. He added:

> The amendments that have embodied a consensus have endured and are a living part of the Constitution. But where we amended the Constitution without a national meeting of minds, we were forced to retract the amendment, and only after devastating effects on the society.[6]

This is an obvious reference to the 18th Amendment.

12. AN ABSOLUTELY PROHIBITIVE LAW ON ABORTION IS NOT ENFORCEABLE

By "absolutely prohibitive" I include two specifications. First, it prohibits all abortions, even in cases of rape, incest and when the life of the mother is at stake. Second, it includes under "abortion" destruction of the human being *from the moment of conception.* This latter was the intent of the Human Life Statute (S.158) introduced by Jesse Helms, January 19, 1981. It sought by a simple majority of both Houses to declare the fetus a human being from the moment of conception. Thus in effect it sought to redefine the terms "person" and "life" to bring them under the protective clauses of the 14th Amendment.

I say that such an "absolutely prohibitive" law is unenforceable. There is no consensus to support it for one thing. Poll after poll over the years has established this. Even religious groups with strong convictions against abortion have noted this. For example, the Conference of German Bishops (Catholic) and the Council of the Evangelical Church (EKD, Protestant) issued a remarkable joint statement on abortion some years ago.[7] After rejecting simple legalization of abortion in the first three months (*Fristenregelung*), they stated that the task of the lawmaker is to identify those conflict situations in which interruption of pregnancy will not be punished (*straflos lassen*).

I mention this because of the apparently ineradicable American tendency to identify moral conviction with public policy ("there oughta be a law!"). This is visible in the refusal of some pro-lifers to admit any toleration into public policy.

There is another reason why an "absolutely prohibitive" law would not work. It has to do with the second specification, legal protection *from the moment of conception.* If this were enshrined in the penal code and attempts were made to enforce it, we would be embroiled in conspiracy law (the *intent* to abort). How so? For the simple reason that in the pre-implantation period there is no evidence of pregnancy. Lacking such evidence, one could not prosecute another for having done an abortion, but only for having *intended* to do so. That is just not feasible.

13. THERE SHOULD BE SOME CONTROL OF ABORTION IN PUBLIC POLICY

This may seem to have all the bite of statements about motherhood. The fact that those otherwise so polarized could agree on this "middle ground" is an indication of its harmless character. Even *Roe v. Wade* admitted "some" control.

My point, however, is not that this tiny island of agreement is important in itself. It is that by focusing on it discussants will be forced to face the next two questions: 1. What kind of control? 2. Why?

I admit that discussion of these questions could take us right back to square-one stalemates and be self-defeating. However, it could also lead to a more nuanced and sophisticated notion of public policy in a pluralistic society.

14. WITNESS IS THE MOST EFFECTIVE LEAVEN AND MOST PERSUASIVE EDUCATOR WHERE THE QUESTION OF ABORTION IS CONCERNED

I mean in no way to discredit or deemphasize the place of rational discourse in human affairs and controversies. We abandon that at our own risk and very often the result is war of one kind or another.

I mean only that genuine education is eye-opening. The most effective way of opening eyes is often the practical way of witness. We come to understand and appreciate genuine heroism much more by seeing (in some form or other) heroic activity than by hearing or reading a lecture on it. Are we not more selfless and other-concerned when surrounded by selfless and other-concerned people? Are we not more fearlessly honest (especially about ourselves) when friends we deeply admire exhibit such honesty? Etc.

The point should be clear. Those with deep convictions about freedom of choice for women or, on the other hand, about the sanctity of life, would be considerably more effective if they emphasized much more what they are for than what they are against, and did so *in action*. Concretely, that means that pro-lifers (whether individuals, institutions such as dioceses, or organizations) should put resources (money, personnel) into preventing problem pregnancies and supporting them in every way when they occur. The very same thing is paradoxically true of those who approach the matter in terms of the primacy of free choice. For if the choice is truly to be free, genuine alternatives must exist (cf. my next point). In summary, putting one's money where one's mouth is can be done in ways at least as effective (and far more so, I believe) as picket lines.

15. ABORTION IS FREQUENTLY A SUBTLY-COERCED DECISION

Daniel Callahan pointed out twenty years ago that "a change in abortion laws, from restrictive to permissive, appears—from *all data* and in *every country*—to bring forward a whole class of women who would otherwise not have wanted an abortion or felt the need for one."

The most plausible interpretation of this phenomenon, according to Callahan, is that the "free" abortion choice is a myth. Once again Callahan:

> A poor or disturbed pregnant woman whose only choice is an abortion under permissive laws is hardly making a "free" choice, which implies the possibility of choosing among equally viable alternatives, one of which is to have the child. She is being offered an out and a help. Nor can a woman be called free where the local mores dictate abortion as the conventional wisdom in cases of unmarried pregnancies, thwarted plans and psychological fears.[9]

Interestingly agreement on the coerced character of many abortion decisions might bring about the unexpected result of cooperation between pro-choicers and pro-lifers. For pro-choicers their concern for true freedom would lead them to attempt to reduce or abolish the coercive forces by offering genuine alternatives. Pro-lifers should rejoice at this because the provision of alternate options would reduce the felt need for abortion, and thus the number of abortions.

16. THE AVAILABILITY OF CONTRACEPTION DOES NOT REDUCE THE NUMBER OF ABORTIONS

I mention this because I have been exposed to discussions of abortion that are soured by introduction of statements like the following: "The Catholic Church, being so staunchly opposed to abortion, should be in the forefront of those backing contraception to prevent it. Yet by condemning contraception it inconsistently adds to the number of abortions." This supposes that approval of and support for contraception will reduce abortions.

One of a group of "minor" truths listed by Daniel Callahan in 1973 was the following: "There is no evidence yet from any country that, with enough time and availability of effective contraceptives, the number of abortions declines."[10] Clearly "availability of effective contraception" is one thing; official approval of their use is quite another. But with the number of Catholics who either disagree with or depart from official Church teaching on contraception, official disapproval (or approval) does not seem to make that much difference. Therefore, Callahan's assertion should operate as a rebuttal to the statement cited above about Catholic inconsistency.

I do not attach much conciliatory significance to this except that it does clear the air of distracting and one-sided statements.

17. PERMISSIVE LAWS FORFEIT THE NOTION OF "SANCTITY OF LIFE" FOR THE UNBORN

This is a hard saying; but that does not make it less true. Here Daniel Callahan is at his best and most tortured. He wants and does grant the woman the right not to have (via abortion) a child she does not want. But he is unflinchingly honest about what this means. "Under permissive laws," he notes, "any talk whatever of the 'sanctity of life' of the unborn becomes a legal fiction. By giving women the full and total right to determine whether such a sanctity exists, the fetus is, in fact, given no legal or socially established standing whatever."[11] Callahan does not like being backed into this corner. But he is—as he always has been—utterly honest. His legal position does not allow for any "pious doublethink." The law "forces a nasty either-or choice, devoid of a saving ethical ambiguity."

I wish that all discussants, on both sides, were so honest. Conversation about this seventeenth point might encourage them to be so.

18. HOSPITALS THAT DO ABORTIONS BUT HAVE NO POLICY SHOULD DEVELOP ONE

I introduce this as a piece of "unexplored middle ground" because of my personal experience. Some health care facilities—obviously non-Catholic—have approached the problem almost exclusively in terms of patient autonomy. And I know some that have grown nervous about this, because it amounts to simple capitulation to patient preferences. They have begun to see that this is not a carefully analyzed moral stance on abortion, but really abdication of the responsibility to work through to one.

The counsel to "develop a policy" is, therefore, promising even though it is relatively non-threatening (because it leaves totally open what that policy ought to be). It is promising because it suggests that ethical complexity and ambiguity might become more explicit. That is an advance.

19. THE "CONSISTENT ETHIC OF LIFE" SHOULD BE TAKEN SERIOUSLY

I happily borrow the term "consistent ethic of life" from Cardinal Joseph Bernardin. It has long been fairly clear to many people that those who are most vociferous about fetal rights are amongst our most hawkish fellow citizens. That something is amiss here is clear to most people, hawks excepted. We have a long way to go to entice many people of both sides of the abortion debate to view that problem within the larger context of other life problems.

20. WHENEVER A DISCUSSION BECOMES HEATED, IT SHOULD CEASE.

This is my final middle ground. I am not suggesting, of course, that abortion is so trivial a concern that heat is inappropriate. Not at all. Rather the idea—based on long experience—is that shouting sessions on abortion only alienate and divide the shouters. Nothing is illumined, not because the offerings are not illuminating, but because nobody is listening or being heard.

I expect the idea of an unexplored middle ground and the invitation to explore it to please very few. Yet the abortion problem is so serious that we must grasp at any straw. A nation that prides itself on a tradition of the dignity and equality of all persons and civil rights to protect such equality cannot tolerate a situation where a very significant number of citizens are convinced that between 1.3 and 1.5 million human beings are factually being denied this equality and these rights. That nation must at least continue to discuss the problem openly. Quite simply the soul of the nation is at stake. If abortion is what many think it is, its pervasiveness in a society represents a horrendous racism of the adult world. When it is justified in terms of the rights of others, then all of our rights are endangered because their foundations have been eroded by arbitrary and capricious application.

For this reason alone—and for many others—I think it important that abortion continue to occupy a prime place in the public consciousness and conversation, even though we are bone-weary of the subject. If we settle for the *status quo*, we may well be presiding unwittingly and tearlessly at the obsequies of some of our own most basic and treasured freedoms. The very possibility that that is the case means that any strategy—even the modest one of keeping a genuine conversation alive by suggesting a middle ground as its subject—has something to recommend it.

CHAPTER 16

Surrogacy:
A Catholic Perspective

A few prenotes are in order prior to my substantial presentation. First, I have entitled this chapter *a* Catholic perspective, not *the* Catholic perspective. I do this not because there is not an official Catholic perspective. There is. It is presented briefly in *Donum vitae* ("Instruction on Respect for Human Life in its Origin and on the Dignity of Procreation"[1]). Rather I do it because the theologian's task is not simply to repeat official formulations, but to assimilate them critically so that the very assimilative effort contributes to the purification of these formulations. To say anything else would be to wrap these formulations in a non-historical immobility that is untrue to reality.

Second, "a Catholic perspective" means to underline the fact that the perspective is not merely presented by a Catholic, but is one that attempts to draw on the riches and worldview identified with a historical believing community. As we say in theological shorthand, "reason informed by faith." This is not to suggest that all Catholics will or must share these analyses and conclusions. Nor is it to suggest that non-Catholics will not or cannot share them. It simply means that "Christ . . . through his life, death and resurrection has given a new meaning to human existence,"[2] and that this meaning will shape our consciousness as we deliberate together about what is morally appropriate human conduct.

A sound Catholic methodology will begin by stating its criterion of judgment when dealing with new technologies. Vatican II is of great help here. Dealing with marital morality it stated that the "moral aspect of any procedure . . . must be determined by objective standards which are based on the nature of the person and the person's acts."[3]

Let me repeat briefly here what I noted in Chapter 1. The official commentary on this wording noted two things: that in the expression there is formulated a general principle that applies to all human actions, and that the choice of this expression means that "human activity must be judged insofar as it refers to the human person integrally and adequately considered."[4]

I fully accept this criterion. Indeed I take responsibility for its use in the American Fertility Society's *Ethical Considerations of the New Reproductive Technologies*.[5] That document stated:

> "Integrally and adequately" refers to the sum of dimensions of the person that constitute human well-being: bodily health; intellectual and spiritual well-being, which includes the freedom to form one's own convictions on important moral and religious questions; and social well-being in all its forms: familial, economic, political, international and religious. Actions (policies, laws, omissions, exceptions) that undermine the human person, integrally and adequately considered, are morally wrong. Actions that are judged to be promotive and supportive of the human person in the sum of his or her essential dimensions are morally right.[6]

The document notes of this criterion that "in principle it calls for an inductive approach based on experience and reflection." I note here that *Donum vitae* reproduced this personal criterion. Repeatedly it refers to the integral good of the human person, or some such phrase. In this sense it is one with Vatican II. One may legitimately question, however, whether *Donum vitae* actually uses this criterion when it draws concrete conclusions about reproductive technologies.

Now let us turn to surrogacy. At the very outset we should distinguish surrogate gestational mothers from surrogate mothers. A surrogate gestational mother provides the gestational but not the genetic component for reproduction. A surrogate mother provides both the female genetic component and the gestational component. Once this distinction has been made it may be temporarily shelved because most of the ethical pros and cons apply quite similarly to both forms of surrogacy. One can see this by reviewing the American Fertility Society's document on surrogacy.

There are at least two general approaches to our subject that can be identified. The first views surrogacy under the rubric of the use of third parties *in genere,* as but a single example of a general practical. The second views surrogacy *in specie* and underlines the advantages and drawbacks of this specific instance of third party usage.

1. THIRD PARTY PARTICIPATION IN GENERAL

Under the title of "Third party participation" several different procedures are possible: donated sperm, donated ovum, donated embryo, donated uterus or combinations of these. Most discussions have centered around donated sperm (AID) because this is by far the most common of these procedures; so I will use it to review some of the issues of third party participation in reproductive technologies.

The most thoughtful and stimulating recent study on AID is that of Paul Lauritzen.[7] Lauritzen examines some contemporary works on AID. One is by Lisa Sowle Cahill.[8] Cahill rejects third party participation in reproductive technologies because they separate genetic and social parenthood. There are moral responsibilities that are directly contingent on genetic connection. They are inalienable and cannot be completely transferred to others. Thus, in Lauritzen's words:

> Thus it could never be morally acceptable to create a child with the intention of separating genetic and social parenthood, for to do so would require an individual to create a set of moral obligations he or she had no intention of discharging.[9]

For Cahill, the responsibilities of parenthood do not root entirely in human choice. They root also in biological (genetic connections). For this reason "biological relationships can and should exercise some constraints upon freedom to choose (or not to choose) the parental relation."[10] And for Cahill, biological restraints restrict the freedom to choose AID and surrogate motherhood.

Lauritzen criticizes this view on the ground that it assumes that to separate genetic and social parenthood is to abandon *all* constraints on reproductive choice. As he says:

> Yet in disagreeing with Cahill about the normative ideal, I am not abandoning all restraints on reproductive choice. Rather I am simply drawing the line of acceptable choice at a different place.[11]

What is not clear to me in Lauritzen's fine study is where he is drawing the line and above all why. The major ethical obstacles he sees to the responsibility of parenthood in AID are secrecy (deception at the heart of the parent-child relationship) and the problem of asymmetry. When dealing with secrecy he cites the work of Baran and Pannor:

> For most of the men we interviewed, the choice of donor insemination had been an acute response to the pain they were experiencing. They never permitted themselves the time and op-

portunity to explore their feelings about the devastating ego blow. They prevented themselves from becoming comfortable with and accepting of their handicap. Instead, they cast the handicap in concrete, and their feelings of inadequacy were continuously reinforced by visual proof: their donor offspring.

With this enormous deficit in place, the relationship between the husband and wife had to be realigned. The husband became weaker and more passive; the wife became stronger and more powerful. The wife was the real mother of the children, and this message, although never spoken, was clearly given to the husband in many ways. The husband could be devoted and caring toward the children, while, at the same time, recognizing the difference between his parental role and his wife's.[12]

Lauritzen seems to treat this scenario as a problem of secrecy and therefore one that could be dispersed by candid revelation and discussion. Actually I believe it will be seen by many as an intrinsic problem and as inseparable from AID itself, whether secrecy is there or not. Whatever the case, if secrecy and asymmetry are the two obstacles to responsible parenthood in using AID, and if both can be overcome, it is not clear where and why Lauritzen would "draw the line of acceptable choice."

This exchange between Cahill (emphasizing the basic importance of genetic connections) and Lauritzen (emphasizing the superior importance of the parenting function) is a kind of symbol of the way the ethical discussion is conducted.

For instance, *Donum vitae* regards the use of third party gametes as "a violation of the reciprocal commitment of the spouses and a grave lack in regard to that essential property of marriage which is its unity."[13]

How is this unity to be understood? There are at least two possibilities. The first is at root nonconsequentialist in character. It appeals to the nature of marriage—or at least that is how I read *Donum vitae's* presentation of the argument. After noting that the child must be the fruit and sign of the mutual self-giving of the spouses, of their love and fidelity, it states: "The fidelity of the spouses in the unity of marriage involves reciprocal respect of their right to become a father and a mother only through each other."[14] A certain notion of marriage as exclusive at all levels seems to undergird that statement, though I admit that if one pushes hard enough (e.g., "Why must unity be so understood?") one gets to consequentialist considerations.

The second possibility is that of Lauritzen. AID introduces life experiences that cannot be fully shared and "this lack of mutuality may interfere with the couple's ability to care for and to love the child that is created."[15] But is this disunity an overwhelming obstacle? Lauritzen thinks not.

At this point I would like to introduce a consideration I have rarely heard discussed. It will be recalled that *Donum vitae* rejected any reproductive technology that is a substitute for sexual intercourse. My own experience with couples who have undergone IVF and ET is that they do not regard these procedures as a *substitute* for sexual intimacy, but as a kind of technological continuation or extension of it. Now if that is indeed the case, then we must ask: Is it appropriate for third parties to be involved in such continuation?

Let me summarize here. There are two key issues on which there is likely to continue to be strong disagreement: (1) Does third party involvement (via gametic donation or surrogate gestation) infringe on conjugal exclusivity? (2) Does having a jointly raised child justify such infringement? My own answer is yes to the first, no to the second. I hold these positions because I believe the notion of conjugal exclusivity should include the genetic, gestational and rearing dimensions of parenthood. Separating these dimensions (except through rescue, as in adoption) too easily contains a subtle diminishment of some aspect of the human person.

To argue that marital exclusivity ought to include the genetic, gestational and rearing components can be argued in at least two different ways. First, it could be argued that third party involvement is itself violative of the marriage covenant independent of any potential damaging effects or benefits. This is the thrust of Lisa Cahill's analysis, as well as that of Pius XII. The view might be argued in purely ethical terms (Cahill) or in religious terms. An example of the latter is the distinguished Paul Ramsey. He writes: "To put radically asunder what God joined together in parenthood when He made love procreative, to procreate from beyond the sphere of love . . . or to posit acts of sexual love beyond the sphere of responsible procreation (by definition, marriage) means a refusal of the image of God's creation in our own."[16]

As I just noted above, there is a simpler way of making this point. Many couples regard in vitro fertilization not as a *replacement* for their sexual intimacy, but as a kind of *continuation* or *extension* of it. On that view, third party presence (via egg or sperm) is presence of another in the intimacy itself, a thing that ought not to be. One need not call this adultery to make the point.

The second form of the argument is that any relaxation in marital exclusivity will be a source of harm to the marriage (and marriage in general) and to the prospective child. For instance, the use of donor semen means that there is a genetic asymmetry in the relationship of husband and wife to the child, with possible damaging psychological effects. If a surrogate mother is used, conflicts could arise that damage both the marriage and the surrogate.

William J. Winslade and Judith Wilson Ross recently raised some of the questions I have in mind.

> Is the child to know about the method of its birth? If so, how much information should the child have—only that which is deemed to be health-related data, or all of the other biological information about its heritage that most of us value? Whose interests, whose preferences, whose needs count here? Born into a society that is already fragmented by divorce and confused about alternative life styles, morals and sexual choices, the child may well have serious identity problems at a later time. Does such a possibility have to be seriously considered by those who want to undertake unusual reproductive methods?

The Winslade-Ross essay concludes:

> The interests and well-being of the baby-to-be-made seem to be the last issues considered, and sometimes (when physicians promise anonymity to the donor or parents require it of the surrogate) seem not to be considered at all.[17]

Another form of this first approach is the assertion that third party involvement separates procreation from marriage *in principle*. That opens the door, both by human proclivity and the logic of moral justification, to a litany of worrisome problems such as single-women insemination and insemination of a lesbian couple.

An argument built on possible harmful consequences is one subject to empirical verification. It must be admitted in all honesty that the data are thin at best, often even conjectural. Fears of what might happen once marital exclusivity is relaxed are legitimate even if they do not always lead to clearly established absolute prohibitions. In the past I have argued that the risks and potential harms involved would support a safeside moral rule (procreation should be restricted to marriage at all levels—genetic, gestational, social) against the slide to abuse. This is a prudential calculus which gives greater weight to *institutional* risk of harm than to individual benefit.

2. SURROGACY *IN SPECIE*

There are two levels at which one might approach this problem, the individual and the social. By "this problem" I am referring to surrogate motherhood, not surrogate gestation only since the circumstances for this latter are likely to be extremely rare.

First the individual level. I will simply list here some of the concerns noted by the American Fertility Society. The AFS report lists potential harms under these categories: the surrogate, the couple, the child.[18]

1. The surrogate.

- Physical hazards in carrying a pregnancy for other persons.
- Psychological harm in giving up one's own genetic child.
- Exploitation of the surrogate, especially if she is poor.

2. The couple.

- Woman could be harmed by not having access to medical advice that could help her solve infertility in other ways.
- Risk of harassment from surrogate.
- Continued involvement of surrogate could harm couple's relationship.
- Financial risk to couple because of uncertain legal status of the procedure.
- Pain if surrogate decides to keep the child.

3. The child.

- Child could be physically harmed by a surrogate's genetic defect.
- Surrogate who knows she has no rearing responsibility might be careless during pregnancy.
- Concerns about child's sense of identity and clarity about parenthood.

The benefit to be expected is that a surrogate arrangement would allow the otherwise infertile (because of lack of a uterus, for example) couple to rear a child with a genetic relationship to one of them.

Weighing the pros and cons of this procedure, the AFS's ethics committee concluded that if surrogate motherhood is to be pursued, it should be "pursued as a clinical experiment." By this the committee meant to designate "an innovative procedure that has a very limited or not historical record of whether any success can be achieved."[19] Being a member of this committee I can confidently assert that this is about as close as the committee would come to outright condemnation. Indeed, committee member C. Alvin Paulsen stated his dissent by noting that "the risk/benefit ratio of the surrogacy procedures does not justify their support."[20]

There is one important aspect of surrogate motherhood that should be noted: the potential harms are inherent in the procedure. They are not the result of inadequate protocols, etc. This point has been noted by others.[21]

Now let me turn to the social level. There will naturally be some overlap here with considerations already mentioned. At the time of the Baby M. case Daniel Callahan wrote: "We are caught in the middle of a major social experiment without the faintest idea how it should be conducted. The case reveals why the attendant problems are so hard and why surrogate motherhood was probably a bad idea from the outset."[22] By the "attendant problems" Callahan refers to the kinds of problems our society would be better off without. He refers to three above all. 1) Surrogacy represents yet another mode of producing children that is less than desirable, and that at a time when we are not underpopulated. 2) Furthermore we court confusion about parentage with the accompanying uncertainty about responsibility for the welfare of the child. 3) We introduce a cadre of women whose prime virtue is what we now take to be a vice—"the bearing of a child one does not want and is prepared not to love."

These considerations of Callahan's open on another issue of social concern: The impoverishment of women by their reduction to their child-bearing capacity. I find it difficult to see how any surrogacy arrangement does not reduce a woman to a means.

It is considerations like the above that led me to entitle the only article I have written on this subject "Surrogate Motherhood: A Stillborn Idea."[23]

One response to this presentation might well be: How is this a Catholic perspective? What makes it Catholic? Could not any humanist espouse a similar analysis? Such questions reflect a misunderstanding about the nature of moral reflection in the Catholic community. This reflection has never yielded to the sometimes comforting enticements of sectarianism, as if "Catholic" contained an implied reference to a *secretum arcani* in the moral sphere.

It is here that I return to the criterion of the person integrally and adequately considered. If that is truly the appropriate criterion, as I believe it is, then whatever will throw light on the impact of the reproductive technologies on the well-being of persons is necessarily part of human reflection on the matter. The Catholic Church, with its centuries-old tradition of natural law in moral matters, is quite comfortable with Aquinas' saying that "we offend God only in so far as we offend our own good."[24] If surrogate motherhood offends—on balance—our own good as persons, Catholics would reject it. I believe they should.

CHAPTER 17

The Cruzan Decision: Missouri's Contribution

The Missouri Supreme Court decision on Nancy Cruzan is, in my judgment, so bad that it may prove to be pedagogically useful.[1] It is muddled, confused and/or downright wrong on virtually every key issue.

Imagine the following scenario. There are four one-thousand-bed long-term-care facilities strategically placed near population centers in Missouri. Each bed contains a patient in a persistent vegetative state (PVS). Each is sustained by a gastrostomy feeding tube at state expense for an average of 20 to 25 years, many of them outliving their families and dear friends.

Is this an impossibly fanciful caricature? Not at all, if the pivotal tenets of *Cruzan v. Harmon* are valid and allowed to stand. Yet our sense of the fitting, indeed our common sense, is powerfully assaulted by this scenario. I mentioned "pivotal tenets." Note the following. (1) The Court explicitly adverted to the fact that it was deciding the case "not only for Nancy, but for many, many others." It was establishing precedent for Missouri. (2) It disallowed *any* quality of life considerations in adjudicating such cases. "The state's interest is not in quality of life"(31), but in life itself. "Life is precious and worthy of preservation without regard to its quality."(23) (3) This interest "is an unqualified interest in life."(31, 27) (4) Even merely vegetative life (PVS) is a benefit to the patient and must be preserved by artificial nutrition-hydration. (5) The Court *seems* to believe that withdrawal of Nancy's gastrostomy tube would be tantamount to killing her. It refers to a "decision to cause death"(32). This matter, however, remains unclear in the *dicta* of the decision.

In the remainder of this commentary, I want to raise six substantive issues and conclude by pointing out what I believe to be the philosophical root of the Court's misguided judgment.

SUBSTANTIVE ISSUES

1. THE STATE'S INTEREST

As noted, the Cruzan Court sees the state's interest in life itself, not its quality and this interest is "unqualified." The Court nowhere defines quality of life. It should have looked at the literature. It would have discovered two senses of that term and tempered its rationale accordingly. The first refers to the value of a life to society in terms of functional contributions, social usefulness, etc.—and therefore to the valuation of that life by a society using such a criterion. That quality of life in this sense—an arbitrarily defined level of functioning—has no legitimate place in cases like that of Cruzan is obvious.

But there is another sense to the term and one that apparently escaped the Court's notice. It refers to the biological condition of the individual and its relationship to the pursuit of life's goods and goals. Quality of life in this second sense is critical to good decision-making. This was acknowledged by the President's Commission for the Study of Ethical Problems in Medicine and Biomedical and Behavioral Research when it defined the patient's best interest broadly to "take into account such factors as the relief of suffering, the preservation or restoration of functioning and the quality as well as the extent of the life sustained."[2] The Baby Doe rules imply a quality-of-life dimension when they exempt from aggressive life-sustaining treatment babies who will be permanently unconscious. Both the Herbert and the Conroy court did the same. For instance, the Conroy court (New Jersey Supreme Court) acknowledged that "although we are condoning a restricted evaluation of the nature of a patient's life in terms of pain, suffering and possible enjoyment under the limited-objective and pure objective tests, we expressly decline to authorize decision-making based on assessments of the personal worth or social utility of another's life, or the value of that life to others."

The Cruzan Court rejects any—even restricted—quality of life ingredient as pertaining to the state's interest. In doing so, it achieves two remarkable results. First, it puts itself at odds with most persons whose best interests it proposes to protect. Human persons have an enormous stake in the quality of their lives—how they live, how they die, and how they live while dying. That is the assumption that under-girds living wills and durable power of attorney arrangements for medical decisions. For instance, I myself, along with countless others I am sure, have specified in my living will that, if I am in a PVS, I do not want artificially administered nutrition and hydration. I judge this to pertain to my personal well-being. Yet the logic of the Cruzan Court would sweep this directive aside. Its interest is in life, not its quality and this interest is "unqualified." I take that to mean that per-sonal preferences—and the moral and religious soil that nourishes them—are not in any way a state interest. If "unqualified" does not mean this, what does it mean?

Weigh carefully these words of the Court: "Given the fact that Nancy is alive and that the burdens of her treatment are not excessive for her, we do not believe her right to refuse treatment, whether that right proceeds from a constitutional right of privacy or a common law right to refuse treatment, outweighs the immense, clear fact of life in which the state maintains a vital interest."(36) Those words are abso-lute. They state quite astonishingly: given life (even PVS life) and the absence of burden in maintaining it, the state's "vital interest" over-whelms and negates any other consideration or putative right. One has to wonder why the Court even bothered to discuss the adequacy or inadequacy of information about Nancy's preferences and intent, as it did on p. 35.

The second result of the Court's blanket refusal to consider *any* quality of life ingredient in these cases is that it reduces overall per-sonal well-being and best interests to its biological component. That is vitalism, a point I shall return to below. The Court states (43) that it chooses "to err on the side of life." Actually it is erring on the side not of life, but of biologism. When we conflate the complex notion of personal "best interests" into sheer medical effectiveness, we equate the *personally* beneficial with the *medically* effective and thereby give powerful analytic support to the noxious idea that whatever *can* be done *ought* to be done.

2. THE GUARDIAN'S AUTHORITY

When an individual is presently incompetent (and has not reliably expressed her preferences previously) or has always been in-competent, decisions about that person's care must fall to others. The analytic basis for this proxy responsibility has varied from court to court depending on the circumstances (e.g., right of privacy in *Quin-lan*, common law right of self-determination in *Fox*, best interests in

Storar, etc.). In other words, if no third party could make decisions about termination of treatment, either the patient's right of privacy, or right of self-determination or best interests would be frustrated.

The Cruzan Court rejects the right of privacy as a basis for withdrawing Nancy's gastrostomy tube. Such a right cannot be exercised by third parties. It also denies that the "common law right to refuse treatment—founded in personal autonomy—is exercisable by a third party absent formalities." Why? Because "a guardian's power to exercise third party choice arises from the state's authority, not the constitutional rights of the ward. The guardian is the delegate of the state's *parens patriae* power."(39-40) And, of course, the state has this "unqualified" interest in life, even PVS life.

It is the source of the guardian's power that interests me here. The Cruzan Court says it is delegated by the state. That confuses *origin* with *recognition*—at least for previously competent patients—a confusion traceable to the Court's utterly legalistic approach to these matters. The logical upshot of this confusion: it becomes impossible to get patients off of useless or even burdensome treatment (for if this state's interest in life is "unqualified," what matters the burden?). What the Court has done is to place *all* third party decision-making responsibilities under the notion of guardianship.

I want to argue that the common law notion of self-determination, which is valid for the competent patient, must lead spontaneously to a notion of *family* self-determination for the incompetent one, if best interests and ultimately human dignity are to be served. In other words, the state does not exactly *originate* third party power as it does in some instances of guardianship; it merely *recognizes* (or notarizes) it, at least for cases like the Cruzan case.

There are two good reasons for arguing this: first, the family is normally in the best position to judge the real interests of the incompetent patient. The family knows those treatments that might be particularly disturbing and those that the patient may have accepted without distress in the past.

Second, and more importantly, our society places great value on the family. The family is a basic moral community affirmed to have not only rights, but also responsibilities in determining how best to serve the interests of its incompetent members. For this reason the principle of self-determination can best be understood to extend beyond the individual to encompass the notion of familial self-determination. This familial autonomy or self-determination is a value highly treasured. While it perhaps should not take precedence over individual autonomy in cases where patients are or were competent, it certainly justifies a prominent role for family members in helping to assess what is in the best interests of the incompetent one. Family members are given enormous responsibility for moral nurture, theological and secular education, and decisions about the best interests of their incompetent members throughout the lifetime of the family unit. It should be no different in the case when the incompetent family member is seriously or terminally ill. Occasionally this may lead a family to decide that the incompetent one's interests can best be served by declining a medical intervention.

To me this means that "familyness" and the kinship bonds we call family are the basic source or foundation of a proxy's power, not the state's grant. Of course, the principle of familial self-determination cannot ride unchecked. Society's responsibility to assure that the interests of its incompetent members are served will place some limits on familial self-determination. However, the state should intervene only when the familial judgment so exceeds the limits of reason that the compromise with what is objectively in the incompetent one's best interest cannot be tolerated.

This is the thrust of much of what Charles B. Blackmar says in his dissent. In his words: "I believe that decisions about Nancy's future should be made by those near and dear to her . . ." Exactly. This is, as a matter of fact, done all the time and it is done by people who would be shocked to learn that they may do so because they have been empowered by the state. As Blackmar stated: "Decisions of this kind are made daily by the patient or relatives . . ." That *fact* should have alerted the Cruzan Court that its understanding of the source of third party responsibility was incomplete.

3. THE NOTION OF A DYING PATIENT

The Court repeats several times that Nancy is not dying or "terminally ill"(5, 36, 32, 23, etc.). I suggest that the notion of a "dying patient" or "terminally ill" one is ambiguous. Who is said to be terminally ill or not is often a function of the technology available. A person with end-stage renal disease is a dying patient—if no dialysis is available. A patient without spontaneous respiration is a terminal patient—if no respirator is at hand. A person who cannot take food and water in normal ways is a dying patient—unless we intervene technologically with an N.G. tube or gastrostomy tube.

"Terminally ill" is, therefore, capable of two readings. First, it can refer to an incurable condition that will lead to death in a short time whether interventions are used or not. I will call this the *narrow* sense. Missouri adopted it in its living will statute when it specified "terminal condition" as "a death will occur within a short time *regardless of the application of medical procedures*" (emphasis added). The second sense is *broader*. The Uniform Rights of the Terminally Ill Act (URITA) defined "terminal illness" as follows: "an incurable or irreversible condition that, *without the administration of life-sustaining treatment*, will, in the opinion of the attending physician, result in death within a relatively short time" (emphasis added). In the first sense Nancy Cruzan is not terminal. In the second sense she is.

This is a crucial issue for two reasons. First, if Nancy is said to be nondying, that assertion strengthens the state's interest in her fate in the face of a decision that could leave her dead. Second (and this buttresses the first point), if she is non-dying but dies as a result of nutrient withdrawal, that makes such withdrawal look positively causative, a killing act. This seems to be the approach of the Cruzan Court. For it refers to "a decision to *cause* her death"(32) and "seeks to *cause* death of an incompetent"(39).

That language assumes the answer to a serious philosophical issue—the difference between an *occasion* and a true *cause*. Take an analogy. Suppose hurricane winds bend and break a sapling tree. We prop it up, hoping to revive it, but see that it will never return to full budding form, even though it will stand and possibly produce a few anemic leaves. So we remove the prop and the tree dies. What killed the tree? Was it not the hurricane winds? Analogously, if we remove nutritional props from Nancy, was it not the original anoxic trauma or insult that *caused* her death, that killed her?

This matter is only muddied by the usage "starve." I have heard physicians adamantly assert that the term is an exclusively medical term. I question that. While the term can be parsed in terms of medical effects and phenomena, it is a value term. "To starve another" means to withhold food and water from one *to whom it ought to be given.* That leaves totally untouched the question of "to whom it ought to be given" and the criteria for this determination. To jump ahead a bit, "ought to be given" assumes that the person will derive genuine benefit from feeding. More of this below.

4. THE NATURE OF ARTIFICIAL NUTRITION-HYDRATION

The Cruzan Court, in contrast to virtually every other authoritative source, regards this issue as irrelevant. "The issue is not whether the continued feeding and hydration of Nancy is medical treatment; it is whether feeding and providing liquid to Nancy is a burden *to her.*"(35)

Here I believe the Court is both right and wrong. It is right in thinking that too much emphasis has been put on the question of whether a gastrostomy tube constitutes medical treatment or so-called "ordinary care." The unexpressed assumption is that if it is not medical treatment, it must always be provided. Otherwise we would be killing the patient. Thus, the conclusion of the President's Commission, the American Medical Association and the American Academy of Neurology to view artificial nutrition-hydration as medical treatment. I confess I adopted this line of reasoning myself.

But that assumption is not necessarily correct. I believe we should argue that any interventions—whether they be classified as medical treatment or not—may be omitted if they are excessively burdensome or *if they provide no benefit.* And here is where the Court is wrong or at least incomplete. It says the issue concerns *only the burden.* By implication, we may not cease any interventions even if they are humanly useless.

Even if one agrees with the Court that the matter is a "semantic dilemma" and one to be avoided, still I think we must admit that the Court failed, and in two ways.

First, it does indeed take a position—the position that artificial nutrition-hydration is not medical treatment. It states: "Common sense tells us that food and water do not treat an illness, they maintain a life." In short, it is not medical treatment because it does not treat a disease. This is similar to the argument of some philosophers that artificial nutrition-hydration is not medical treatment because it merely provides "what all need to live."

This is analytically at least incomplete and, I believe, ultimately wrong. It assumes that *how* nutrients are supplied and *why* their artificial provision is necessary is irrelevant to the idea of treatment. Is it not the case that the inability to eat is caused by Nancy's cerebral anoxia and the subsequent ongoing cerebral cortical atrophy? Is not such atrophy and dysfunction a disease? When we use medical technology to bypass the inability to eat normally, in a broad sense we *treat* that disease even though we do not cure it. We should not, I think, equate all treatment with cure; otherwise many medical modalities that we commonly regard as treatment would not merit the name (prostheses, bypass surgery, analgesics for pain, some infertility interventions, etc.).

The second move by the Cruzan Court is to assert that the "medical argument" (artificial nutrition-hydration = medical treatment) is dangerous. "It seems to say that treatment which does not cure can be withdrawn." That is a thudding *non sequitur*. It need say or imply nothing of the kind. All it need say is that *any* treatment may be withheld or withdrawn when it is, in human estimate, nonbeneficial to the patient. There are many treatments that cannot cure but ought to be used and not withdrawn, e.g., analgesics for pain in terminal illness, as noted above.

5. THE BURDENS-BENEFIT CALCULUS

Everyone—from the Congregation for the Doctrine of the Faith[3] to the President's Commission—agrees that the criterion for treatment decisions is the burdens-benefit calculus. Briefly, if a proposed treatment will offer no benefit, or the benefit will be outweighed by the burdens, the treatment is morally optional.

The Cruzan Court focuses only on the burden of the treatment(35). In doing so it supposes that preservation of life in a PVS is a benefit to the patient. Indeed, it says so explicitly. This point constitutes my most crucial disagreement with the decision. Furthermore, it is the point that sharply divides opinion on this and similar cases.

In my view, those who take the position that indefinite preservation in a PVS is beneficial to the patient have departed from the substance of the Catholic tradition on this matter. That tradition never counted mere vegetative life a patient-benefit. The Cruzan Court does.

6. THE MAJOR CONCERN OF THE CRUZAN COURT

In any number of places (e.g., 27, 32) the Court leads us to believe that withdrawing artificial nutrition-hydration from Nancy will expose others with a reduced quality of life to similar withdrawals. In other words, allowing any quality of life consideration here would open the door to abuses of the weak.

This is certainly a legitimate concern and I do not wish to minimize it. But the proper response to it is not the safeside victimization of Nancy Cruzan and her family. It lies rather in hard and fast exception-stoppers. Concretely, third-party decisions to withdraw nutrition-hydration should be rigidly controlled by two conditions: irreversible PVS and the dying condition. (It is here that the notion of "the dying patient" becomes urgently relevant—and possibly divisive.)

THE PHILOSOPHICAL ROOTS OF THE CRUZAN COURT

At the outset I stated that I believe the Court to be "muddled, confused and/or downright wrong on virtually every key issue." I have tried to list some of these issues. But perhaps more important is the underlying philosophy that has guided the Court's deliberations.

That philosophy is what I will call "legal positivism." The Court has faced and decided the Cruzan case only on the narrow basis of constitutional or legal precedent. Finding analytical soft spots in the *dicta* of previous courts, it has ignored the wisdom and plain common sense struggling for expression in those decisions.

I can put this another way by saying that the Cruzan Court gave no weight to moral tradition. It faced profound human problems with only legal tools and categories. Equivalently this means that it was attempting to decide *human* problems without benefit of the values that inform the human. This is like facing medical dilemmas with only medical tools and expertise, as if medical good is simply identified with personal good. The case of Nancy Cruzan goes far deeper than the reach of constitutional and legal precedent. If we deny that, we freeze the ability of courts to face new and profoundly human problems. We paralyze their ability to be wise.

CHAPTER 18

The Case of Nancy Cruzan: A Reflection

My initial reaction to the Supreme Court decision in the case of Nancy Cruzan was quite critical.[1] Why? Four reasons especially. First, I judged that one of the first repercussions would be to remove families from participation in decisions concerned with the best interests of their dear ones. I view such distancing as highly undesirable. There should be in morality and public policy a presumption that family members are best positioned to determine what an incompetent family member would choose or what is in the incompetent's best interest. A presumption yields, of course, to contrary evidence. But to disallow Joe and Joyce Cruzan's testimony to qualify as a source of clear and convincing evidence struck me as a presumption in the opposite direction, and therefore divisive of families.

My second reason for a critical response was that the Supreme Court, very much as Missouri had done, left totally unprotected those who have been incompetent from birth and babies. Missouri's Supreme Court had asserted that its interest in the preservation of life was "strong enough to foreclose any decision to refuse treatment for an incompetent person unless that person had previously evidenced, in clear and convincing terms, such a decision for herself" (Justice Stevens in his dissent). Absent that previous evidence, the interest in preservation of life prevails. This means that the always incompetent (e.g., Joseph Saikewicz, John Storar) must be kept alive no matter what. When the Supreme Court says that such an evidentiary requirement (clear and convincing, from the patient herself) is not unconstitutional, it means that it does not violate the liberty interest of the incompetent contained in the due process provisions of the 14th

Amendment. But that seems to imply that the always incompetent have no such liberty interest. Strictly speaking, I suppose, they do not. That is, those who were never really free hardly have liberty interests. But at the root of the liberty interest is the dignity interest. And they certainly have that.

My third reason for an initial negative response was the lack of a sustained and enlightening analysis of the state's interest in the preservation of life. Justice Stevens adverted to this in his dissent. Indeed, by failing to make this analysis, the Supreme Court seemed to equate the preservation of life with the preservation of the biological persistence of Nancy's bodily functions.

Finally, if evidence must be clear and convincing from the patient herself, it struck me that the *Cruzan* decision would foster a general reluctance to start life-preserving interventions if it is to be so difficult to stop them when they are no longer beneficial to the patient.

My second reaction was much less critical. Once again, for several reasons. First, it is clear that the decision was crafted along the most narrow grounds. It stated only that Missouri's heightened evidentiary requirement was not unconstitutional. It did *not* say it was necessary or wise or the only available approach. In other words, the Constitution permits, but does not require, a heavy burden of proof. I believe it was to be expected that the Court's ruling would be strictly constructionist. That did not help the Cruzans very much; but it leaves a lot of room for future development, what Justice O'Connor refers to as "the more challenging task of crafting appropriate procedures for safeguarding incompetents' liberty interests."

Second, the Court explicitly acknowledged for competent persons the existence of a constitutionally protected (14th Amendment) liberty interest in refusing unwanted medical treatment. Indeed it agrees that such a liberty interest perdures into incompetency when it, along with Missouri, supports a surrogate's decision to reject treatment as long as there is clear and convincing evidence of the patient's wishes.

Third, there are indications in the dicta that the Court would find lesser evidentiary demands and other arrangements constitutionally acceptable. For instance, writing about surrogate decision-makers and the duty of a state to accept such decisions, Justice O'Connor states: "In my view, such a duty may well be constitutionally required to protect the patient's liberty interest in refusing medical treatment."

Finally, I am relieved that the Court did not anchor the right to refuse treatment in the right to privacy. Indeed it explicitly rejects such a basis when it notes (footnote 7) that "we believe this issue is more properly analyzed in terms of a Fourteenth Amendment liberty interest."

At this juncture it is appropriate to make two points. First, I am not a constitutional lawyer or historian. Therefore, I read the constitutional aspects of this decision as an amateur. Second, however, it is remarkable how indistinguishable is so-called constitutional reasoning from straight-out moral reasoning. Because of this considerable overlap I am emboldened to continue the discussion and raise some philosophical issues that seem to me to be incomplete.

The Supreme Court has clearly acknowledged a liberty interest in refusing unwanted medical treatment. It has also acknowledged relevant state interests. It describes the constitutional problem as follows (citing *Youngberg vs. Romeo*): "Whether respondent's constitutional rights have been violated must be determined by balancing his liberty interests against the relevant state interest."[2] This is the structure not only of the constitutional issue, but also the structure of the moral issue. Central to both the constitutional and moral issue is a *balancing* of interests, specifically those of Nancy and those of the state. Before a balancing of interests can be successfully accomplished, an accurate statement of those interests must be made. It is here that I find the Court's analysis quite vulnerable.

Let me begin with the state's interest. As the Court notes, "Missouri relies on its interest in the protection and preservation of human life, and there can be no gainsaying this interest."

Realizing that this is a very general statement, the Court tries to particularize it by noting that the state's interest is really in safeguarding "the personal element of this choice [between life and death] by heightened evidentiary requirements." These "heightened evidentiary requirements" refer, of course, to the patients' own earlier statements made while competent. One can bicker all day whether clear and convincing personal statements are the best way to protect the "personal element." Obviously, Justice O'Connor thinks other ways would be constitutionally acceptable. She notes that the *Cruzan* decision does not "prevent States from developing other approaches for protecting an incompetent individual's liberty interest in refusing medical treatment."

But this is not my concern. It is rather "the personal element of this choice" as the state's interest to be protected. What does this phrase mean? The Court notes that "the choice between life and death is a deeply personal decision of obvious and overwhelming finality" and it wants to protect this personal dimension. True enough, but perhaps not enough of the truth. Decisions that can lead to life or death are indeed *ordinarily* "of obvious and overwhelming finality." The Court includes the removal of Nancy's gastrostomy tube in this category. But Nancy's situation is not ordinary. She is in a persistent vegetative state. Release from this state is hardly a matter of "overwhelming finality." What is or was of overwhelming finality, I would argue, was the original cerebral insult that left Nancy in this condition. Let me put this in another way. The Court professes an interest in "the personal element of this choice." It was precisely this "element" that led it to support the constitutionality of Missouri's heightened evidentiary requirements. At this point, however, I want to question the significance of this "personal element" *in these circumstances.* Once a person is in a persistent vegetative state, there would seem to be no "personal element of this choice" remaining to protect. What I am suggesting is that the analytic soft spot in the Court's approach is the equation of a decision about the persistently vegetative Nancy Cruzan with an "ordinary" decision between life and death.

The point I am making can be urged from several different perspectives. For instance, in allowing Missouri's heightened evidentiary requirements, the Court asserts that "we think a State may properly decline to make judgments about the 'quality' of life that a particular individual may enjoy, and simply assert an unqualified interest in the preservation of human life to be weighed against the constitutionally protected interests of the individual." In short, no "quality-of-life" judgments. Paradoxically, in refusing to allow *any* quality-of-life dimension, the Supreme Court (with Missouri) is actually making precisely such a judgment. It is saying that preserving a life even *in that condition* represents a value to the person and a state interest.

But does it really? I believe Justice Brennan is much closer to the truth when he argues that "no state interest could outweigh the rights of an individual in Nancy Cruzan's position." Brennan immediately continues: "The only state interest asserted here is a general interest in the preservation of life. But the State has no legitimate general interest in someone's life, completely abstracted from the interest of the person living that life, that could outweigh the person's choice to avoid medical treatment." Justice Stevens is getting at the same idea when he asserts that Missouri's policy "is an effort to define life, rather than to protect it." He continues: "Missouri insists, without regard to Nancy Cruzan's own interests, upon equating her life with the biological persistence of her bodily functions." He sees this an aberrant. So do I. And it is at the very heart of every key notion in this discussion (state's interest, patient benefit).

The urgent question is the evaluation of life in a persistent vegetative state. Is such a life a value to the one in such a condition? Is its preservation a benefit to the patient and therefore a state interest? Avoiding this question is obviously the more comfortable path. But it cannot be avoided, it can only be delayed. Missouri gave its answer when it referred to "the immense, clear fact of life in which the state maintains a vital interest." Obviously, then, the "immense clear fact of life" is identified with *any* life regardless of condition.

Some philosophers also take this point of view. Writing about artificial nutrition and hydration for permanently vegetative patients, William May and others stated: "In our judgment, feeding such patients and providing them with fluids by means of tubes is *not* useless in the strict sense because it does bring to these patients a great benefit, namely, the preservation of their lives." This "great benefit" and Missouri's "immense, clear fact of life" strike me as examples of biologism or vitalism. By these terms I refer to a positive evaluation of circulation—ventilation regardless of what personal goals it enables for the individual.

We are understandably afraid of allowing a quality of life ingredient a role in decision-making for the incompetent. It is dangerous. But I agree with Bernard D. Davis, professor emeritus at Harvard Medical School, that "irreversible coma is so clearly definable, as a special class, that it could be given special treatment without starting on a slippery legal slope."[4] What is that special treatment? A reversal of the presumption currently honored. At present, absent a prior expression of preference. we must presume an interest of the patient, or the state, in continuing life support. Davis proposes that in this extreme case (persistent vegetative state) evidence of a prior request should no longer be required. With appropriate safeguards we should presume a preference for termination of treatment.

What is the basis for this shift of presumptions? Davis refers to a "meaningful estimate . . . of public attitudes" and suspects that a survey of such attitudes would find a large majority opposed to continuing life-preservation for persistently vegetative patients. I do not have to suspect this. I am convinced of it. For several years I have asked audience after audience if they would want artificial nutrition and hydration were they irreversibly unconscious. With virtual unanimity the answer has been no. These people were saying that they did not regard *continuance in that condition* a benefit to them. For if they regarded this as a benefit, especially a "great benefit," they would be inconsistent in rejecting it if the treatment were otherwise not burdensome. If the vast majority of people do not regard existence in a persistent vegetative state as a genuine benefit, why should the state assert such continuance as an interest? In Justice Stevens' words, "life, particularly human life, is not commonly thought of as a merely physiological condition or function." For that reason Stevens concluded "there is no reasonable ground for believing that Nancy Beth Cruzan has any *personal* interest in the perpetuation of what the State has decided is her life."

The Supreme Court has judged that Missouri's heightened evidentiary requirements are not unconstitutional, that they are not an infringement of Nancy's liberty interest. Implied in such a view, I believe, is a further judgment that continuance in a persistent vegetative state is a patient benefit and therefore a state interest. I cannot accept that. So, while the *Cruzan* opinion has in my view analytic soft spots, it does leave the door wide open for further development. In that there is hope.

CHAPTER 19

"Moral Considerations"
Ill-Considered

Controversies are at times like house pests: just when you think they have died out, they reappear. So it is with the ethical discussion of artificial nutrition and hydration for patients in a persistent vegetative state (PVS).

The majority of philosophers and theologians—along with most courts—had concluded that the provision of such nutrition and hydration is not morally mandatory because it can no longer benefit the patient.

Now along comes the December 12, 1991 statement of the bishops of Pennsylvania entitled "Nutrition and Hydration: Moral Considerations."[1] What have the bishops said? First, they have stated that "in almost every instance there is an obligation to continue supplying nutrition and hydration to the unconscious patient." Second, the only exceptions to this conclusion are instances when death is imminent or the patient is "unable to assimilate what is being supplied." Third, outside of these two cases of "futility," withdrawal of nutrition and hydration from a PVS patient is "euthanasia by omission," "killing by omission." As the bishops word it:

> Sad to say, the intent is not to relieve suffering but, rather to cause the patient to die. Nor can it be argued that it is merely the intention to "allow" the patient to die, rather than to "cause his death." The patient in the persistent vegetative state is not thereby in a terminal condition, since nutrition and hydration and ordinary care will allow him to live for years. It is only if that care is taken away—and barring any other new disease or debilitation—that the patient will die. It is the removal of the nutrition and hydration that brings about the death. This is euthanasia by

omission rather than by positive lethal action, but it is just as really euthanasia in its intent.[2]

Finally, the bishops turn to advance directives such as the living will and durable power of attorney. "Neither the patient nor the surrogates of the patient have the moral right to withhold or withdraw treatment that is ordinary." But artificial nutrition and hydration for a PVS patient is (except in the two instances noted above) ordinary care. Therefore, it may not be withheld or withdrawn. Briefly, the bishops state that it is immoral to specify in one's living will or to one's durable attorney "no artificial nutrition and hydration if I am in a PVS." For this would be to refuse an ordinary means, one that is neither futile (in the bishops' sense) nor excessively burdensome.

Now, what have the bishops of Pennsylvania done? As I read their document, they have (1) appealed to their teaching prerogatives and responsibilities (2) to impose a concrete application of more general principles (3) that represents one side of a disputed question (4) and used a questionable analysis (5) to arrive at extremely questionable conclusions. A word about each is in place if my criticism is to stand up.

1. A TEACHING STATEMENT

"Nutrition and Hydration: Moral Considerations" is not a casual white paper floated to facilitate discussion groups. It is, as Cardinal Anthony Bevilacqua states in the Foreword, "an effort on our part to fulfill our responsibilities as bishops to give guidance to all the Catholic faithful of this state who are entrusted to our care." He concludes: "Our statement is intended to express, as well as we are currently able, the teaching of the Catholic Church as it affects these admittedly difficult cases."[3] These statements are self-explanatory. The bishops view their reflections as a teaching statement.

2. A CONCRETE APPLICATION

Catholic moral teaching, at the level of general principle, maintains that life is a basic good but not an absolute one and that, therefore, not all means must be used to preserve it. As Pius XII noted in 1957:

> But normally one is held to use only ordinary means—according to the circumstances of persons, places, times, and culture—that is to say means that do not involve any grave burden for oneself or another. A more strict obligation would be too burdensome

for most and would render the attainment of the higher, more important good too difficult. Life, health, all temporal activities are in fact subordinated to spiritual ends.[4]

When these general statements are fit to specific instances, we are dealing with applications.

The Florida bishops noted this in their statement on treatment of the dying: "The application of these principles to a patient who has been diagnosed with medical certainty to be permanently comatose, but whose death is not imminent, has aroused controversy."[5]

Why is it important to note that discussion surrounding treatment of PVS patients is an application? For the simple reason that the bishops do not, indeed cannot, claim the same authority for applications as they do for their statement of general principles. They noted this in "The Challenge of Peace."

> We stress here at the beginning that not every statement in this letter has the same moral authority. At times we reassert universally binding moral principles (e.g., noncombatant immunity and proportionality). At still other times we reaffirm statements of recent popes and the teaching of Vatican II. Again, at other times we apply moral principles to specific cases.[6]

The bishops then note that where applications are concerned "prudential judgments are involved based on specific circumstances which can change or which can be interpreted differently by people of good will." They note that their judgments of application should be taken seriously but are "not binding in conscience." Notwithstanding its juridical ring, this last statement wisely withdraws from the type of magisteriolatry that would expect the pope or bishops to dot every moral "i" and cross every moral "t" regardless of specificity.

Yet phrases used by Cardinal Bevilacqua such as "fulfill our responsibilities as bishops," "give guidance to all of the Catholic faithful of this state" and "express . . . the teaching of the Catholic Church" fairly droop with authoritative accents. That is why above I used the word "impose." Such weighted phrases could easily mislead people into thinking that what the bishops say is "the teaching of the Catholic Church." It is not. It is an application that involves us in circumstances that "can be interpreted differently by people of good will." Judgments of application should, as "The Challenge of Peace" notes, be "taken seriously." One of the ways to do that is to point out their weaknesses and inadequacies where they exist. And that brings us to the next point.

3. ARTIFICIAL NUTRITION AND HYDRATION AS A CONTROVERTED SUBJECT

By saying that withdrawal of nutrition and hydration is controverted, I refer to philosophical-theological controversy. Most courts and several medical groups (e.g., the American Medical Association, the American Academy of Neurology) have approved such withdrawal, as did the President's Commission for the Study of Ethical Problems in Medicine and Biomedical and Behavioral Research.

I noted in the previous chapter that a group of ethicists (including William May, Germain Grisez, William Smith, Mark Siegler, Robert Barry, O.P., and Orville Griese) argued that "in our judgment, feeding such patients [permanently unconscious] and providing them with fluids by means of tubes is not useless in the strict sense because it does bring to these patients a great benefit, namely, the preservation of their lives."[7] They go on to note that the damaged or debilitated condition of the patient has been the key factor in recent court cases and conclude that decisions to withdraw food have been made "because sustaining life was judged to be of no benefit to a person in such poor condition. These decisions have been unjust."

On the other hand bioethicists such as Dennis Brodeur, Kevin O'Rourke, O.P., Albert S. Moraczewski, O.P., John Paris, S.J., James Walter, James Bresnahan, S.J., Daniel Callahan, Albert Jonsen, Thomas Shannon, George Annas, and James Drane—to mention but a few—have come to a different conclusion.

Let Dennis Brodeur be a single example here. Artificial nutrition-hydration that "simply puts off death by maintaining physical existence with no hope of recovery . . . is useless and therefore not ethically obligatory."[8] It is "vitalism" to think otherwise. Brodeur correctly rejects a notion of quality of life that states that a certain arbitrarily defined level of functioning is required before a person's life is to be valued. But if it refers to the relationship between a person's biological condition and the ability to pursue life's goals, it is critical to good decision-making. "In some circumstances" he concludes, "science's ability to respond helpfully to allow a person to pursue the goals of life is so limited that treatment may be useless."

This controversy is manifested even at the episcopal level. The Texas bishops do not agree with the Pennsylvania bishops.[9] Neither do the bishops of Washington and Oregon. After noting the two different approaches outlined above, these latter urge that there "should be a presumption in favor of providing patients with these necessities of survival." They finally conclude: "In appropriate circumstances, the decision to withhold these means of life support can be in accord with

Catholic moral reasoning and ought to be respected by medical caregivers and the laws of the land." The same conclusion is drawn by Bishop John Leibrecht (Springfield-Cape Girardeau) in his comments on the Nancy Cruzan case. He discusses the two different approaches and says of the second that it is "a valid Catholic position which approves removal of Nancy Cruzan's tube." He concludes: "Unless there is an official and binding decision from church authorities, Catholics would be mistaken to hold that only one or the other line of Catholic moral reasoning is correct."[11]

I recently discussed the Pennsylvania document with nineteen physicians responsible for ethics committees around the country. They were in unanimous disagreement with the conclusions of the Pennsylvania bishops.

Why underline the controverted character of withdrawal of nutrition-hydration from PVS patients? The answer can be found in the old (1948) *Ethical and Religious Directives for Catholic Hospitals* drawn up by the eminent Gerald Kelly, S.J. Directive 3 reads: "As now formulated, the Directives prohibit only those procedures which, according to present knowledge of facts, seem certainly wrong. In questions legitimately debated by theologians, liberty is left to physicians to follow the opinions which seem to them more in conformity with the principles of sound medicine."

This directive may sound a little quaint to contemporary ears. But it embodies the centuries-old wisdom of probabilism. As Kelly explains in his commentary: "The provisions of directive 3 are but concrete applications of the sound general principle that obligations (i.e., precepts and prohibitions) are not to be imposed unless they are certain."[12]

We must remember that the question of artificial nutrition-hydration is extremely practical. It impacts physicians, nurses, families, hospitals, legislators, etc. It touches every individual who constructs advance directives. If it is indeed "legitimately debated"—as it is—it is beyond the competence of a group like the Pennsylvania bishops to settle the debate.

4. QUESTIONABLE MORAL REASONING

The guidance provided by the Pennsylvania bishops is based on very questionable reasoning. They argue that withdrawal of artificial nutrition-hydration involves in most cases the intent to kill. It is "murder by omission." How do they arrive at that stark judgment? As follows: the PVS patient is not in a terminal condition. It is only if nutrition-hydration is removed that the patient will die. "It is the removal of the nutrition and hydration that brings about the death." This is not merely "allowing to die." The bishops believe it involves the "clear intent to bring about death."

Is this the proper way the situation of PVS should be analyzed? Not according to the Texas bishops. They note that life-sustaining means, including artificial nutrition and hydration, may be omitted "under conditions which render those means morally non-obligatory." Certainly diagnosed PVS is one of those conditions in their view. They then add interestingly:

> In those appropriate cases the decision maker is not guilty of murder, suicide, or assisted suicide, since there is no moral obligation under these circumstances to impede the normal consequences of the underlying pathology. The physical cause of death is ultimately the pathology which required the use of those means in the first place. [13]

The Texas bishops, then, do not view the PVS patient as non-terminal. They see such a person as "stricken with a lethal pathology which, without artificial nutrition and hydration, will lead to death." The moral question is when should we intervene to prevent the "normal consequences of a disease or injury." When it is decided that the patient can no longer benefit from the intervention, the underlying pathology is allowed to take its natural course. This does not involve the intent to bring about death.

This is the analysis proposed by Kevin O'Rourke, O.P. [14] O'Rourke, in an analysis almost identical to that of the Texas bishops, observes that "withholding artificial hydration and nutrition from a patient in an irreversible coma does not induce a new fatal pathology; rather it allows an already existing fatal pathology to take its natural course." Therefore, O'Rourke argues that we should not be discussing whether death is imminent, but "whether a fatal pathology is present." If it is, the key moral question is "whether there is a moral obligation to seek to remove the fatal pathology or at least to circumvent its effects."

This is also the approach of Daniel Callahan in his book *What Kind of Life?* Dealing with exactly these cases Callahan asks:

> On the level of physical causality, have we killed the patient or allowed him to die? In one sense, it is our action that shortens his life, and yet in another sense it is his underlying disease that brings his life to an end. I believe it reasonable to say that, since his life was being sustained by artificial means (respirator or

tube), and that was necessary because of the fact that he had an incapacitating disease, his disease is the ultimate reality behind his death.[15]

Because of this decisive causal role played by the underlying disease, Callahan states: "To allow someone to die from a disease we cannot cure (and that we did not cause) is to *permit the disease to act as the cause of death*" (my emphasis). In brief, those who argue that in withdrawing nutrition-hydration we introduce a new cause of death and therefore kill the patient have overlooked the lethal causal character of the underlying pathology. This is precisely the point urged by Sidney Callahan. Persons who believe we must sustain a body in an endless limbo "confuse withdrawing the feeding tube with active killing partly because they refuse to take into account that it is an injury or disease that has ended the person's human future."[16]

The origin of the analysis adopted by the Pennsylvania bishops must remain somewhat speculative. But one would not be too far off in thinking that the late John R. Connery, S.J., was influential here. Connery argued that when quality of life is the central focus, then "the intention is not to free the patient of the burden of using some means, but the burden (or the uselessness) of the life itself. The only way to achieve this goal is by the death of the patient." Therefore, "the intention is the death of the patient" which Connery regarded as "euthanasia by omission"—though I am told that he changed his view shortly before his death.

Actually the situation need not be conceptualized in terms of *life as a burden.* All we need say is that life in a PVS is not a benefit or value to the patient. Therefore, withdrawing nutrition-hydration is withdrawing something from which the patient does not benefit.

This brings us to the central issue in this debate, the notion of benefit. May, *et al.,* see nutrition-hydration for a PVS patient as providing a "great benefit," the preservation of life. So do the Pennsylvania bishops. Kevin O'Rourke, on the contrary, believes that mere "physiological function bereft of the potential for cognitive-affective function does not benefit the patient" and is, in this sense, useless.[18] Daniel Callahan, Dennis Brodeur, John Paris, the Texas bishops and many others share O'Rourke's assessment. So do I.

In deciding what is truly beneficial to a patient it is useful to distinguish with Lawrence Schneiderman, Nancy S. Jecker, and Albert R. Jonsen between an effect and a benefit.[19] The authors argue that the goal of medical treatment is "not merely to cause an effect on some portion of the patient's anatomy, physiology or chemistry, but to benefit the patient as a whole." They believe that nutritional support can effectively preserve a host of organ systems of a PVS patient but remain futile. This they conclude because "the ultimate goal of any treatment should be improvement of the patient's prognosis, comfort, well-being or general state of health. A treatment that fails to provide such a benefit—even though it produces a measurable effect—should be considered futile."

This point was made recently by Bishop William Bullock of Des Moines.[20] Noting that God gives us life to carry out human activities, Bullock asserts that "the benefit of care or treatment to prolong the life of a dying person or of a person for whom these human activities have become very difficult or even no longer possible diminishes in proportion to what remains possible for them." Benefit, he states, refers to "possible recovery or a prolongation of at least minimally conscious life." When such a benefit is absent, to omit nutrition-hydration "is not to intend the patient's death but to permit nature to take its inevitable course."

The determination of what is truly beneficial to us as human persons is a broad human judgment. In all the groups I have polled on this matter, I have found only one person (of thousands) who wished to be maintained indefinitely in a PVS, and he did not understand the condition. This should not be taken to suggest that we determine right and wrong by head-counting. That misses the point. The significance of this virtual unanimity is that people do not regard continuance in a PVS through artificial nutrition-hydration a genuine benefit. Effect, yes. Benefit, no.

Let me conclude with a fanciful scenario. Imagine a 300-bed Catholic hospital with all beds supporting PVS patients maintained for months, even years by gastrostomy tubes. Fanciful? Not if the guidelines of the Pennsylvania bishops are followed. Appalling? In my judgment, yes—not least of all because an observer of the scenario would eventually be led to ask: "Is it true that those who operate this facility actually believe in eternal life?"

Endnotes

Chapter 1

1. *Theological Studies* 1 (1940) 412-443.
2. One thinks immediately of John C. Ford's "The Morality of Obliteration Bombing," *Theological Studies* 5 (1944) 261-309. Interestingly, one finds reference in *Theological Studies* 5 (1944) 511-513 to an article by John Rock and Miriam F. Menkin entitled "In Vitro Fertilization and Cleavage of Human Ovarian Eggs," in *Science* (August 4, 1944) 105-107.
3. *Theological Studies* 9 (1948) 105.
4. *Theological Studies* 10 (1949) 70.
5. *Theological Studies* 10 (1949) 71-74.
6. John R. Connery, S.J., "Steady Dating Among Adolescents," *Theological Studies* 19 (1958) 73-80.
7. *Theological Studies* 11 (1950) 76 and 15 (1954) 101.
8. Francis V. Courneen, S.J., "Recent Trends with Regard to Fasting," *Theological Studies* 7 (1946) 464-470.
9. Anthony F. Zimmerman, S.V.D., "Morality and the Problems of Overpopulation," *Proceedings* of the C.T.S.A. (Fourteenth Annual Convention, 1959) 5-27.
10. Antonius Lanza and Petrus Palazzini, *Theologia Moralis.* Appendix: *De Castitate et luxuria* (Romae: Marietti, 1953) 225.
    "Likewise, masked balls offer a fairly facile opportunity for disaster; for there are some who hide their faces so that, no longer restrained by the bridle of shame, they may do incognito what they would not dare to do if recognized. Today, however, the situation has degenerated badly with more recent dances: one stoep [sic], paso doble, turquey-trot, pas de l'ours, spiru, charleston, fox-trot, rumba, carioca, boogie-woogie, samba, etc."
11. Richard A. McCormick, S.J., "Self-Assessment and Self-Indictment," *Religious Studies Review* 13 (1987) 37. Chapter 3 of this volume.
12. Gérard Gilleman, S.J., *Le primat de la charité en théologie morale* (Paris: Desclée, de Brouwer, 1952).

13. Daniel Callahan, "Authority and the Theologian," *Commonweal* 80 (1964) 319-323.
14. For a discussion cf. Ronald Modras, "The Implications of Rahner's Anthropology for Fundamental Moral Theology," *Horizons* 12.
15. For example cf. M. Flick, S.J., and Z. Alszeghy, S.J., "L'Opzione fondamentale della vita morale et la grazia," *Gregorianum* 41 (1960) 593-619; P. Fransen, S.J., "Pour une psychologie de la grâce divine," *Lumen Vitae* 12 (1957) 209-240.
16. Joseph Fuchs, S.J., *General Moral Theology* (Rome: Gregorian University, 1963). This is my translation of Fuchs' *Theologia Moralis Generalis*. Fuchs has also discussed the matter elsewhere, for instance, in "Basic Freedom and Morality," in *Human Values and Christian Morality* (Dublin: Gill and Macmillan, 1970) 92-111. B. Schüller, S.J., "Zur Analogie sittlicher Grundbegriffe," *Theologie und Philosophie* 41 (1966) 3-19.
17. I believe the C.D.F.'s *Persona humana* (*The Pope Speaks* 21 [1976] 60-73) presents the notion inaccurately. Cf. Charles E. Curran, "Sexual Ethics: Reaction and Critique," *Linacre Quarterly* 43 (1976) 147-164.
18. Peter Knauer, S.J., "La détermination du bien et du mal moral par le principe du double effet," *Nouvelle revue théologique* 87 (1965) 356-376.
19. Germain Grisez, *Abortion: The Myths, the Realities and the Arguments* (Washington: Corpus Books, 1970) 331.
20. *Theological Studies* 12 (1951) 60.
21. There are others such as Benedict Ashley, O.P., and Kevin O'Rourke, O.P., in *Health Care Ethics* (St. Louis: Catholic Health Association, 1977). Their treatment is too sketchy to be considered substantial.
22. Bernard Hoose, *Proportionalism: The American Debate and its European Roots* (Washington: Georgetown University Press, 1987).
23. As in Robert Blair Kaiser, *The Politics of Sex and Religion* (Kansas City: Leaven Press, 1985) 177.
24. André Hellegers said much the same thing as DeLocht. Cf. LeRoy Walters, "Religion and the Renaissance of Medical Ethics in the United States: 1965-1975," *Theology and Bioethics*, ed., Earl E. Shelp (Dordrecht: Reidel Publishing Co., 1985) 9-10.
25. AAS 58 (1966) 218-229 at 219.
26. *Notes on Moral Theology 1965-1980* (Lantham, Maryland: University Press of America, 1981) 212.
27. J. Massingberd Ford, "Toward a Theology of Speaking in Tongues," *Theological Studies* 32 (1971) 3-29.
28. "Partners in the Mystery of Redemption," *Origins* 17 (April 21, 1988) 757, 759-788.
29. C.J. McFadden, *Medical Ethics* (Philadelphia: F.A. Davis, 1967); Gerald Kelly, S.J., *Medico-Moral Problems* (St. Louis: Catholic Health Association, 1949-1954); T.J. O'Donnell, S.J., *Morals in Medicine* (Westminster: Newman, 1956); Edwin F. Healy, S.J., *Medical Ethics* (Chicago: Loyola University Press, 1956).

30. Walters as in note 24, 4.
31. Gustavo Gutiérrez M., "Notes for a Theology of Liberation," *Theological Studies* 31 (1970) 243-261.
32. Gutiérrez, 255.
33. *Catholic Mind* 69 (1971) 37-58.
34. *Octogesima adveniens* (cf. note 33) n. 7.
35. The Documents of Vatican II, ed. by Walter M. Abbott, S.J. (New York: America Press, 1966) 256.
36. *Schema constitutionis pastoralis de ecclesia in mundo huius temporis: Expensio modorum partis secundae* (Vatican Press, 1965) 37-38.
37. Louis Janssens, "Artificial Insemination: Ethical Considerations," *Louvain Studies* 8 (1980) 3-29 at 24.
38. Found in R.A. McCormick, S.J., "L'Affaire Curran," *America* 154 (1986) 267.
39. I go out of my way here to point out that this in no way impugns the quality or integrity of professors presently at Catholic University. It seems to me to be a judgment about institutional policy.
40. Charles E. Curran, "Public Dissent in the Church," *Origins* 16 (1986) 178-184. Cf. also Curran, *Faithful Dissent* (Kansas City: Sheed and Ward, 1986) 61.
41. Cf. note 38, 266.
42. Cf. Giancarlo Zizola, *La restaurazione di papa Wojtyla* (Roma: Laterzae Figli, 1985) 3.
43. Richard A. McCormick, S.J., "The Chill Factor: Recent Roman Interventions," *America* 150 (1984) 475-481. I cannot avoid the conclusion that the C.D.F. has somehow been isolated from contemporary discussions and therefore in significant respects misunderstands them.
44. As an example cf. Walter Kerber, S.J., ed., *Sittliche Normen* (Düsseldorf: Patmos, 1982).
45. *Sollicitudo rei socialis*, *Origins* 17 (March 3, 1988) 642-660 at 653.
46. Documents of Vatican II, 246.
47. Documents of Vatican II, 244.
48. Karl Rahner, S.J., "A Basic Interpretation of Vatican II," *Theological Studies* 40 (1979) 716-727.
49. Rahner, 718.
50. Johannes Metz, *Followers of Christ* (Mahwah, New Jersey: Paulist, 1978) 40.
51. Joseph Sittler, *The Structure of Christian Ethics* (Baton Rouge: Louisiana State University Press, 1958). Unfortunately this book is out of print.
52. Such an emphasis may help to *recognize* obligation, but it does not *justify* it. Cf. James Childress, "Scripture and Christian Ethics," *Interpretation* 34 (1980) 371-380.
53. Documents of Vatican II, 209.

Chapter 2

1. Peter Hebblethwaite, "Synod Dreams," *National Catholic Reporter*, October 24, 1980.
2. Karl Rahner, "Dream of the Church," *The Tablet* 180 (1981) 52-55.
3. I-II, q. 91, a. 2. "Fit providentiae particeps, sibi ipsi et aliis providens."
4. Cited in Eugene Kennedy's *Re-Imagining American Catholicism* (New York: Vantage Books, 1985) 19.
5. Andrew M. Greeley, "Defection Among Hispanics," *America* 159 (1988) 61-62.
6. John Mahoney, S.J., *The Making of Moral Theology* (Oxford: Clarendon Press, 1987).
7. Don Peppers, "Make Money, Have Fun, Be Ethical," *New York Times*, July 24, 1988, F3.
8. Enrico Chiavacci, "The Grounding for the Moral Norm in Contemporary Theological Reflection," in *Readings in Moral Theology No. 2*, ed. by Charles E. Curran and Richard A. McCormick, S.J. (Ramsey, New Jersey: Paulist Press, 1980) 18.
9. Chiavacci, 288.
10. Joseph Sittler, *The Structure of Christian Ethics* (New Orleans: Louisiana State University Press, 1958) 18.
11. Chiavacci, 288.
12. Chiavacci, 288.
13. Sittler, 50-51.
14. John Courtney Murray, *We Hold These Truths* (Kansas City: Sheed & Ward, 1960) 296.
15. Karl Rahner, S.J., "A Basic Interpretation of Vatican II," *Theological Studies* 40 (1979) 716-727.
16. *Documents of Vatican II* (New York: America Press, 1966) 209. Hereafter *Documents*.
17. *Documents*, 240.
18. Cf. James Bresnahan, S.J., "Rahner's Christian Ethics," *America* 123 (1970) 351-354.
19. John H. Yoder, "The Hermeneutics of Peoplehood: A Protestant Perspective on Practical Moral Reasoning," *Journal of Religious Ethics* 10 (1982) 40-67.
20. Stanley Hauerwas, "Story: Ethics and the Pastoral Task," *Chicago Studies* 21 (1982) 59-71.
21. Roger L. Shinn, "Homosexuality: Christian Conviction and Inquiry," in Ralph W. Weltge, ed., *The Same Sex* (Philadelphia: Pilgrim, 1969) 43-54 at 51.
22. Pius XI, *Quadragesimo anno*, para. 79, 80 as in Terence P. McLaughlin, ed., *The Church and the Reconstruction of the Modern World: The Social Encyclicals of Pope Pius XI* (Garden City: Doubleday Image Books, 1957) 246-247.
23. *Documents*, 199, footnote 2.

24. *Documents*, 244.
25. *Documents*, 232.
26. *The Challenge of Peace* (Washington, D.C.: USCC, 1983).
27. *Documents*, 244.
28. Murray, *We Hold These Truths*, 296.
29. F. Hürth, S.J., "La fécondation artificielle: Sa valuer morale et juridique," *Nouvelle revue théologique* 68 (1946) 402-426 at 416.
30. John C. Ford, S.J. and Gerald Kelly, S.J., *Contemporary Moral Theology: Marriage Questions* (Westminster: Newman, 1963) 288.
31. Rahner, as in note 2.
32. Congregation for the Doctrine of the Faith, *Inter insigniores* as in Austin Flannery, ed., *Vatican Council II: More Postconciliar Documents* (Northport, New York: Costello Publishing Co. 1982) 338.
33. *Documents*, 349.
34. *Documents*, 214.
35. "Dalla 'Rerum novarum' ad oggi," *Civiltà cattolica* 132 (1981) 345-357.
36. Charles E. Curran, "Public Dissent in the Church," *Origins* 16 (1986) 178-184 at 181-82.
37. Murray, *We Hold These Truths*, 297.

Chapter 3

1. Yves Congar, O.P., "A Brief History of the Forms of the Magisterium and Its Relations with Scholars," in *Readings in Moral Theology No. 3*, edited by Charles E. Curran and Richard A. McCormick, S.J. (Mahwah: Paulist Press, 1982) 325.
2. Daniel Callahan, "Authority and the Theologian," *Commonweal* 80 (1964) 319-323.
3. Documents of Vatican II, 209.

Chapter 4

1. Eugene Kennedy, "The End of the Immigrant Church," *Illinois Issues*, August, 1982, 15-21.
2. *Documents of Vatican II*, 244.
3. *Documents of Vatican II*, 48.

Chapter 5

1. I borrow liberally in this paper from the writings of Thomas Clarke, S.J., especially (but not exclusively) his chapter "Public Policy and Christian Discernment" in *Personal Values and Public Policy* edited by John C. Haughey, S.J. (Mahwah: Paulist Press, 1979).

2. Karl Rahner, *Foundations of Christian Faith* (New York: Seabury, 1978) 93-94.
3. Rahner, *loc. cit.*, 94.
4. *Loc. cit.*, 96.
5. *Loc. cit.*, 97.
6. *Loc. cit.*, 98-99.
7. Ronald Modras, "The Implication of Rahner's Anthropology for Fundamental Moral Theology," *Horizons* 12 (1985) 70-90 at 72.
8. Karl Rahner, *Theological Investigations* III (Baltimore: Helicon, 1967) 113.
9. Modras, *loc. cit.*, 74.

Chapter 6

1. *Chicago Sun Times*, September 14, 1986.
2. *The New York Times*, September 27, 1986.
3. *Chicago Sun Times*, September 28, 1986.
4. NC release.
5. NC release.
6. Yves Congar, O.P., "A Brief History of the Forms of the Magisterium and Its Relations with Scholars," in *Readings in Moral Theology n. 3*, ed. by Charles E. Curran and Richard A. McCormick, S.J. (Mahwah: Paulist, 1982) 325.
7. *Humanae vitae*, n. 28.
8. *The New York Times*, September 27, 1986.
9. NC release.
10. Documents of Vatican II, 270.
11. Documents of Vatican II, 268-269.
12. *The New York Times*, October 3, 1986.
13. Cf. Charles E. Curran, *Faithful Dissent* (Kansas City: Sheed and Ward, 1986) 268.
14. NC release.

Chapter 7

1. *Origins* 19 (1989) 97-109.
2. Eugene Kennedy, *Tomorrow's Catholics Yesterday's Church* (New York: Harper & Row, 1988).
3. Karl Rahner, S.J., "Theologie und Lehramt," *Stimmen der Zeit*, n. 198 (1980) 363-375 at 373.
4. Karl Rahner, S.J., "Dream of the Church," *Tablet* 180 (1981) 52-55.
5. André Naud, "Les voix de l'Église dans les questions morales," *Science et Esprit* 32 (1980) 161-176.
6. *Documentation catholique*, n. 1511, 1968, col. 321-324.

7. Francis A. Sullivan, S.J., "Note sulla nuova formula per la professione di Fede," *Civiltà Cattolica*, n. 3338 (1989) 130-139.

8. Charles E. Curran, *Faithful Dissent* (Kansas City: Sheed and Ward 1986) 269.

9. AAS 42 (1950) 568.

10. *L'Osservatore Romano*, English edition, n. 27, July 6, 1987, 12-13.

11. Richard A. McCormick, S.J., *The Critical Calling* (Washington: Georgetown University Press, 1989).

12. Yves Congar, O.P., "A Brief History of the Forms of the Magisterium and Its Relations with Scholars," in *Readings in Moral Theology n. 3*, Charles E. Curran and Richard A. McCormick, S.J., eds., Mahwah: Paulist Press, 1982) 327.

13. Avery Dulles, S.J., "The Theologian and the Magisterium," *Proceedings of the Catholic Theological Society of America*, 31 (1976) 235-246 at 241-242.

14. André Naud, *Le magistère incertain* (Montreal: Fides, 1987) 227.

15. Karl Rahner, S.J., see note 4.

16. G. Ermecke, "Die Bedeutung von 'Humanwissenschaften' für die Moraltheologie," *Munchener Theologische Zeitschrift* 26 (1975) 126-140.

17. Joseph Fuchs, S.J., "Moral Truths—Truths of Salvation?" *Christian Ethics in a Secular Arena* (Washington: Georgetown University Press, 1984) 57-58.

18. Karl Rahner, S.J., "Basic Observations on the Subject of Changeable and Unchangeable Factors in the Church," *Theological Investigations* (New York: Seabury, 1976) 14.

19. Fuchs, as in note 17, 61.

20. Documents of Vatican II, 209.

21. Cf. Richard A. McCormick, S.J., *Notes on Moral Theology 1981-1984* (Lanham: University Press of America, 1984) 108.

22. As in Naud, note 14, 240.

23. Bernard Häring, "The Encyclical Crisis," *Commonweal* 88 (1968) 588-594.

24. As cited in Robert Blair Kaiser, *The Politics of Sex and Religion* (Kansas City: Sheed and Ward, 1985) 170.

25. James Malone, "How Bishops and Theologians Relate," *Origins*, 16 (1986) 169-174.

26. John R. Quinn, "New Context for Contraception Teaching," *Origins* 10 (1980) 104.

27. Documents of Vatican II, 270.

28. Clifford Longley, "Cynicism and Sexual Morality" (London) *Times* August 4, 1986.

29. *Origins* 19 (1989) 104.

30. Cf. *The Wanderer*, July 27, 1989.

31. *The Tablet* 243 (June 10, 1989) 660.

Chapter 8

1. Kenneth Untener, "What a Prophet Does and Does Not Do," *Origins* 21 (May 23, 1991) 38.
2. Documents of Vatican II, ed. by Walter M. Abbott, S.J. (New York: America Press, 1966) 270.
3. Congregation for the Doctrine of the Faith, "Instruction on the Ecclesial Vocation of the Theologian," *Origins* 20 (July 5, 1990) 117-126.
4. *Loc. cit.,* 123.
5. *The New Yorker,* July 22, 1991, 52.
6. Avery Dulles, S.J., "Authority and Conscience," *Church* (Fall 1986) 8-15 at 15.
7. Rembert Weakland, "The Price of Orthodoxy," *Catholic Herald,* September 11 and 18, 1986.
8. Walter J. Burghardt, S.J., *Woodstock Report,* June, 1991.
9. Joseph Ratzinger, "The Church and the Theologian," *Origins* 16 (May 8, 1986) 769.
10. Avery Dulles, S.J., *A Church to Believe In* (New York: Crossroad, 1982) 118-132.
11. Dulles, 126.

Chapter 9

1. The exchanges between Curran and the Congregation for the Doctrine of the Faith, including the letter of July 25, 1986, can be found in Curran's *Faithful Dissent* (Kansas City: Sheed and Ward, 1986).
2. Bernard Quelquejeu, O.P., "Acceptance of the Rights of Man, Disregard for the 'Rights of Christians': The Inconsistency of Rome," *The French Revolution and the Church,* ed. by Claude Geffré and Jean-Pierre Jossua (Edinburgh: T. and T. Clark, 1989) 122-123.
3. Congregation for the Doctrine of the Faith, "Instruction on the Ecclesial Vocation of the Theologian," *Origins* 20 (July 5, 1990) 117-126.
4. Paul Sieghart, Cardinal Heenan Memorial Lecture, Heythrop College, December 1988.
5. "Correspondence on 'L'Affair Curran,'" *America* 154 (May 3, 1986) 363.
6. *Faithful Dissent,* 268.
7. I take this from the Documentary Service of the United States Catholic Conference, September 30, 1968.
8. *Faithful Dissent,* 268.
9. From an NC news release.
10. *Human Life in Our Day,* United States Catholic Conference, November 15, 1968.
11. *Faithful Dissent,* 283.
12. Ladislas Orsy, S.J., "An Oath Too Far," *Tablet* 244 (April 7, 1990) 442-443.
13. *Faithful Dissent,* 280.

14. "Academic Freedom and Tenure: The Catholic University of America," *Academe: Bulletin of the AAUP* 75 (September-October, 1989) 27-38.
15. *Origins* 18 (1989) 671.
16. American Association of University Professors, *Policy Documents and Reports* 1984 ed. (Washington, D.C.: AAUP, 1984) 3.
17. Cf. note 14 for citations of the AAUP Investigating Committee.
18. Cf. Charles E. Curran, *Catholic Higher Education Theology and Academic Freedom* (Notre Dame: University of Notre Dame Press, 1990) 127.
19. College and University Department of the NCEA, *Catholic Mind* 74 (October 1976) 51-64.
20. National Conference of Catholic Bishops, "Catholic Higher Education and the Pastoral Mission of the Church," *Origins* 10 (1980) 378-384.

Chapter 10

1. Janet E. Smith, "*Humanae Vitae* at 20: New Insights into an Old Debate," *Crisis* 6 (June, 1988) 16.
2. "Taking it on the Chin—For Life: Reflections on a Vatican Instruction," *America* 156 (April 11, 1987) 295-296.
3. Documents of Vatican II, 250, 254.

Chapter 11

1. Alisdair MacIntyre, "Theology, Ethics and the Ethics of Medicine and Health Care," *Journal of Medicine and Philosophy* 4 (1979) 435-443.
2. Johannes B. Metz, *Followers of Christ* (Ramsey, New Jersey: Paulist, 1978) 39-40.
3. Joseph Sittler, *The Structure of Christian Ethics* (New Orleans: Louisiana State University Press, 1958).
4. Sittler, 45.
5. John 1:3.
6. Walter Kasper, *An Introduction to Christian Faith* (Ramsey, New Jersey: Paulist, 1980) 82.
7. Sittler, 46.
8. Cf. Edmund Pincoffs, "Quandary Ethics," *Mind* 80 (1971) 552-571.
9. I take these distinctions from Norbert Rigali, S.J., "On Christian Ethics," *Chicago Studies* 10 (1971) 227-247.
10. A good presentation of this discussion is Vincent MacNamara's *Faith and Ethics* (Washington: Georgetown University Press, 1985).
11. James M. Gustafson, *Ethics From a Theocentric Perspective. V. II Ethics and Theology* (Chicago: University of Chicago Press, 1984) 98.
12. *Declaration on Euthanasia* (Vatican City: Vatican Polyglot Press, 1980); also in *Origins* 10 (1980) 154-157.

13. Karl Barth, *The Knowledge of God and the Service of God According to the Teaching of the Reformation* (London: Hodder and Stoughton, 1938) 95.

14. Thomas E. Clark, S.J., "Public Policy and Christian Discernment," in John Haughey, S.J., (ed.) *Personal Values in Public Policy* (Ramsey, New Jersey: Paulist, 1979) 232-242.

15. L. Cerfaux, O.P., "La charité fraternelle et le retour du Christ," *Ephemerides Theologicae Lovanienses* 24 (1958) 326.

16. Joseph Fuchs, S.J., *Christian Morality: The Word Becomes Flesh* (Washington: Georgetown University Press, 1987) 204.

17. *The Documents of Vatican II* (New York: America Press, 1966) 209.

18. MacNamara, 120.

19. *Ibid.,* 117.

20. *Ibid.,* 116.

21. *Ibid.,* 119.

22. *Ibid.,* 121.

23. Philip Rieff, *The Triumph of the Therapeutic: Uses of Faith After Freud* (New York: Harper and Row, 1966).

24. Daniel Callahan, "Living with the New Biology," *Center Magazine* 5 (July-August, 1972) 4-12.

25. Cf. Richard A. McCormick, S.J., *Health and Medicine in the Catholic Tradition* (New York: Crossroad, 1984) 37-38.

26. Karl Barth, *Church Dogmatics* (Edinburgh: T.T. Clark, 1958) IV/2, 216.

27. MacNamara, *loc. cit.,* 123.

28. Edmund Pellegrino, M.D., "Agape and Ethics: Some Reflections on Medical Morals from a Catholic Christian," forthcoming as I write.

29. Theodore Minnema, "Human Dignity and Human Dependence," *Calvin Theological Journal* 16 (1981) 5-14.

30. Drew Christiansen, S.J., "The Elderly and Their Families: The Problems of Dependence," *New Catholic World* 223 (1980) 100-104.

31. Christiansen, 102.

32. Christiansen, 104.

33. Cf. Richard A. McCormick, S.J., "Theology and Biomedical Ethics," *Logos* 3 (1982) 25-43.

34. *Declaration on Euthanasia* as in note 19.

35. John 15:13.

36. Pius XII, *AAS* 49 (1957) 1031-32.

37. Franz Böckle, "Glaube und Handeln," *Concilium* 120 (1976) 641-647.

Chapter 12

1. Thomas J. Peters and Robert H. Waterman, Jr., *In Search of Excellence: Lessons from America's Best-Run Companies* (New York: Harper and Row, 1982).

2. Peters and Waterman, 75.

3. Peters and Waterman, 75-76.
4. Peters and Waterman, 76.
5. I borrow this wording from Joseph Sittler's *The Structure of Christian Ethics* (New Orleans: Louisiana State University Press, 1958).
6. Marvin R. Dunn, M.D., *American Medical News*, June 1, 1992, 28.
7. Leon R. Kass, M.D., "The Care of the Doctor," *Perspectives in Biology and Medicine* 34 (Summer, 1991) 553-560. *American Medical News* (May 4, 1992) reported a statement of Kevin Sullivan, a consultant to medical groups, on physician performance standards: "Quality improvement is a tool for achieving business objectives. It is a means to an end." This elicited a scathing response from David L. Wishart, M.D. in the June 22 issue. He noted that the Sullivan approach "puts the business cart before the service horse." And in an analysis close to Kass he stated: "The rewards to the practitioner come as a consequence of the satisfaction of the patient and those who support him (third parties)."
8. Several New York hospitals have hired carefully trained impostors to play patient roles in an effort to improve doctors' ability to communicate. The program originated as a "response to concerns that today's doctors are more adept with technology and jargon than with compassion." (*New York Times*, June 4, 1992).
9. Cf. *New York Times*, February 17, 1992.
10. *American Medical News*, June 1, 1992, 15.
11. *American Medical News*, June 1, 1992, 7.
12. *New York Times*, February 18, 1990.
13. *New York Times*, February 20, 1990.
14. *New York Times*, February 18, 1990.
15. *New York Times*, February 18, 1990.
16. *New York Times*, February 18, 1990.
17. Edmund Pellegrino, "Altruism, Self-Interest and Medical Ethics," *Journal of the American Medical Association* 258(1987) 1939-1940.
18. *New York Times*, January 12, 1992. It is also this ethos that prompted Journalist J. Taylor Buckley to state of his stay at a Helsinki hospital: "A stay in the surgical hospital of Helsinki last month provided ample proof that at least Finland's brand of subsidized, universal care would never fly here. For one thing, their approach is far too mercy-driven and personal-care oriented to merit consideration as a possible replacement for a free-market arrangement like ours. Having people in health jobs because they are dedicated is scary anathema to our rich tradition of economic incentives and government bungling." *USA Today*, May 19, 1992.
19. *Free Inquiry*, Fall, 1991, 14.
20. Leon R. Kass, "Suicide Made Easy," *Commentary*, December, 1991, 22.
21. *American Medical News*, February 10, 1992, 3.
22. Daniel Callahan, "Shattuck Lecture: Contemporary Biomedical Ethics," *New England Journal of Medicine* 302(1980) 1232.

23. John Courtney Murray, S.J., *We Hold These Truths* (New York: Sheed and Ward, 1960) 166.
24. Cf. note 22.
25. Linda H. Aiken and Connie Flynt Mullinix, "The Nurse Shortage: Myth or Reality?" *New England Journal of Medicine* 317(1987) 641-645.
26. I take this list from Aiken and Mullinix.
27. Robert Sokolowski, "The Art and Science of Medicine" in *Catholic Perspectives or Medical Ethics* edited by Edmund D. Pellegrino, John P. Langan, S.J., and John Collins Harvey (Dordrecht: Kluwer Academic Publishers, 1989) 269.
28. Joseph Sittler, *The Structure of Christian Ethics* (New Orleans: Louisiana State University Press, 1958) 64.
29. *Documents of Vatican II,* ed. by Walter Abbott, S.J. (New York: America Press, 1966) p. 498.
30. *Ibid.,* 499.
31. *Ibid.,* 493.
32. *Ibid.,* 493.
33. *Documents,* p. 505.

Chapter 13

1. Karl Rahner, "Über schlechte Argumentation in der Moraltheologie," in H. Boehlaars and R. Tremblay, eds., *In Libertatem Vocati Estis* (Rome: M. Pisani, 1977) 249.
2. Daniel Callahan, *What Kind of Life: The Limits of Medical Progress* (New York: Simon and Schuster, 1990) 23.
3. Joseph A. Califano, Jr., *America's Health Care Revolution: Who Lives? Who Dies? Who Pays?* (New York: Random House, 1986) 104.
4. James D. Lubitz and Gerald F. Riley, "Trends in Medicare Payments in the Last Year of Life," *New England Journal of Medicine* 328 (No. 15, April 15, 1993) 1092-1096.
5. Christopher F. Koller, "Health Care Priorities: Four Things to Keep in Mind" (An Open Letter), *Commonweal* (April 23, 1993) 6.
6. Barbara Katz Rothman, "The Products of Conception: The Social Context for Reproductive Choices," *Journal of Medical Ethics* 11 (No. 4, December 1985) 188-192 at 190.
7. *Turpin v. Sortini* 119 Cal. App. 3d 690; *Harbeson v. Parke Davis* 746 Fed 2d 517; 656 P 2d 483; 98 Wash 2d 460.
8. *The New York Times,* "Whether to Make Perfect Humans" (Editorial, July 22, 1982) A22.
9. *Doe v. Bolton,* 410 U.S. 179, 192 (1973).
10. Califano, *America's Health Care Revolution,* 187.
11. Koller, "Health Care Priorities," 6.
12. Nicole Carroll, "On Death and Dignity: Patients Seek Control Over Their Lives," *USA Today* (February 23, 1993) 1D.

13. Callahan, *What Kind of Life*, 147-148.
14. *Free Inquire* Interview, "Medicide: The Goodness of Planned Death," *Free Inquiry* 11 (No. 4, Fall 1991) 14-18, at 14.
15. Bruce Jennings, "Active Euthanasia and Foregoing Life-sustaining Treatment: Can We Hold the Line?" *Journal of Pain and Symptom Management* 6 (Number 5, July 1991) 312-316, at 316.
16. Nicole Carroll, "On Death and Dignity," 1D.
17. General Synod Board of Social Responsibility, Church of England, *On Dying Well: An Anglican Contribution to the Debate on Euthanasia* (London: Church Information Office, 1975) 22.
18. Melinda Beck, "Doctors Under the Knife," *Newsweek* (April 5, 1993) 28.
19. Lisa Belkin, "Doctors in Distress: Many in Medicine See Rules Sapping Profession's Morale," *The New York Times* (February 19, 1990) Al.
20. Joseph Fletcher, "Ethical Aspects of Genetic Controls: Designed Genetic Changes in Man," *New England Journal of Medicine* 285 (September 30, 1971) 776-783, at 781.
21. Richard Scheinin, "Love, Justice, Sex: These Three," *San Jose Mercury News* (October 31, 1992) 10.

Chapter 14

1. *The Tablet*, February 10, 1990, 181.
2. Clifford Grobstein, *Science and the Unborn* (New York: Basic Books, 1988) 61.
3. Cf. "Ethical Considerations of the New Reproductive Technologies," *Fertility and Sterility* 46 (1986, Supplement 1) 295.
4. Ethics Advisory Board: HEW Support of Research Involving Human In Vitro Fertilization and Embryo Transfer: Report and Conclusions (Washington, D.C., U.S. Department of Health, Education and Welfare, 1979); *Federal Register* 35033-58, June 18, 1979.
5. Great Britain: Department of Health and Social Security: Report of the Committee of Inquiry into Human Fertilisation and Embryology, edited by M. Warnock (London: Her Majesty's Stationery Office, 1984) 27, 63.
6. Cf. LeRoy Walters, "Ethical Issues in Human In Vitro Fertilization and Embryo Transfer," in *Genetics and the Law* III, ed. by A. Milunsky, G. Annas (New York: Plenum Press, 1985) 215.
7. *Documents of Vatican II*, ed. by Walter M. Abbott, S.J. (New York: America Press, 1966) 256.
8. *Charter of the Rights of the Family* (Vatican City: Vatican Polyglot Press, 1983) 9.
9. *Catholic Standard*, October 28, 1982, 6.
10. *The Tablet*, February 3, 1990, 158.
11. *Declaration on Procured Abortion* (Vatican City: Vatican Polyglot Press, 1974).

12. *Instruction on Respect for Human Life in its Origin and on the Dignity of Procreation* (Vatican City: Vatican Polyglot Press, 1987). Because of its cumbersome title this document is after referred to as *Donum vitae* after its first two Latin words.

13. Note 11, 9.

14. *Loc. cit.*, 10.

15. *Donum vitae*, 13.

16. *Loc. cit.*, 13.

17. *Loc. cit.*, 10, endnote 19.

18. I draw upon Clifford Grobstein as in note 2, the pages of *Fertility and Sterility* as in note 3, and an unpublished study of a research group of the Catholic Health Association entitled "The Status and Use of the Human Preembryo."

19. *Fertility and Sterility* as in note 3, 265.

20. *Loc. cit.*, 275.

21. *Loc. cit.*, 275.

22. Howard W. Jones, M.D., "And Just What is a Pre-embryo?" *Fertility and Sterility* 52 (1989) 189-191.

23. Grobstein as in note 2, 25.

24. Jones, *loc. cit.*, 190.

25. *Loc. cit.*, 10.

26. Grobstein, 27.

27. Bioethics, *De duabus naturis*, 3. Cf. *Sacramentum Mundi*, edited by Karl Rahner (New York: Seabury, 1975) 1207.

28. *Summa Theologica I*, q. 30, a. 4, ob. 2; *Summa contra Gentiles* IV, 49.

29. *Sacramentum Mundi*, 1207.

30. John Mahoney, S.J., *Bioethics and Belief* (London: Sheed & Ward, 1984) 60.

31. Cited in Richard A. McCormick, S.J., *How Brave a New World?* (Washington: Georgetown University Press, 1981) 134.

32. Cited in *The Tablet*, March 3, 1990, 270.

33. *The Tablet*, January 6, 1990, 12.

34. Grobstein, 27.

35. *The Tablet* as in note 33.

36. *The Tablet*, February 3, 1990, 141.

37. *The Tablet*, January 13, 1990, 46.

38. In this connection cf. the interesting study of Carol A. Tauer, "The Tradition of Probabilism and the Moral Status of the Early Embryo," *Theological Studies* 45 (1984) 3-33

39. A. Vermeersch, S.J., *Theologiae Moralis Principia-Responsa Consilia* (Rome: Gregorian University Press, 1945) II, 456.

40. Cf. Mahoney, 83.

41. *The Tablet*, February 3, 1990, 142.

42. Mahoney, 79.

43. Mahoney, 80.

44. Mahoney, 82.
45. Mahoney, 85.
46. *Fertility and Sterility* as in note 3, 575.
47. Cited in *Theological Studies* 48 (1987) 95, endnote 40.

Chapter 15

1. Cf. Richard A. McCormick, S.J., "Public Policy on Abortion" in *How Brave a New World?* (Washington: Georgetown University Press, 1981) 189-206.
2. *Origins* 13 (1983-84) 491-494; 14 (1984-85) 705, 707-709.
3. *The New York Times,* August 19, 1988.
4. Cited in Franz Scholz, "Durch ethisce Grenzsituationen awfgeworfene Normen probleme," *Theologisch-praktische Quartalschrift* 123 (1975) 342. Original is found in *Kirchenzeitung für die Diözese Augsburg.*
5. "Déclaration des évêques belges sur l'avortement," *Documentation catholique* 70 (1973) 432-438.
6. Opening statement of Sen. Patrick J. Leahy (D.-Vt.): Hearings before the Subcommittee on the Constitution of the Senate Judiciary Committee. U.S. Senate, 97th Congress, first session October 5, 1981. Cited in Mary C. Segers, "Can Congress Settle the Abortion Issue?" *Hastings Center Report* 12 (June, 1982) 2028.
7. "'Fristenregelung' entschieden abgelehnt," *Ruhrwort* (December 8, 1973) 6.
8. Daniel Callahan, "Abortion: Thinking and Experiencing" *Christianity and Crisis* (January 8, 1973) 295-298.
9. Callahan, *loc. cit.,* 296.
10. Callahan, *loc. cit.,* 297.
11. Callahan, *loc. cit.,* 297.

Chapter 16

1. *Instruction on Respect for Human Life in its Origin and on the Dignity of Procreation* (Vatican City: Vatican Polyglot Press, 1987).
2. *Declaration on Euthanasia* (Vatican City: Vatican Polyglot Press, 1980) 4; see also *Origins* 10 (1980) 154-157.
3. *Documents of Vatican II,* ed. Walter Abbott, S.J., (New York: America, 1966) 256.
4. *Schema constitutionis pastoralis de Ecclesia in mundo huius temporis: Expensio modorum partis secundae* (Rome: Typ. pol. Vat., 1965) 37-38.
5. *Fertility and Sterility,* Supplement 2, vol. 53 (n.6, 1990) 1 S.
6. Cf. note 5.

7. Paul Lauritzen, "Pursuing Parenthood: Reflections on Donor Insemination," *Second Opinion* (July 1990) 57-75. For responses to Lauritzen see *Second Opinion* (January 1992) 95-107.
8. Lisa Sowle Cahill, "The Ethics of Surrogate Motherhood: Biology, Freedom and Moral Obligations," *Law, Medicine and Health Care* 16 (1988) 65-71.
9. Lauritzen, *loc. cit.*, 64.
10. Cahill, *loc. cit.*, 65.
11. Lauritzen, *loc. cit.*, 65.
12. Annette Baran and Rubin Pannor, *Lethal Secrets: The Shocking Consequences and Unsolved Problems of Artificial Insemination* (New York: Warner Books, 1989) 51.
13. Cf. note 1, 24.
14. *Ibid.*, 23.
15. Lauritzen, *loc. cit.*, 72.
16. Paul Ramsey, *Fabricated Man: The Ethics of Genetic Control* (New Haven: Yale University Press, 1970) 89.
17. William J. Winslade and Judith Wilson Ross, *New York Times* (February 21, 1986) 27.
18. Cf. note 5 at 59 S.
19. *Ibid.*, vii.
20. *Ibid.*, 73 S.
21. For example Karen H. Rothenberg, "Gestational Surrogacy and the Health Care Provider: Put Part of the 'IVF Genie' Back into the Bottle," *Law, Medicine and Health Care* 18 (1990) 345-352 at note 38.
22. Daniel Callahan, "Surrogate Motherhood: A Bad Idea," *New York Times* (January 20, 1987) 25.
23. Richard A. McCormick, S.J., "Surrogate Motherhood: A Stillborn Idea," *Second Opinion* v. 5, 1987, 128-132.
24. *Summa contra gentiles* 3, 122.

Chapter 17

1. *Cruzan v. Harmon*, 760 S.W. 2d 408 (Mo. 1988).
2. *Deciding to Forego Life-Sustaining Treatment* (Washington: U.S. Government Printing Office, 1983) 135.
3. Congregation for the Doctrine of the Faith, *Declaration on Euthanasia* (Vatican City: Vatican Polyglot Press, 1980).

Chapter 18

1. *Nancy Beth Cruzan v. Director, Missouri Department of Health*, U.S. Supreme Court No. 88-1503 (Argued: December 6, 1989, Decided: June 25, 1990).
2. *Youngberg v. Romeo*, 457 U.S. 307, 321 (1982).

3. William E. May, *et al.*, "Feeding and Hydrating the Permanently Unconscious and Other Vulnerable Persons," *Issues in Law and Medicine* 3 (Winter, 1987) 203-211.
4. *Wall Street Journal,* (July 31, 1990).

Chapter 19

1. "Nutrition and Hydration: Moral Considerations," *Origins* 21 (1992) 541-552.
2. *Loc. cit.*, 550.
3. *Loc. cit.*, 541.
4. Pius XII, AAS 49 (1957) 1031-1032.
5. "Treatment of Dying Patients," *Origins* 19 (1989) 47-48.
6. *The Challenge of Peace* (Washington, D.C.: U.S. Catholic Conference, 1983).
7. William E. May *et al.*, "Feeding and Hydrating the Permanently Unconscious and Other Vulnerable Persons," *Issues in Law and Medicine* 3 (Winter, 1987) 203-211.
8. Dennis Brodeur, "Feeding Policy Protects Patients' Rights, Decisions," *Health Progress* 66 (June, 1985) 38-43.
9. "On Withdrawing Artificial Nutrition and Hydration," *Origins* 20 (June 7, 1990) 53-55.
10. "Living and Dying Well," *Origins* 21 (November 7, 1991) 345-352.
11. John Leibrecht, "The Nancy Cruzan Case," *Origins* 19 (January 11, 1990) 525-526.
12. Gerald Kelly, S.J., *Medico-Moral Problems* (St. Louis: Catholic Health Association, 1958) 21.
13. *Loc. cit.*, 54.
14. Kevin O'Rourke, O.P., "The A.M.A. Statement on Tube Feeding: An Ethical Analysis," *America* 155 (November 22, 1986) 321-331.
15. Daniel Callahan, *What Kind of Life?* (New York: Simon and Schuster, 1990) 234.
16. Sidney Callahan, "Timely Arguments," *Health Progress* 72 (April, 1991) 73.
17. John R. Connery, S.J., "Quality of Life," *Linacre Ouarterly* 53 (1986) 26-33.
18. *Loc. cit.*, 322.
19. Nancy S. Jecker, Lawrence J. Schneiderman, and Albert R. Jonsen "Medical Futility: Its Meaning and Ethical Implications," *Annals of Internal Medicine* 112 (June 15, 1990) 949-954.
20. William Bullock, "Assessing Burdens and Benefits of Medical Care," *Origins* 21 (January 30, 1992) 553-555.

Index